Greek Tragedy in 20th-Century Italian Literature

Bloomsbury Studies in Classical Reception

Bloomsbury Studies in Classical Reception presents scholarly monographs offering new and innovative research and debate to students and scholars in the reception of Classical Studies. Each volume will explore the appropriation, reconceptualization and recontextualization of various aspects of the Graeco-Roman world and its culture, looking at the impact of the ancient world on modernity. Research will also cover reception within antiquity, the theory and practice of translation and reception theory.

Also available in the series

Alexander the Great in the Early Christian Tradition: Classical Reception and Patristic Literature, Christian Thrue Djurslev

Ancient Magic and the Supernatural in the Modern Visual and Performing Arts, edited by Filippo Carlà and Irene Berti

Ancient Greek Myth in World Fiction since 1989, edited by Justine McConnell and Edith Hall

Anne Carson/Antiquity, edited by Laura Jansen

Antipodean Antiquities, edited by Marguerite Johnson

Classical Antiquity and Medieval Ireland: An Anthology of Medieval Irish Texts and Interpretations, edited by Michael James Clark, Erich Poppe and Isabelle Torrance

Classics in Extremis, edited by Edmund Richardson

Faulkner's Reception of Apuleius' The Golden Ass in The Reivers, by Vernon L. Provencal

Frankenstein and Its Classics, edited by Jesse Weiner, Benjamin Eldon Stevens and Brett M. Rogers

Gender, Creation Myths and their Reception in Western Civilization: Prometheus, Pandora, Adam and Eve, edited by Lisa Maurice and Tovi Bibring

Greek and Roman Classics in the British Struggle for Social Reform, edited by Henry Stead and Edith Hall

Greeks and Romans on the Latin American Stage, edited by Rosa Andújar and Konstantinos P. Nikoloutsos

Homer's Iliad and the Trojan War: Dialogues on Tradition, Jan Haywood and Naoíse Mac Sweeney

Imagining Xerxes, Emma Bridges

Julius Caesar's Self-Created Image and Its Dramatic Afterlife, Miryana Dimitrova
Kinaesthesia and Classical Antiquity 1750–1820: Moved by Stone, Helen Slaney
Once and Future Antiquities in Science Fiction and Fantasy, edited by Brett M. Rogers and Benjamin Eldon Stevens
Ovid's Myth of Pygmalion on Screen, Paula James
Performing Gods in Classical Antiquity and the Age of Shakespeare, by Dustin W. Dixon and John S. Garrison
Reading Poetry, Writing Genre, edited by Silvio Bär and Emily Hauser
Sex, Symbolists and the Greek Body, Richard Warren
The Classics in Modernist Translation, edited by Miranda Hickman and Lynn Kozak
The Classics in South America: Five Case Studies, by Germán Campos Muñoz
The Codex Fori Mussolini, Han Lamers and Bettina Reitz-Joosse
The Gentle, Jealous God, Simon Perris
The Thucydidean Turn: (Re)Interpreting Thucydides' Political Thought Before, During and After the Great War, Benjamin Earley
Translations of Greek Tragedy in the Work of Ezra Pound, Peter Liebregts
Truth in the Late Foucault: Antiquity, Sexuality and Psychoanalysis, edited by Paul Allen Miller
Victorian Classical Burlesques, Laura Monrós-Gaspar
Victorian Epic Burlesques, Rachel Bryant Davies
Virgil's Map: Geography, Empire, and the Georgics, Charlie Kerrigan

Greek Tragedy in 20th-Century Italian Literature

Translations by Camillo Sbarbaro and Giovanna Bemporad

Caterina Paoli

BLOOMSBURY ACADEMIC
LONDON • NEW YORK • OXFORD • NEW DELHI • SYDNEY

BLOOMSBURY ACADEMIC

Bloomsbury Publishing Plc, 50 Bedford Square, London, WC1B 3DP, UK
Bloomsbury Publishing Inc, 1359 Broadway, 12th Floor, New York, NY 10018, USA
Bloomsbury Publishing Ireland, 29 Earlsfort Terrace, Dublin 2, D02 AY28, Ireland

BLOOMSBURY, BLOOMSBURY ACADEMIC and the Diana logo
are trademarks of Bloomsbury Publishing Plc

First published in Great Britain 2024
This paperback edition published 2026

Copyright © Caterina Paoli, 2024

Caterina Paoli has asserted her right under the Copyright,
Designs and Patents Act, 1988, to be identified as Author of this work.

For legal purposes the Acknowledgements on p. viii constitute
an extension of this copyright page.

Cover design: Terry Woodley
Cover image © Paul Klee, 1879–1940, *The Tight Rope Walker (Seiltänzer)*, 1923.
Artokoloro/Alamy Stock Photo

All rights reserved. No part of this publication may be: i) reproduced or transmitted in any form, electronic or mechanical, including photocopying, recording or by means of any information storage or retrieval system without prior permission in writing from the publishers; or ii) used or reproduced in any way for the training, development or operation of artificial intelligence (AI) technologies, including generative AI technologies. The rights holders expressly reserve this publication from the text and data mining exception as per Article 4(3) of the Digital Single Market Directive (EU) 2019/790.

Bloomsbury Publishing Inc does not have any control over, or responsibility for, any third-party websites referred to or in this book. All internet addresses given in this book were correct at the time of going to press. The author and publisher regret any inconvenience caused if addresses have changed or sites have ceased to exist, but can accept no responsibility for any such changes.

A catalogue record for this book is available from the British Library.

Library of Congress Cataloging-in-Publication Data
Names: Paoli, Caterina, 1984- author.
Title: Greek tragedy in 20th-century Italian literature: translations by Camillo Sbarbaro and Giovanna Bemporad / Caterina Paoli. Other titles: Bloomsbury studies in classical reception ; v. 34. Description: New York: Bloomsbury Academic, 2024. | Series: Bloomsbury studies in classical reception; vol 34 | Includes bibliographical references and index. Identifiers: LCCN 2023053571 (print) | LCCN 2023053572 (ebook) | ISBN 9781350186163 (hardback) | ISBN 9781350186484 (paperback) | ISBN 9781350186170 (pdf) | ISBN 9781350186187 (ebook)
Subjects: LCSH: Sbarbaro, Camillo, 1888-1967. | Bemporad, Giovanna. | Greek drama (Tragedy)—Translations—History. | Italian literature—20th century—History and criticism. Classification: LCC PA3071.9 P36 2024 (print) | LCC PA3071.9 (ebook) | DDC 809–dc23/eng/20240105 LC record available at https://lccn.loc.gov/2023053571
LC ebook record available at https://lccn.loc.gov/2023053572

ISBN: HB: 978-1-3501-8616-3
PB: 978-1-3501-8648-4
ePDF: 978-1-3501-8617-0
eBook: 978-1-3501-8618-7

Series: Bloomsbury Studies in Classical Reception

Typeset by RefineCatch Limited, Bungay, Suffolk

For product safety related questions contact productsafety@bloomsbury.com.

To find out more about our authors and books visit www.bloomsbury.com
and sign up for our newsletters.

Contents

Acknowledgements		viii
Note on Translations		x
	Introduction	1
1	Poetic Translations in Context: The Reception of Greek Tragedy in the Italian *Novecento*	9
2	*Parole precise e ispirate*: Camillo Sbarbaro and the Regenerative Function of Translating Greek Tragedy	39
3	Giovanna Bemporad's Early Translations of Greek Tragedy	85
4	Creative Pedagogy and Poetic Translation: Camillo Sbarbaro's, Pier Paolo Pasolini's and Giovanna Bemporad's Commitment to Education	123
	Conclusion	165
Notes		173
Bibliography		211
Index		227

Acknowledgements

I am grateful to the Heath Harrison Award of the Faculty of Medieval and Modern Languages, University of Oxford, the Random House Scholarship, UK, and St Catherine's College, UK, which funded my doctoral studies at the University of Oxford. I would like to thank the Christina Drake Fund of the Faculty of Medieval and Modern Languages, University of Oxford, for awarding me the scholarship that allowed me to travel to Italy and undertake research on Giovanna Bemporad's archive. I offer sincere thanks to the 2019 MHRA Research Scholarship committee, UK, and to the Italian Department at the University of Warwick, UK, for awarding me the Research Scholarship in the Modern European Languages that enabled me to publish this book.

My most heartfelt gratitude goes to my supervisor, Nicola Gardini, for his guidance at every step of my doctoral research. I wish to express my thanks to the people who helped me complete this project: Martin McLaughlin for his precious advice over the years, and for having examined, together with Stefano Jossa, my PhD thesis, providing critical feedback on how to improve this work; Jennifer Burns for her mentorship during my time at the University of Warwick; Vilma De Gasperin for the possibility to gain teaching experience for the Italian Department at the University of Oxford during my doctorate; to Ruth Chester for translating quotations from Italian and French into English; to Lily MacMahon and Zoe Osman at Bloomsbury, for their assistance throughout the realization of this book.

I met Giovanna Bemporad in 2011, who encouraged me to pursue this research, generously devoting time to the discussion of this work from its initial stage. An invaluable point of reference has been Maria Pia Diamanti, Giovanna Bemporad's assistant, who supported her until the very end of her life. Together with her, Nicola Gardini and Giorgio Montecchi, in 2013 we finalized the donation of Giovanna Bemporad's archive to Centro Apice, University of Milan, Italy.

Many thanks to Valentina Gosetti for her friendly support throughout these years. To Cecilia Piantanida for discussing aspects of this work. To Alberica Bazzoni for our stimulating discussions and collaborations on the intersections between women's writing and translation studies. To Alastair James for welcoming me in Oxford when I first arrived. Finally, I would like to thank my family for their ongoing support.

Note on Translations

Unless otherwise stated, extracts in Italian and French have been translated into English by Ruth Chester.

Introduction

The twentieth-century interest in the rediscovery of Greek tragedy in Italy can be considered an extension of the centuries-long transnational debate interrogating the reception of the Moderns and the Classics as an opportunity for comparison, literary and cultural advancement, and source of poetic inspiration.[1] Within the history of Italian literature and culture, the period of Humanism saw a strong revitalization of translations from Greek and Latin into vernacular, together with the advent of textual criticism and philology. Romanticism, with the debate ignited by Mme de Staël's *De l'esprit des traductions*, must also be remembered as a key moment in which theoretical reflection on the role of Ancient and Modern languages and cultures was supported by a blossoming of translation activity.[2] The wider debate on the identity of national literatures, the role of translations in the shaping of new identity models and the need to challenge cultural archetypes by means of translation not only provide a historical context for the poetic translations of Greek tragedy discussed in this book, but they also function as a dynamic comparative framework for the Italian reception of the tragic genre. From its early years, the twentieth century saw almost a rebirth of the tragic genre fuelled by an intensification of translation practice from the classical languages. The corpus of Greek tragedy was specifically re-translated by many individuals (professional and amateur translators, academics, poets) for the stage, an approach that found in Gabriele D'Annunzio and Ettore Romagnoli two leading exponents.[3] Ettore Romagnoli, following D'Annunzio's manifesto on *La Rinascenza della Tragedia* and imbued with Nietzschean enthusiasm for the unity of the arts represented by Greek tragedy, re-translated almost the entire tragic corpus. Alongside this monumental work, Romagnoli collaborated with the Istituto Nazionale del Dramma Antico (INDA), an institution that came to life in 1914 thanks to the initiative of a group of wealthy Sicilian patrons led by

Mario Tommaso Gargallo, who wanted to make Syracuse the living centre of a theatrical event to which, every year, different intellectuals would contribute. The INDA project was officially launched in 1914 with Aeschylus' *Agamemnon*, directed by Romagnoli, who also provided the translation and wrote the music for the play.[4] The ancient theatre in Syracuse became the official site where Greek tragedy was brought back to life via freshly minted translations. The aestheticizing nature of Romagnoli's translations was informed by his ideas on the function of the translator, whom he saw as the 'Demiurge' on which the reception of the genre depended. Although in stark contrast with Romagnoli's opinion on the potential of translation, the community of Italian classicists also contributed significantly to this rebirth by producing new translations for the INDA, thus making the performance of the genre the dominant feature of the Italian reception of Greek tragedy. The antinomies between the two approaches, here briefly mentioned, are often encompassed within the so-called debate between the *eruditi* and the *estetizzanti*.[5]

The Fascist regime also exerted its influence on this reception, encouraging translation from the Classics. Pinpointing to what extent the revitalization of the Classics was contaminated by Fascist ideology is still an object of study and research. The example of Ettore Romagnoli represents well the grey area in which many intellectuals of this period dwell. On the one hand, Romagnoli significantly contributed to the development of INDA – an institution that works to this day and has produced an incredibly rich archive – drawing attention to the importance of the translator in a time in which translation was still considered an ancillary practice. On the other hand, Romagnoli tangentially collaborated with the Fascist regime regarding its cultural agenda on the use of the Classics.[6] Addressing the complex issue of cultural appropriation deployed by the regime goes beyond the remits of this monograph, which instead focuses on the encounter between Greek tragedy and two poet-translators, Camillo Sbarbaro (1888–1960) and Giovanna Bemporad (1923–2013). These authors, somewhat eccentric personalities who worked from the margins though without being isolated within the literary landscape, are here presented as an original pair of the Italian *Novecento* on the grounds of elective affinities, key analogies between their personal and professional choices, and their approach to the translation of Greek tragedy. The two poet-translators met for the first time at Villa Solaia in the 1950s, a few kilometres from Siena, during one of Bemporad's stays with the Vivante family in Tuscany. Camillo Sbarbaro, impressed and fascinated by one of Bemporad's famous readings of her *Odyssey* translation, started a lifelong friendship with her.[7] Born in 1888 in Santa Margherita Ligure, Sbarbaro was mostly active within the Ligurian literary scene, publishing his first poems in the journal *La Riviera Ligure*. He also contributed poems to the Florentine journal *La Voce*, internalizing key elements of the fragmentism that defined his subsequent poetic collections. Beyond any desire to impose his own authority, Sbarbaro exerted his influence on, among others, the literary critic of Hermeticism, Carlo Bo, while teaching him Greek and on the poet Eugenio Montale.[8] Sbarbaro also enjoyed a second period of literary success, mostly defined by his activity as a translator and revived by the republishing of his early poetry collections thanks to the relentless work of his publisher and friend Vanni Scheiwiller in the 1950s. Among the poets on whom he exerted an influence and by whom he was fascinated in this second period was Giovanna Bemporad. From a later generation, Giovanna Bemporad, an Italian poet of Jewish origin and a translator of classical and modern languages, was born on 19 November 1923 in Ferrara. Bemporad devoted her entire life to poetic translation, which she considered a way of being rather than simply an activity or practice. She conceived of poetry and translation as a mode of existence which required exclusiveness and lifelong commitment. Such a choice led to a very unconventional life. She was only a teenager when she became famous for a translation of Virgil's *Aeneid* in *endecasillabi sciolti*, miraculously completed – so the story goes – in thirty-six nights.[9] The child prodigy and her translation drew the attention of the most influential figures of the Italian literary scene, who remained central to Bemporad's life. Pier Paolo Pasolini, for instance, was the first to approach the young translator when she was still a student at the Liceo Galvani in Bologna. Among her mentors, intellectuals, critics and poets like Carlo Izzo, Leone Traverso, Mario Praz, Vincenzo Errante and Giuseppe Ungaretti must be remembered as key figures who recognized her potential, were instrumental in providing contacts with publishing houses and oversaw her literary journey from its youthful beginnings. Almost in opposition to Sbarbaro, her life was defined by a mobility that approaches the nomadic and that saw her moving back and forth between Bologna, Venice, Florence and Rome, without forgetting the Friulian period with Pier Paolo Pasolini where she collaborated in the didactic experiment of the *scuola irregolare*. Bemporad entered the literary world as a child prodigy and remained as a formidable translator, refined poet and original performer, appreciated for her public readings of her own translations.

Sbarbaro and Bemporad took the less travelled road within the scenario that characterized the reception of Greek tragedy in twentieth-century Italy. Both poet-translators distanced themselves from the aestheticizing or hyper-erudite approaches to antiquity, often aimed at performance in a traditional sense, which largely dominated the century. Sbarbaro and Bemporad sought instead to open a dialogue with the tragic genre that would enhance their poetic awareness, holding translation as an experience that would trigger poetic reflection and ignite creative experience.[10] This perspective is evidently indebted to the theoretical assumptions of the poetics of Hermeticism, a literary movement active in the 1930s, which held poetic translation, both from the Classics and the Moderns, as a form of privileged interdisciplinary dialogue between poetry, translation, criticism and metapoetic thought.[11] Another of Bemporad's mentors, Leone Traverso, translator of Aeschylus and Rilke, is a telling example embodying this approach which assigned great importance to the rhythmic equivalence between the languages involved in translation, an aspect that Bemporad internalized with her own research on the hendecasyllable, both in her poetry and translations. Though from an earlier period, Sbarbaro's take on translation, that of the fragmentism of *La Voce*, prefigures the Hermetic sensibility. He translated both from the Moderns and the Classics (in his specific case from French and Greek) and even enriched his own translations with prefaces, which are also pieces of criticism on the poetics of the authors that he translated. In this respect Sbarbaro embodies the trilogy of the poet, translator and critic put forward by Hermeticism as a key figure that could engender a truly interdisciplinary dialogue between these fields. Sbarbaro and Bemporad's translations reassert the fundamental importance of translating both from Moderns and the Classics as a key moment in the dialogue between literatures and poetics.

Another similarity links these two poet-translators when it comes to the translation of Greek tragedy. As theorized by Leopardi, whose influence looms large in the poetic discourse of both Sbarbaro and Bemporad, their approach to the tragic paradigm is informed by an awareness of the otherness represented by the Classics, holding translation from the ancient languages to be a fundamental stage of poetic apprenticeship.[12]

Sbarbaro's and Bemporad's teaching commitment is a further point of convergence in the way in which they thought about the transmission of classical literature. They eschewed institutional channels and sought instead a way that would allow them to develop their own peculiar pedagogy. Sbarbaro's ideas on teaching were put into practice via his so-called *metodo della partecipazione*, as described by Carlo Bo in his memories of Sbarbaro as a teacher of Greek. Bemporad's emphasis on the transmission of classical poetry via her oral performances was first developed and consolidated during her time as a teacher of Latin and Greek in Pier Paolo Pasolini's school in Casarsa, where her students were engaged as an audience, participating to the daimonic experience of the poet-translator-performer. Sbarbaro and Bemporad's didactic experience has a common thread that unifies the way in which they conceived the role of Classics in education. Both poets assigned an ethical and creative function to the Classics whereby translation played a key role within the process of awakening the students' creativity and poetry was the catalyst within their pedagogic thinking.

Their kindred connection becomes all the more evident when compared to the context wherein either aestheticizing or erudite approaches to the reception of antiquity were the dominant modes in a discourse that was tied to the performance of the genre. By comparison with other twentieth-century Italian poets who devoted their attention to the translation of Greek tragedies – for example Pier Paolo Pasolini, Salvatore Quasimodo and Edoardo Sanguineti – Sbarbaro and Bemporad stand out for a wholly peculiar approach to the dramatic texts. While all other poets mostly produced translations for performance's sake and devoted a great deal of attention to the cultural implications of the tragic texts on stage which at times resulted in mimetic endeavours or attempts to rewrite the genre, Sbarbaro and Bemporad focused purely on the textual dimension of tragedy, neglecting the theatrical component of the translated text as well as any consideration of the staging process, fully aware that the tragic word has its own internal theatricality beyond the staging apparatus. Such similar approaches reflect the influence the translation experience had on their lyrical dimension. While for other poets translating Greek tragedies spurred an interest in dramatic writing per se or informed novel ideologies on the Classics, Sbarbaro and Bemporad's engagement with Greek drama contributed to the modelling of their poetic identites, the negotiation of key themes of their oeuvre and the articulation of metapoetic thoughts.

Similarly, and once more against the twentieth century's prevailing approach towards the tragic paradigm, their versions of the Sophoclean dramas, as well as the sources where such versions are referenced and discussed, do not reveal an ideological interest in the use of the tragic paradigm.[13] There is also a further difference when considering Sbarbaro and Bemporad in comparison to other poet-translators of Greek tragedies. All primary critical studies on Greek tragedy and its reception cross paths with the philosophical debate on the concept of the tragic. As Peter Szondi has notably pinpointed in his seminal essay on the tragic, the stark separation of the concept from the genre has a tradition of its own and speculation on this theme progresses alongside the intellectual advancement of the discipline of dialectics.[14] Both Sbarbaro and Bemporad's appropriations of Greek tragedies can be considered to stand entirely outside this critical approach. While their poetic translations of Greek tragedies appear to redefine an idea of the tragic within its dramatic form, their approach actually focuses solely on the linguistic and textual nature of the original. Equally distant from the anthologizing approach, Sbarbaro and Bemporad translated entire tragedies, resisting the temptation to select extracts and, in a sense, rewriting the text according to their preference. Selecting from a number of translations of Greek tragedies they completed in the 1940s, I particularly focus on Sbarbaro's version of Sophocles' *Antigone* and on Bemporad's rendering of Sophocles' *Electra*. While I argue that their versions of Sophocles are representative of a wider engagement with the tragic genre, in the chapters devoted to Sbarbaro and Bemporad I also demonstrate how both authors developed a fascination of sorts with the mythical cycles treated in the tragedies of *Antigone* and *Electra*. My analysis of their appropriations demonstrates that both authors conceived the translations of Sophocles' plays as an occasion to explore their own poetic voices, hence charging translation with creative and inspirational meanings; but most importantly, they enriched the reception of Sophocles with their novel interpretations that unveil new aspects of the texts translated. I trace the influence and effects of these translations on their original opuses as a whole and the shaping of their poetic personae. As a result, my analysis sheds new light on Sbarbaro and Bemporad's poetic worlds and on their relationship with the classical legacy.

The book is structured in four chapters. The first chapter offers a historical contextualization of Bemporad and Sbarbaro's translations while placing them in dialogue with other twentieth-century poet-translators who dealt with the tragic genre. Taking into account the aforementioned affinities between the two poet-translators, the second and third chapters are structured similarly and they examine, respectively, Sbarbaro and Bemporad's poetic translations in detail. In chronological order, in Chapter 2, I discuss Sbarbaro's version of Sophocles' *Antigone* and its relationship with his poetic opus. In Chapter 3, I focus on Bemporad's version of Sophocles' *Electra* and investigate its influence on her poetic work. From a methodological viewpoint, I combine a comparative approach with historical and textual analysis. I have avoided applying a fixed theoretical framework, in the conviction of a method which starts from close reading and analysis of the texts and then derives its interpretative categories from a scrutiny of these results. Among the ever-growing scholarship on translation studies, I have selected the theoretical works of authors who focused on the poetic significance of the translation practice. As I discuss in the relevant chapters of the book, the theoretical works of Giacomo Leopardi, Walter Benjamin, Antoine Berman and Yves Bonnefoy informed my discussion of Sbarbaro and Bemporad's poetic translations. The novelty and originality of this study is twofold. The comparative framework provides a fresh perspective on two poets who are here studied together for the first time. At the same time, the two poets' works are investigated through the new focus of poetic translation of the tragic genre. In addition to this, thanks to archival research, I bring to the fore and discuss original and completely unpublished material. Chapter 4 is divided into two broad sections. In the first section I consider Sbarbaro's pedagogic commitment both from an historical and from an interpretative perspective. For the first time in Sbarbaro scholarship, I analyse the poet's thoughts on didactics, tracing a connection between the practice of translation, the role assigned to the Classics in education and his poetic work. In the second section, I focus on Bemporad's experience as a teacher of Classics in Pier Paolo Pasolini's school and take into account how this experience had a lasting influence in Bemporad's negotiation of classical literature. Chapter 4 therefore offers a novel perspective on Sbarbaro and Bemporad's didactic commitments with the aim of highlighting how their engagement with the Classics held an ethical significance in their literary views. I then conclude by summarizing my findings with the aim of highlighting the *fil rouge* unifying Sbarbaro and Bemporad's relationships with the Classics as it emerges from the joint study of their poetic translations of Greek tragedies and their pedagogical commitments. This is done in the hope of encouraging future research both on the individual authors and, more generally, on the history of classical reception in the Italian *Novecento*.

1

Poetic Translations in Context

The Reception of Greek Tragedy in the Italian *Novecento*

This chapter focuses on the reception of Greek tragedy in Italy in the twentieth century, contextualizing Camillo Sbarbaro and Giovanna Bemporad's poetic translations. Although poetic translations of Greek tragedy represent a quantitatively smaller practice when compared to the tens and tens of professional and amateur translators of Greek tragedy blooming in the twentieth century, they significantly contributed to the reception of the genre and still await critical attention. Paolo Zoboli's seminal book *La rinascita della tragedia. Le versioni della tragedia greca da D'Annunzio a Pasolini* first drew attention to the reception of Greek tragedy in Italy with a specific focus on translation. Targeting a chronological span of sixty years (1900–60), this study highlighted an ever-increasing number of translations of Greek tragedy, identifying a peak in the 1930s. In light of remarkable numbers, appropriately recorded in a *regesto* at the end of the monograph, Zoboli argued for a rebirth of the genre in twentieth-century Italy, assigning a key role to translation.[1] The book underlined the lack, and therefore the necessity, of a study discussing poetic translations of Greek tragedy and their role in such a rebirth. Understanding how the poets positioned themselves in this debate provides a meaningful framework for studying Camillo Sbarbaro's and Giovanna Bemporad's translations, and understand their commitment to translate Greek tragedy in relation to the rest of the poetic community. The most evident analogy between poetic and non-poetic translations of Greek tragedy is an engagement with theatrical performance. Poets, like the majority of classical scholars, translated for the theatre. While the overarching argument of this book addresses the contribution of poets to the reception of Greek tragedy by taking into account the case studies of Camillo Sbarbaro's and Giovanna Bemporad's translations, the scope of this chapter is to highlight how these poets' work represent a novelty for their interest in developing a theatricality of sorts among the poet-translators of Greek tragedy. By abstaining from any kind of interaction with the stage, Sbarbaro's and Bemporad's poetic versions stand out within a period that witnessed the collaboration of scholars and poets with the Istituto Nazionale del Dramma Antico (INDA) and its festivals. In light of this partnership, which characterized the entire century, the first section of this chapter explores the influence exerted by the work of a poet, Gabriele D'Annunzio, and that of a classical philologist, Ettore Romagnoli, on the reception of Greek tragedy.

Gabriele D'Annunzio's *La rinascenza della tragedia* (1897), with its call to poets to revive Greek tragedy in ancient theatres, was enabled by the creation of the Istituto Nazionale del Dramma Antico (INDA), based in Syracuse (1914). The classical philologist Ettore Romagnoli played a paramount role in the creation of INDA and translated a significant number of tragedies for the Syracuse festivals. Romagnoli's interest in translation and his active commitment to the representation of Greek tragedy as part of a cultural ritual was an exceptional case. The Italian academia, the official institution for the transmission of classical antiquity, had a conflicting approach towards the 'rebirth' and the role of translations. By considering the works of three distinguished classical scholars, Giorgio Pasquali, Manara Valgimigli and Gennaro Perrotta, I intend to highlight some of the salient aspects of the twofold attitude of classical philology. Classicists did not dismiss occasional collaboration with INDA. However, they remained firmly anchored to the principles of historical philology, which considered translation solely a practical activity not to be encouraged per se without a solid knowledge of classical literature and civilization. In addition to this, the aesthetics of Benedetto Croce and Giovanni Gentile – very influential among the community of classical scholars – held translation, especially that of poetry, as an almost impossible act not deserving any theoretical speculation or particular critical attention.

The Italian reception of Greek tragedy is profoundly indebted to the contemporary European cultural scene, especially to the major evolution undergone by classical scholarship during the nineteenth and twentieth centuries. Both historical philology (Pasquali) and the approach inspired by Aestheticism (D'Annunzio and Romagnoli) owe their models to the European intellectual scene, of which the second section of this chapter will outline the major trends.

Mapping the impact that the European cultural scene had on the classical reception in Italy allows for the discussion of another major aspect concerning the reception of Greek tragedy in twentieth-century literature: the concept of tragic. A philosophical category that found its origin within the tradition of German Idealism, this concept crosses the path of the reception of Greek tragedy in many ways. Understanding the scope and the influence that such a category had on the Italian scene is fundamental to situate Sbarbaro's and Bemporad's poetic translations in relation to the critical debate on the tragic.

In the third and last section of this chapter, I compare the approach of other Italian poets who translated Greek tragedy in the twentieth century (Pier Paolo Pasolini, Salvatore Quasimodo and Edoardo Sanguineti) with that employed by Sbarbaro and Bemporad, highlighting analogies and differences.[2] While appearing to be part of a wider movement, Sbarbaro's and Bemporad's versions constitute a countertrend against the most common tendency of translating for the stage. Despite the chronological difference between the case studies (Sbarbaro and Bemporad translated Greek tragedy in the 1940s, whereas Pasolini, Quasimodo and Sanguineti did so after 1960) the comparative analysis proves helpful to pinpoint the peculiarity of these undertakings. From a critical viewpoint, Yves Bonnefoy's considerations on the nature of the tragic text and the challenges it poses to a poet-translator can help to further address the difference in Sbarbaro's and Bemporad's translations of Greek tragedy and their decision to engage only with the text, dismissing the implications embedded in the translation of the theatrical text. Bonnefoy, a poet himself and a translator of Shakespeare, suggested that the only interpretation capable of reactivating the dialogic nature, thus the performativity of the tragic text, relies on a rhythmical quest. Sbarbaro's and Bemporad's translations, by focusing solely on the text, seemed to have addressed the dialogical nature of tragedy as expressed by Bonnefoy. By finding a new rhythm, Sbarbaro and Bemporad viewed the translation of Greek tragedy as a means by which to explore the potential of their own poetic abilities – and not intended for the stage.

Greek Tragedy on Stage: Gabriele D'Annunzio's *Rinascenza della Tragedia*, the INDA Project and the Contribution of Classical Scholarship

The reopening ceremony of the Roman Theatre of Orange (1869), after its partial restoration, and the performance of Sophocles' *Antigone* profoundly inspired Gabriele D'Annunzio. The influence of this performance on D'Annunzio's poetic imagination emerges in his emblematic pamphlet 'La rinascenza della tragedia', written a few years later (1897):

> Oggi risonano ancora i versi dei tragedi e scrosciano gli applausi della moltitudine assisa nell'ordine dei gradi aperti sotto il cielo estivo. Costruito contro il fianco petroso d'un colle, a simiglianza del Teatro di Dioniso contro il fianco dell'acropoli ateniese, il vasto e fulvo monumento aduna nei suoi cerchi una gente diversa, convenuta quivi dai borghi prossimi e dalle città lontane per udire la lamentazione d'Antigone e l'ululo delle Erinni. [...] Ho voluto rappresentare questo avvenimento straordinario – che forse passerà sotto silenzio in Italia ove ogni gusto della cultura è smarrito – poiché mi sembra significativo come indizio d'una tendenza nuova, come annunzio di un impreveduto risveglio nello spirito latino, che finalmente riconosce tra la nebbia estranea di cui si era avvolto i segni dell'antica luce.[3]

Today the verses of the tragedies resound and the applause of the multitude seated on the ordered open steps peals out under the summer sky. Built against the rocky side of a hill, in likeness of the Theatre of Dionysus against the side of the Athenian Acropolis, the vast and ruddy monument brings a varied populace together in its circles, gathered here from the local neighbourhood and from distant cities to hear the lamentations of Antigone and the wails of the Furies. [...] I wanted to show this extraordinary event, which will perhaps go unnoticed in Italy where all taste for culture has disappeared, since it seems to me a significant sign of a new tendency, an announcement of an unexpected reawakening in the Latin spirit, which finally discerns the signs of the ancient light through the extraneous clouds in which it has wrapped itself.

It is evident that revived representations of Greek tragedy in ancient theatres held a symbolic meaning for D'Annunzio: the poet saw not only the rebirth of a genre but also that of a community assembling for a ritual event.[4] The arrival of *gente diversa* (varied populace) from neighbourhoods and cities to listen to

Antigone's lament reminded D'Annunzio of the Athenian crowd, coming from the polis and its districts to celebrate the festivals in which Greek tragedy was originally performed. The excerpt is imbued with references to ancient Greece and its cultural festivals. D'Annunzio read Greek tragedy festivals as the powerful archetype on which Italian modernity (the one that descended from Rome, as the phrase 'spirito latino' suggests) should mould its own cultural events. He felt that his duty was to encourage Italy to follow such an example, thus reconnecting the history of Rome to that of ancient Greece. As Zoboli rightly pointed out, behind the reference to the reawakening of the 'spirito latino' (Latin spirit) in opposition to the 'nebbia estranea' (extraneous clouds) is to be read an allusion to the polemic of Friederich Nietzsche on Richard Wagner's Bayreuth theatre.[5] Following Nietzsche's call, D'Annunzio did reclaim the Mediterranean context of tragedy.[6] He went as far as to promote an actual programme for the rebirth of Greek tragedy in Italy, where poets had a leading role:

L'opera dramatica [sic] resta l'unica forma vitale con cui i poeti possono manifestarsi alla folla e darle la rivelazione della Bellezza, comunicarle i sogni virili ed eroici che trasfigurano subitamente la vita. Sarà gloria dei poeti risollevare quella forma a dignità primitiva, infondendole l'antico spirito religioso.[7]

The dramatic work remains the only living form with which poets can show themselves to the crowd and give them the revelation of Beauty, communicate to them the virile and heroic dreams which immediately transform life. It will be the glory of the poets to raise that form to its original dignity again, instilling in it the ancient religious spirit.

In the *opera dramatica*, namely Greek tragedy, D'Annunzio identified the only possibility of a dialogue between poets and the rest of the community. Such a dialogue is possible only if the genre is brought back to the ritual dimension of its origins. Modern poets, therefore, must resurrect the ritual function of the *parola tragica* (tragic word). Towards the end of *La Rinascenza*, D'Annunzio quotes Aeschylus' lines: 'Colui che canta al dio un canto di speranza, vedrà compiersi il suo voto' (The one who sings a song of hope to the God, he will see his vow granted).[8] Ultimately, the *Rinascenza della tragedia* is to be read as a sort of religious vow.

Although the modes in which Italian poets ought to make Greek tragedy live again were not specified, it is evident that performance in ancient theatrical sites occupied a critical role in D'Annunzio's project. The theatrical performance signified the re-enactment of the cultural rite. Specifically, D'Annunzio was very keen on Graeco-Roman theatres in Italy. The poet's trips to Greece, prior to the writing of *La rinascenza della tragedia*, had a significant impact on his poetic imagination and on his project. By 1897 – when *Rinascenza della tragedia* was first issued – the poet had already completed his first visit to Greece (1895). D'Annunzio participated in the ceremony celebrating the discovery of Delphi's charioteer with an oration titled *Discorso agli Ateniesi* (1898)[9] proclaiming the sisterhood between Greek and the Italian languages. During another visit to Greece with Eleonora Duse (1899), he wrote a memorable letter to Piero Treves describing the epiphany he had in Mycenae: his mission was to make the tragedies of Aeschylus, Sophocles and Euripides live again in Italian culture.[10] The Latin theatre in Albano, conceived as the Italian, and consequently Mediterranean, answer to Wagner's theatre (opened in Bayreuth in the year 1876), was supposed to be the place where D'Annunzio would revive the work of ancient tragedians.[11] D'Annunzio advertised his 'new' mission with an extensive campaign on the cultural pages of Italian and European newspapers in order to attract public interest.[12] His enthusiasm for the rebirth of Greek tragedy stimulated visible effects also on his work as a playwright.[13]

The poet never translated a Greek tragedy nor did he accomplish his project for the Albano theatre.[14] His tragic engagement, in the end, remained prophetic. Indeed, the reception of Greek tragedy in the twentieth-century Italy was to be mainly a history of dramatic performances in festivals. However, the rebirth of Greek tragedy, as we will see, did not happen thanks to the work of poets, as D'Annunzio had hoped.

It was mostly due to the work of a classical philologist, Ettore Romagnoli, that Greek tragedy was reintroduced into Italian theatres. Romagnoli is a key figure if one is to understand the interconnection of translation and theatre in the reception of Greek tragedy in twentieth-century Italian literature.[15] Romagnoli's work has three fundamental merits. Firstly, he was extraordinarily committed to bringing Greek tragedy back to the stage. Romagnoli played a paramount role in the foundation of the National Institute of Ancient Drama (INDA) at the Greek theatre in Syracuse. Secondly, his work as a translator was unprecedented: Romagnoli translated the whole canon of Greek poetry, devoting particular attention to Greek tragedy, besides most Greek poetry. Thirdly, Romagnoli devoted significant attention to the theorization of translation as practice.

According to Romagnoli, the revival of Greek tragedy restored the tragic genre to its origins. In an essay on Greek music (1905), Romagnoli pinpointed the origin of Greek tragedy in these terms:

> I Greci ebbero dunque dalla musica la rivelazione nubilosa e balenante d'uno stato sovrumano più intenso e vibratile. Indi la concezione d'una umanità eletta che sempre ardesse di quella vita, che parlasse sempre quel linguaggio alato: indi la origine della tragedia, che presenta in forma obiettiva quella umanità ideale. In questi limiti la tragedia è figlia della musica. Bene Federico Nietzsche ne ebbe l'intuizione ma la mortificò poi fin da principio, inserendovi il germe della dottrina schopenaueriana. Dunque, la musica dà la forma a ogni genere di poesia, suggerisce gli spunti e i voli alla lirica, ispira l'anima alla tragedia.[16]
>
> From music the Greeks had the obscure and sudden revelation of a more intense and vibrating godlike state. Thence the idea of an elected humanity which always burned in that life, which always spoke that winged language; thence the origin of tragedy, which presents that ideal humanity in objective form. Surely Friedrich Nietzsche had an intuition of it but he demeaned it from the start, inserting into it the germ of Schopenhauerian doctrine. Therefore, music gives form to every kind of poetry, it prompts the sparks and flights of lyric, inspires the soul of tragedy.

Evidently indebted to Nietzsche's work, this excerpt depicts the importance attributed by Romagnoli to the relationship between music and tragedy.[17] Romagnoli wanted to re-create this connection in modern performance. His first translation for the INDA clearly shows this agenda. In 1914 he translated, directed and composed the music for the choruses of Aeschylus' *Agamemnon* for the opening of the INDA and its festivals of Greek tragedy in Syracuse.[18] This was a turning point for the reception of the tragic genre in Italy: the festival had an enormous impact on the public and has remained successful throughout the whole twentieth century to this day.[19] Dramatic performances of Greek tragedies in the Greek theatre of Syracuse held a symbolic meaning: Greek tragedy was celebrated as the core of classical civilization as a whole, the most refined expression of Greek culture. Moreover, through this project Romagnoli also had the opportunity to propose his *moderno concetto di ellenismo* (modern concept of Hellenism):

> È dissipata la nebbia dalle nostre pupille. Quasi ogni opera letteraria dell'Ellade lascia cadere il suo drappeggiamento classico, e rivela, ora, la viva sprezzatura popolaresca, ora l'accesa policromia o la sognante sfumatura romantica.[20]

> The fog has lifted from our eyes. Almost every literary work from Hellas lets its classical drapery fall and reveals, now lively popular disdain, now vibrant technicolour or dreamy romanticism.

Interestingly, Romagnoli opposed all Classicizing or neoclassical interpretation, ultimately resting on Winckelmann's reading of ancient art.[21] Romagnoli's translations and staging of Greek tragedy in INDA's festivals – inspired by his *moderno concetto di ellenismo* (modern concept of Hellenism) – promoted a new way of interpreting Greek antiquity, which found its guiding principles in the cultural agenda of Aestheticism and Romanticism. Romagnoli's Nietzschean opposition to Classicism, as we will see, was not unique to him. The entire community of classical scholars, as well as poets who dealt with classical reception, challenged the model of Classicism and called for a different approach.

The agonal structure of INDA proposed by Romagnoli in the wake of ancient competitions, prompted an outpouring of translations. A special series was created with the purpose of hosting the translations of the tragedies staged at INDA. Romagnoli worked relentlessly as a translator, overseeing almost all the tragedies staged at INDA up to 1928.[22] Such a commitment was the practical realization of Romagnoli's ideas on the task of translator. He believed that every period has its own translators.[23] The vitality of the classical paradigm is therefore strictly dependent on the historical nature of language. Interpreters, commentators and translators are fundamental mediators in this process.[24] The translator is the most important figure, the best version of the commentator. The translator is, in Romagnoli's view, the 'Demiurge' throughout the ages and only in virtue of his work can classical poetry be transmitted to modernity.

In accordance with his theories, Romagnoli chose verse rather than prose for translation. For him, rhythmical evolution is the sole connection between past and present:

> Il verso, dalla uniformità ritmica originale, ha aspirato, a mano a mano, alla libera modulazione, alla omniritmia. In nessuna forma l'aspirazione ha trovato compimento più perfetto che nell'endecasillabo, il quale, nella

> generica cornice giambica, fissata e solidamente mantenuta dai due accenti delle sedi principali, permette la combinazione e il contrasto di tutti gli altri disegni ritmici.²⁵
>
> From its original rhythmic uniformity, verse has strived, bit by bit, for free modulation, for *omniritmia* (an all-encompassing rhtymic design). In no form has this ambition found a more perfect fulfilment than in the hendecasyllable which, in the generic iambic frame, fixed and solidly maintained by the two stresses on the main positions, enables the combination and contrast of all the other rhythmic patterns.

As is evident from this passage, rhythm is the point of connection between different historical periods. The hendecasyllable is the chosen verse not only in virtue of its rhythm flexibility, but especially because it is considered the final result of the evolution of the iambic trimeter. In other words, the hendecasyllable is the symbol of the historical development of the ancient verse. Like the translator, rhythmical evolution is the 'Demiurge' allowing communication between different historical stages.

Romagnoli's positions on the role of the translator triggered a vigorous debate in the Italian cultural scene. His perspective was in stark contrast both to the standpoint of the most prominent exponents of Idealism and to classical historical philology. It is worth briefly considering Benedetto Croce's and Giovanni Gentile's positions on translation. George Steiner, in his well-known periodization of translation, placed Croce's thought in the period of untranslatability.²⁶ To fully understand Croce's positions on the matter of poetic translation one has to consider the separation between the work of art and everything else, between what is poetry and what is not, which is at the heart of Croce's aesthetics. In his *L'estetica come scienza dell'espressione e linguistica generale: Teoria e storia* (1902), the philosopher described poetic translation as follows:

> La traduzione, che si dice buona, è un'approssimazione, che ha valore originario di opera d'arte e può stare da sé.²⁷
>
> Translation, which is called good, is an approximation which has original value as a work of art and can stand alone.

This excerpt shows how Croce did not conceive poetic translations as possible, because as soon as they came into existence, they immediately became works of their own. Things change for prose texts. In his *Poesia* (1936), Croce admitted translation as far as prose texts are concerned:

> Non v'ha dubbio che la sfera in cui ha luogo il tradurre sia quella dell'espressione prosastica, che si adempie per simboli e segni. Questi segni sono permutabili, secondo che torna comodo; e non solo quelli della matematica, della fisica e delle altre scienze, ma anche quelli della filosofia e della storia.[28]
>
> There is no doubt that the sphere in which translation has a place is that of prosaic expression which is fulfilled through symbols and signs. These signs are changeable according to what is convenient; and not only those of mathematics, physics and the other sciences, but also those of philosophy and history.

The untranslatability of poetry is underscored even more strongly in this passage where translation is confined to the realm of prose and its essence compared to the more general concept of exchange.

Giovanni Gentile developed Croce's positions in the *Estetica* even more radically. Beginning from the assumption that language is not a fact but an act, Gentile arrived at a conclusion which is a complete aporia. In his study *Croce, Gentile e Gramsci sulla traduzione*, Domenico Jervolino highlighted the underlying contradiction at the heart of Gentile's ideas on translation:

> Gentile sottolinea che la lingua, in quanto nella sua concretezza è il parlare, non è fatto (oggetto della conoscenza del grammatico e del glottologo) ma è atto, come qualsiasi forma di vita dello spirito. Intesa la lingua in questo modo, essa è una sola, sicché si può arrivare a due conclusioni opposte che sono come le facce di una medaglia: noi non traduciamo mai, perché l'unica lingua è quella vivente; noi traduciamo sempre, perché 'la lingua vera, sonante nell'animo umano, non è mai la stessa, né anche in due istanti consecutivi; ed esiste a condizione di trasformarsi, continuamente inquieta, viva'.[29]
>
> Gentile stresses that language, in as much as its concretization is speech, is not fact (an object of knowledge of the grammarian and glottologist) but act, like any form of life of the spirit. Understood in this way, language is one, thus two opposing conclusions can be arrived at which are like two sides of the coin; we never translate because the only language is the living one; we always translate because 'true language, sounding in the human soul, is never the same, not even in two consecutive moments; and it exists in a condition of transformation, continually restless, alive'.

In so doing, Gentile enormously broadened the field of translation – as Steiner highlighted[30] – thus directly challenging Croce's positions on the matter, as we can judge from this excerpt:

> Tradurre, in verità, è la condizione d'ogni pensare e d'ogni apprendere; e non si traduce soltanto, come si dice empiricamente parlando e presupponendo così lingue diverse, da una lingua straniera nella nostra, ma si traduce altresì dalla nostra, sempre: e non soltanto dalla nostra dei secoli remoti e degli scrittori di cui siamo lettori, ma anche dalla nostra più recente.[31]
>
> To translate, in truth, is the condition of all thinking and all learning; and one not only translates (empirically speaking and presupposing different languages) from a foreign language into our own, but one also translates from our own, always; and not only from our own of centuries past and from the writers we read, but also from our more recent language.

Such positions were discussed in a more organic way in *Il diritto e il torto delle traduzioni* (1920).[32] Gentile founded the futility of translation in the prejudice of considering the work of spirit as a fact and justified the right to translate as an extension of every form of human intellect. Croce's and Gentile's considerations on translation are deeply grounded in their philosophical system.[33] Overall, they did not encourage the debate on poetic translation as practice.[34] Both philosophers, after having framed translation as an aporia or having dissolved it within the eternal evolution of language, restrained critical interest in translation of poetic texts and its theoretical implications.

In *La traduction et la lettre ou l'auberge du lointain*, Antoine Berman devotes an entire chapter – 'L'emprise philologique' – to the effects of the 'philological power'.[35] By the *emprise philologique*, Berman alludes to the hegemonic control of classical philology over the hermeneutics of ancient texts. From his viewpoint, such hegemony can produce a paralysis in communication which prevents other forms of interpretations the text might prompt.[36] Without rejecting the value of textual criticism, Berman observes the necessity of not confining translation to the philologists' technical expertise. Berman's observations on the *emprise philologique* accurately capture the situation of classical reception in the Italian *Novecento* and its relationship with translation. Romagnoli's unremitting dedication to translation was an *unicum* in the Italian academia which was substantially oriented towards the *emprise philologique*. Giorgio Pasquali, a leading figure of classical scholarship in twentieth-century Italy, in a time of an ever increasing practice of translation proposed an opposing philological method based on 'l'interpretazione storica dei testi e nella storia della cultura' (historical interpretation of texts and cultural history).[37] Pasquali conceived translation as only one of the aspects through which the whole text analysis could be articulated. In any case, translation remained but a shadow of the original text:

> Le traduzioni dai classici possono aspirare a risuscitare nel lettore moderno un'ombra dell'impressione estetica che l'originale produce su chi gli si accosti con preparazione adeguata.[38]
>
> Translations from the classics can aspire to revive in the modern reader a shadow of the aesthetic impression which the original produces upon those who approach it sufficiently prepared.

Pasquali asserts that a historical and linguistic knowledge of the *original* language are the sole lens through which to study classical civilization. Pasquali's polemical stand against the 'explosion' of translations from the Classics follows naturally from this belief:

> Negli ultimi anni il numero delle traduzioni, certo per effetto dell'esempio più che dell'insegnamento del Fraccaroli e del Romagnoli [...], è cresciuta a dismisura. Ve ne sono di genere varissimo. Traduzioni poetiche da poesia, alcune tali che il testo greco sembra aver fornito un comodo pretesto, uno spunto per tirar giù versi italiani, brutti i più com'era da attendersi, altre, opera coscienziosa d'interprete, cui le Muse sono state tuttavia avare del loro favore; rare quelle nelle quali senso della lingua poetica italiana e comprensione esatta del testo si diano la mano. [...] Omero, Eschilo, Sofocle, Pindaro, sono stati più spesso tradotti quanto, come avremo occasioni di dire, meno studiati: per un autore così difficile qual'è Eschilo, i risultati sono particolarmente pietosi. Traduzioni in prosa, talvolta in prosa d'arte, da testi poetici: spesso l'originale stampato a fronte. Sono lavori che si propongono di rendere accessibili a un pubblico mezzanamente colto non del tutto sprovvisto di nozioni di greco, i capolavori degli antichi senza soffocarli di note.[39]
>
> In recent years, through the effect of the example more than the teaching of Fraccaroli and Romagnoli, the number of translations [...], has grown excessively. They are very varied in genre. Poetic translations of poetry, some such that the Greek text seems to have supplied a useful pretext, a prompt to bring down Italian verses, most of them ugly as was to be expected, others meticulous works of an interpreter to whom the Muses have nevertheless been stingy with their favour; rare those in which a sense of poetic Italian language and precise understanding of the text join hands. [...] As we will

have occasion to say, Homer, Aeschylus, Sophocles, Pindar were more often translated as much as less studied: for so difficult an author as Aeschylus, the results are particularly pitiful. Translations in prose, at times in lyric prose, of poetic texts: often the original printed opposite. They are works which propose to make the masterpieces of the ancients accessible to a semi-educated public not completely devoid of knowledge of Greek, without suffocating them with notes.

Starting from the translations of Romagnoli and Giuseppe Fraccaroli,[40] Pasquali bemoans the fact that the widespread practice of translations happened more as an imitation of those two professors (*esempio*, example) rather than an actual outcome of what they actually taught (*insegnamento*, teaching).[41] In a word, Romagnoli and Fraccaroli were still acceptable. Their followers were not.[42]

Combining Croce's and Gentile's views, Manara Valgimigli, another influential classical scholar, discussed at length the scope of poetic translation with special reference to Greek tragedy. In his *Del tradurre la poesia antica* (1952), Valgimigli challenged the idea of the translator as the best commentator. In opposition to this, he claimed the irreducible otherness of every translation by comparison to the original, and ultimately denied that translation was at all possible:

> Perché non siamo noi che, ritornando indietro, dobbiamo andare da Eschilo, è Eschilo che viene fino a noi. Il nostro Eschilo non è il povero mortale e corporale Eschilo che poetò in Atene e morì e fu sepolto a Gela nel 476. Il nostro Eschilo è quello che si è gettato, che si è immerso nel fiume dei secoli che a noi lo riportano e lo ricongiungono.[43]
>
> Because it is not we who, going backwards, must go to Aeschylus, it is Aeschylus who comes to us. Our Aeschylus is not the poor mortal and corporeal Aeschylus who wrote poetry in Athens and died and was buried at Gela in 476. Our Aeschylus is he who threw himself, who immersed himself in the river of the centuries which carry and reunite him with us.

In light of such impossibility, Valgimigli therefore considered groundless any effort to create equivalences between Greek metrics and the phonic structure of the Italian language, and opted for plain prose as the only viable kind of rendition.[44] Almost in contradiction with his theories, Valgimigli nonetheless translated several tragedies both for educational publications and for theatrical representations, reducing and adapting the text in various ways. Among the many translations he undertook, his Sophocles' *Oedipus Rex* for the Olympic Theatre in Vicenza in 1946 must be remembered for its resonance. With this play, Valgimigli revived a centuries-old tradition of the Olympic Theatre that hosted *Oedipus Rex* in 1585.[45] Moreover, Valgimigli collaborated with INDA by translating Aeschylus' *Agamemnon* and *Eumenides*.[46]

Gennaro Perrotta's scholarship can be considered another example demonstrating the merging of historical philology with the positions of Italian Idealism. In his famous *Storia della letteratura greca*, and more precisely in a letter addressed to Croce, Perrotta openly declared his intellectual debt to Croce's aesthetic:

> Ho tentato di applicare allo studio della letteratura greca le vostre teorie sull'arte, delle quali sono da vent'anni convinto seguace.[47]
>
> I have tried to apply your theories of art – of which I've been a committed follower for twenty years – to the study of Greek literature.

The influence of Perrotta's *Storia della letteratura greca*, which applied literary criticism to classical philology, was remarkable, as the many editions of the book demonstrate. The *Storia* is often remembered as an incredibly successful pedagogical tool which guided generations of students in learning Greek literature.[48] Perrotta's firm belief in historical philology – it is worth remembering that he had been Pasquali's pupil – is particularly evident in his studies of Greek tragedy. In his seminal volume *I tragici greci* (1931), Perrotta aimed at offering an interpretation of Greek tragedy free from any vestiges of Classicism or Romanticism, grounding his analysis on the historical and philological method.[49] Perrotta considered translation only a minor aspect of a wider analysis of the text comprising the following stages: 'esame della tradizione e dell'apparato critico, analisi linguistica e metrica, traduzione, interpretazione storica ed estetica'.[50] Somewhat contradictory, Perrotta is now often remembered for the modernity of his approach to translation.[51] His translations of Sophocles' *Women of Trachis* (1931) and of Aeschylus' *Prometheus Bound* (1953) are, perhaps, his most famous versions. Interestingly, in his preface to the *Women of Trachis* Perrotta declared that he had attempted to produce an anti-classicist translation, thus connecting his translation to the same agenda that informs his study on Greek tragedy. Unlike Romagnoli,

Perrotta rejected the use of the hendecasyllable for his translation of Greek tragedy, paying attention mostly to the performativity of the text. Aeschylus' *Prometheus Bound*, translated for the stage of Syracuse, is considered the translation where his attention to performativity comes to the fore most evidently.

This overview has shown that the reception of Greek tragedy in twentieth-century Italy knew a significant season mostly thanks to the work of two figures, against the background of a great deal of discussion on translation. Although the poet D'Annunzio warmly encouraged the 'rebirth of tragedy', it was thanks to the classical philologist Romagnoli that Greek tragedy began to be performed on a regular basis in ancient theatres and was indeed reborn. Romagnoli's relentless commitment to translation and theatrical representations of Greek tragedy prompted an increasing number of translations as well as opening a critical debate on the scope and aims of poetic translation. With the exception of Pasquali, the rest of the classicists, in more or less subtle contrast with Romagnoli's ideology, practically contributed to the rebirth of Greek tragedy by offering their expertise and their translations for INDA's festivals. However, the theoretical scope of this rebirth, entirely based on translations, appears largely underdeveloped.[52] The restraint exercised by Croce's and Gentile's theories of 'relative translatability' surely did not encourage the theoretical debate on the scope of literary translation. Similarly, classical scholars never considered translation more than a minor practice useful only within the much wider and articulated analysis of classical literature.

Birth and Rebirth of Tragedy: The Reception of Greek Tragedy in Italy and Its Cultural Relations with the European Classical Scholarship

The changes within the European intellectual community, with specific reference to classical scholarship, in the course of the nineteenth and twentieth centuries, profoundly influenced Italian culture. The twentieth century saw the blooming of a new whole set of critical perspectives, which questioned the Hermeneutics of the Classics and fostered new interpretative methodologies.

The intellectual upheaval began in the second half of the eighteenth-century Germany, when classicists and philosophers interrogated the modes of enquiry of historical philology, thus expressing the need for a more comprehensive, and less compartmental, approach to the study of classical civilization. This was the beginning of the creation of the paradigm known as *Altertumswissenschaft*.[53] Such interrogations culminated in the formation of what we now define as two critical perspectives: the anthropological and comparative method and Hellenocentrism.

Christian Gottlob Heyne (1729–1812)[54] – a figure who has recently received increasing scholarly interest – is considered the founder of the comparative and anthropological school.[55] Heyne addressed the study of classical civilization by comparing the ancient Greek culture with Eastern primitive civilizations. The combination of archaeology, philology and history of religion led him to ask classical antiquity one of the paramount questions of modern anthropology; that is to say the primary causes at the origin of the differentiation process in ancient civilizations.[56]

The ideas of Wilhelm von Humboldt (1767–1835), who was one of Heyne's students at Göttingen University, are at the heart of the other main school of thought that developed in those years, the Hellenocentric approach. Humboldt established a paradigm according to which the Greeks were divine and not comparable to other ancient civilizations. Such a perspective generated the necessity of creating specific interpretative categories for Greek civilization:

> For us the Greeks step out of the circle of history. [...] We fail entirely to recognize our relationship to them if we dare to apply the standards to them which we apply to the rest of world history. Knowledge of the Greeks is not merely pleasant, useful or necessary to us – no, in the Greeks alone we find the ideal of that which we should like to be and produce. If every part of history enriched us with its human wisdom and human experience, then from the Greeks we take something more than earthly – almost godlike.[57]

Such an axiom spread almost like a sacred formula throughout the twentieth century: the 'superiority' of the Greeks exerted an enormous influence both on scholarly approaches and, more generally, on the larger public. It is worth remembering that Humboldt's ideas also played an important role in the way in which education was conceived and organized in Europe in the nineteenth and twentieth centuries. Humboldt's theories,[58] which inspired the *ratio studiorum* in the Prussian school reform of 1809–10, extended their influence also to the Italian scene. The most evident aspect was the introduction into the school system, in 1861, of the study of ancient Greek language.[59] The principle inspiring Humboldt's reforms held Greek thought as the origin of logos from which philosophy and tragedy originated. It was therefore essential for modern society to look to the political, social and intellectual structure of the Greeks and to imitate their excellent model.[60]

Together with Heyne and Humboldt it is worth quoting, also for chronological proximity and for its resonance, the contribution from another classical philologist, James George Frazer (1854–1941). In his *Golden Bough* (1890), the Greeks remain 'special' among ancient civilizations for having exceptionally experienced the three evolutionary steps: magic, religion and democracy. Frazer applied the anthropological category of the conglomerate – a concept borrowed from geology – according to which pre-existing beliefs, instead of being substituted by the new ones, cluster together thus continuing to exist within the same historical period.[61] As Bertelli pointed out,[62] Frazer did not hesitate to institute – which is characteristic of his method – a comparison between Plato's philosophy and animistic thought:

> Now it is quite true that every voluntary action of every man is directed to some good or rather to something that seems to him good. But acting thus for a good implies a mind in which there is a picture of an object to be attained. But from the fact that all our vocabulary actions are prompted by this mental preconception of an object, were we to infer that every change in physical things is prompted by a striving after the good, we would be committing the same mistake into which savages fall when, from the analogy of their own acts, they ascribe the action of inanimate objects to a principle of life, thought, and feeling inherent in these objects.[63]

Humboldt's Hellonocentric approach and Heyne's and Frazer's comparative-anthropological method continued to evolve throughout the twentieth century. Tracking the evolution of these critical perspectives, and the impact they had in Europe, is directly in dialogue with the development of the modes of classical reception in Italy, offering a more comprehensive framework through which poetic translations of Greek tragedy can be examined. Frazer's pivotal lesson on the origins of Greek religion and study of myth inspired the so-called circle of 'Cambridge Ritualists'.[64] The works of Jane Ellen Harrison (1850–1928), Gilbert Murray (1866–1957) and Francis Macdonald Cornford (1874–1943) were profoundly indebted to Frazer's innovative perspective. Harrison's field was Greek religion and its connections with other early religions.[65] Murray applied the anthropological approach to his study of the primitive, explaining its evolution towards the creation of the logos.[66] Cornford mostly delved into Greek historiography, investigating its mythical-religious implications.[67] However different from one another, the 'Ritualists' shared the desire to discover the origins of Greek culture by using an interdisciplinary approach that included anthropology, archaeology, philology and philosophy.[68] In particular, Cornford's approach was influential over the second generation of French historical anthropologists. Among these, Jean-Pierre Vernant (1914–2007) and Pierre Vidal-Naquet (1930–2006) gained great reputations especially through their research on Greek tragedy.[69] Vernant and Naquet identified 'ambiguous speech' as the distinctive feature of tragedy. In so doing, these scholars highlighted the polysemous, and therefore poetic, nature of the tragic text assigning to modern poets the task of reactivating that multiplicity of levels inherent in the tragic word.[70]

The breadth of this set of methodological approaches – which I here could only briefly present – clearly testifies to the relevance of Greeks' thought and culture to modernity, whether we assert the superiority of the Greeks or we compare their civilization with other civilizations of the ancient world.

Classical reception in Italy in the first half of the twentieth century and, in particular, the figures who dealt with Greek tragedy owe to the Germans their interpretative models. Italian classicists remained firmly attached to the modes of enquiry of historical philology. Giorgio Pasquali's philology, which influenced generations of Italian students and academics, was a direct application of the doctrine elaborated by scholars such as Ulrich von Wilamowitz-Moellendorff.[71] However, German culture was to play a fundamental role also in terms of aesthetic ideology,[72] as is particularly evident in D'Annunzio's and Romagnoli's views on the reception of Greek tragedy. D'Annunzio's idealized image of Greece and his call for the rebirth of tragedy are imbued with references to Friedrich Nietzsche's aesthetic theories. The vast echo of Nietzsche's *The Birth of Tragedy* (1872) in twentieth-century European culture found in D'Annunzio a passionate follower, as we have seen in his *Rinascenza della tragedia*. Similarly, Romagnoli's keen interest in the music of the Greeks and the vital connection between music and tragedy cannot be fully appreciated without Nietzsche's lesson. The project of launching Greek tragedy as a modern performance through the foundation of INDA in the Greek theatre of Syracuse is reminiscent of Nietzsche's invitation to restore the unity of the arts (music, dance and poetry) which was a feature of Greek tragedy.[73] When considering the opposition between the comparative anthropological method and the Hellenocentric model, the reception of Greek tragedy in Italy appears to be almost entirely skewed towards the latter. Italy had to wait until the 1970s to witness the employment of the comparative and anthropological approaches to the study of classical civilization.

At this point, I should not fail to mention yet another critical approach that proved essential to the development of the discourse on tragedy: German Idealism.[74] This philosophy added further complexity to the study of Greek tragedy and that of the concept of tragic.[75] The concept of tragic transcends the historicity of the genre. As a result, fragments of the genre, either thematic or stylistic, were often dislocated outside the boundary of its genre. Greek tragedy became a conceptual category which could be dislocated outside its historical reality and placed within other genres and fields of enquiry. Peter Szondi's seminal *An Essay on the Tragic* (1961) showed how, since Schelling, 'there has been a philosophy of the tragic'.[76] Greek tragedy and its reception metamorphosed into a reflection on the tragic as a philosophical concept often detached from its literary genre as well as from the poetics of tragedy expressed by Aristotle.[77] Tragic poetry as a historical genre has been replaced by philosophical definitions of tragic – a notion which has touched nearly all literary genres, allowing for contaminations and mutations of various kinds.[78] The proliferation of critical perspectives prompted by the concept of tragic mirrors indeed the breadth of the concept itself.[79] Twentieth-century Italian literature was remarkably open to the concept of tragic. This is particularly evident in the narrative and fictional genres, as Barberi Squarotti's study demonstrated.[80] It is beyond the scope of this book to discuss the depths of such a vast interdisciplinary area.[81]

Italian Poets and Greek Tragedy: The Connection with INDA and the Innovative Nature of Camillo Sbarbaro's and Giovanna Bemporad's Translations

Sbarbaro's and Bemporad's poetic translations are a far cry both from the philosophical speculation on the tragic and from the newly born ideologies and enquiries of classical scholarship informing the reception of Greek tragedy. Similarly, within the larger cultural debate on classical reception that saw, at the beginning of the century, the contraposition of the philological model to the aesthetic one – a dispute heavily influencing the discourse on translation – Sbarbaro's and Bemporad's versions of Greek tragedy are equally distant both from the erudite and the aestheticizing perspectives.[82] The two poets' engagement with translation reveals instead a proximity with the cultural *milieu* of the Hermeticism, a literary movement that developed in Italy in the 1920s. Reflecting upon his generation's take on translation in the 1930s, literary critic and translator Oreste Macrí pinpointed the poetic agenda behind it. Intended as a privileged form of collaboration between different areas of knowledge and disciplines, translation was conceived, by poets, critics and translators, as a poetic task conducive to literary reformism.[83] According to Macrí translation became increasingly codified as an autonomous literary genre and tasked with the duty of opening a dialogue between poetry and criticism. Translator-poets and critics such as Leone Traverso, Carlo Izzo and Mario Praz, Renato Poggioli and Sergio Baldi (to name just a few of the most representative names) favoured this interdisciplinary dialogue. Likewise, poet-translators such a Mario Luzi, Vittorio Sereni, Piero Bigongiari and Alessandro Parronchi (to name some of the poet-translators) also contributed to the development of this interdisciplinary discourse by engaging with criticism and translations.[84] Sbarbaro's and Bemporad's approaches to translation are indebted, both from a theoretical and practical viewpoint, to the critical perspectives developed by these cultural operators, with whom the authors (especially Giovanna Bemporad) also had personal connections. There are three main elements connecting Sbarbaro's and Bemporad's work on Greek tragedy and the interdisciplinary angle articulated by this group of intellectuals. First, the sacrifice of personal poetry as a consequence of the work of translating: both Sbarbaro and Bemporad paused the writing of their poetic opus while translating. Second, the use of translation as deeply interdisciplinary experience engendering poetic criticism. In a more or less overt manner, and with different degrees of awareness, the experience of translating Greek tragedy, specifically Sophocles, prompted metapoetic reflections touching on their personae and their objectives. Third, Sbarbaro's and Bemporad's rhythmical translations are in tune, from a stylistic viewpoint, with the metrical translations completed by the poet-translators and translator-poets mentioned above. Leone Traverso's poetics of translation and his considerations on the role of rhythm in translation are illuminating in this respect. Traverso's stress on the importance of discovering the rhythm animating the source text (*seguire l'onda ritmica dell'orginale*; to follow the rhythm of the source text) and then his call to re-create that rhythm in translation informs his humanistic-symbolistic idea of translation. Following this intuition, Traverso attempted first to identify the lexical and syntactical substrate common to the languages he was translating from. Secondly, whilst maintain the etymological similarity of the languages (when possible), he worked to re-create the rhythmical colour of the original in translation by means of compensation. This way of proceeding strongly echoes Sbarbaro's etymologizing approach and Bemporad's phono-symbolic compensations in their versions of Greek tragedy which are dominated by a rhythmical quest. In both cases, the assumption is that an equivalent of a text can be found in another language, almost as if there is something that pre-exists both the translation and the original. Within this framework, it is only evident how vital a role rhythm played, being the means via which the *universal* finds its own manifestations. If Sbarbaro's and Bemporad's intellectual debt towards this way of conceiving the links between rhythm and translation is evident from their poetic versions of Greek tragedy, it must be noted that there is also a macroscopic difference separating their poetic versions from the majority of translations of Greek tragedy produced in twentieth-century Italian panorama. Sbarbaro's and Bemporad's translations were never intended as a text to be performed on stage in front of an audience. Their versions can be instead taken as samples – with all the peculiarities of the cases – belonging to a long, and transnational, history of 'translating Greek Tragedy for the page and not for the stage'.[85] Instead of engaging with the staging apparatus of Greek tragedy, both poets channelled their interaction only with the textual dimension of tragedy. In a century that vowed to resuscitate the tragic genre via producing new translations for performance, focusing only on the textual dimension of Greek tragedy is a significant counter trend. Unlike classicists and other poets, Sbarbaro and Bemporad did not approach Greek tragedy as a surviving piece of art missing its historical and aesthetic context which needed to be resuscitated to former glories. Yet, translating Greek tragedy for the page, as Sbarbaro and Bemporad did, does not mean neglecting the performativity embedded in the genre altogether.[86] Their attention to the rhythm of the tragic word and their dismissal of the staging apparatuses resonates with the reflections articulated by another poet-translator, Yves Bonnefoy, who decades later related his experience of translating a key text of modern tragedy.[87] In *L'hésitation d'Hamlet et la décision de Shakespeare*, Bonnefoy pinpointed the specifics of the tragic word and its relation with the staging process:

> Tout à l'heure je disais que Shakespeare n'était qu'une parole qui peut être dite sur scene nue, un dire parfaitement suffisant en ses mots et par ses mots. [...] Car une telle parole, c'est tout ce qui est et tout ce qui vit qu'elle a dans le champ de sa reflexion. Si elle n'a que faire d'un rendu scénique encombré des choses du proche, elle se sent concernée, istinctivemente, par tout ce qui a lieu dans ce monde, per ses us et façons, par la façon don't les êtres vivent. [...][88] Shakespeare, pour moi, c'étaient alors tout comme aujourd'hui ces mots qui par eux-même mènent l'action, sans besoin de décor ni même d'acteurs.[89]
>
> Earlier I said that Shakespeare was only a word that can be said on a bare stage, a word that is perfectly sufficient in and by its words. [...] For such a word is everything that is and everything that lives in the field of its reflection. If it has little use for a cluttered stage rendering of close things, it is concerned, instinctively, with all that takes place in this world, with its habits and ways, with the way in which beings live. [...] For me, Shakespeare was then, as now, those words that by themselves lead the action, without the need for a set or even actors.

According to Bonnefoy, the intrinsic theatricality of the tragic word is self-sufficient and the staging apparatus is almost an obstacle to the strength of the tragic text. The world itself is its natural stage and audience. Having established the ontological theatricality of the tragic word, he tackles the translator's task. Bonnefoy identifies in the rhythm the only viable dialogue with the tragic text:

> Le rythme est alors le facteur le plus important dans cette recherche, c'est à cette respiration des mots dans les vers che je subordonne toute formulation de la signification. [...] C'est seulement dans et par la coïncidence avec soi du traducteur par la voie des rythmes que l'horizon du sens se dégage, que les significations les plus importantes se découvrent.[90]
>
> Rhythm is then the most important factor in this search, it is to this breathing of the words in the verses that I subordinate any formulation of the meaning. [...] Only in and through the translator's coincidence with himself through the rhythms does the horizon of meaning emerge, are the most important meanings discovered.

Rhythm is the leading route through which the translator can access the core of the tragic text. Moreover, rhythm offers another occasion to reassert the internal theatricality of the tragic word:

> Cette attention au vers, c'est aussi un regard sur la mise en scène. Car se recentrer sur le vers met l'accent sur ce qui se joue dans la parole, c'est demander une écoute, c'est préférer la scène nue ou presque nue à tout décor, et surtout c'est refuser à des gestes d'acteurs à l'appui ou en plus du texte.[91]
>
> This attention to verse is also an examination of the staging. For refocusing on the verse puts the emphasis on what is played out in the word, it is to ask for a hearing, it is to prefer the bare or almost bare stage to any decor, and above all it is to refuse to use the actors' gestures in support of or in addition to the text.

The translation of the tragic text, consequently, can only be framed as a dialogue between the rhythms of two voices. The poet translator, before being able to voice the other, must find his own voice and search for his own rhythm. Sbarbaro's and Bemporad's work on Greek tragedy is strongly centred on a rhythmical quest, a vital impulse which subsequently prompted a reflection on their poetics. Although being informed by a similar approach, the two poets' rhythmical quests produced two different outcomes. Bemporad chose the hendecasyllable. As I discuss at length in Chapter 3 of this book, Bemporad's 'tragic hendecasyllables' are structured in a 'waterfall' model with the effect of expanding the verse beyond syllabic limits. Within this metrical measure, Bemporad found her own rhythm and was able to voice Sophocles' poetry. The vocalic finals and the numerous interjections relentlessly recall the essence of Sophocles's *Electra*, that is to say her continuous lament (ll. 1143–1150):

οἴμοι τάλαινα τῆς ἐμῆς πάλαι τροφῆς
ἀνωφελήτου, τὴν ἐγὼ θάμ' ἀμφὶ σοὶ
πόνῳ γλυκεῖ παρέσχον· οὔτε γάρ ποτε
μητρὸς σύ γ' ἦσθα μᾶλλον ἢ κἀμοῦ φίλος,
οὔθ' οἱ κατ' οἶκον ἦσαν, ἀλλ' ἐγὼ τροφός,
ἐγὼ δ' ἀδελφὴ σοὶ προσηυδώμην ἀεί.
νῦν δ' ἐκλέλοιπε ταῦτ' ἐν ἡμέρᾳ μιᾷ
θανόντι σὺν σοί.

Ahi, la mia antica cura ch'io per te,
dolce fatica, sopportai! Tua madre
mai non t'amò quanto t'amavo io!
Fui io la tua nutrice, e non le donne
di casa: io che tu sempre mi chiamavi
sorella: ed ora tutto con te, morto,
in un giorno soltanto è dileguato.[92]

Ah, I grieve at the uselessness of my nursing long ago, the service that I often bestowed on you in sweet labor! For you were never your mother's darling so much as mine, nor was any in the house your nurse but I, and by you I was ever called 'sister'. But now all this has vanished in a day with your death.[93]

Sbarbaro sought a rhythmic prose and found its flow in the strict observation of the original *ordo verborum*, without omitting occasional metrical inserts – which recall the hendecasyllables typical of his poetry. Internal correspondences in Sophocles' language (κακῶν/ὁποῖον) are often transformed into assonances or internal rhymes as is evident from the very beginning of his *Antigone* (ll. 1–10):

Ἀντιγόνη
ὦ κοινὸν αὐτάδελφον Ἰσμήνης κάρα,
ἆρ' οἶσθ' ὅ τι Ζεὺς τῶν ἀπ' Οἰδίπου κακῶν
ὁποῖον οὐχὶ νῷν ἔτι ζώσαιν τελεῖ;
οὐδὲν γὰρ οὔτ' ἀλγεινὸν οὔτ' ἄτης ἄτερ
οὔτ' αἰσχρὸν οὔτ' ἄτιμόν ἐσθ', ὁποῖον οὐ
τῶν σῶν τε κἀμῶν οὐκ ὄπωπ' ἐγὼ κακῶν.
καὶ νῦν τί τοῦτ' αὖ φασι πανδήμῳ πόλει
κήρυγμα θεῖναι τὸν στρατηγὸν ἀρτίως;
ἔχεις τι κεἰσήκουσας; ἤ σε λανθάνει
πρὸς τοὺς φίλους στείχοντα τῶν ἐχθρῶν κακά;

> Mia compagna di destino, sorella cara,
> Ismene, del retaggio di Edipo sai un male,
> sai quale, Zeus non avvererà mentre noi
> due siamo ancora in vita? Se né dolore
> né calamitá né onta né ignominia vi è
> che già io non abbia vista tra i tuoi ed
> i miei mali.
> E adesso che cos'è questo editto che, dico-
> no, ha or ora emanato a tutta la città
> quello che comanda? Sai qualche cosa,
> hai sentito dire? Oppure ignori che i mali
> che si infliggono ai nemici stanno per ab-
> battersi sui nostri cari?[94]

> Ismene, my sister, true child of my own mother, do you know any evil out of all the evils bequeathed by Oedipus that Zeus will not fulfil for the two of us in our lifetime? There is nothing—no pain, no ruin, no shame, nor dishonor—that I have not seen in your sufferings and mine.[95]

The uniqueness of Sbarbaro and Bemporad's approach to the reception of Greek tragedy appears all the more evident if they are compared to other Italian poets who engaged with the reception of the genre. To this end, it will be worthy reflecting on other poets who translated Greek tragedies. In order to see a fully-fledged poetic involvement with the genre we have to look at the later years of the twentieth century, shying therefore away both chronologically and methodologically from the erudite and aestheticizing approaches which characterized the first half of the century. As we have seen in the first section of this chapter, the majority of translations of Greek tragedies were in fact commissioned for the stage, and until the end of the 1950s, INDA festivals staged Greek tragedies as translated by classical scholars.[96] Pier Paolo Pasolini's translation of Aeschylus' *Oresteia* (1960) is a turning point opening up a new era of collaborations and aims for the reception and staging of Greek tragedy.[97] Pasolini translated Aeschylus' *Oresteia* after the commission by Vittorio Gassman and Luciano Lucignani. The tragedy was staged in 1960 in Syracuse prompting a new phase in INDA, one where poets and theatre directors were going to replace classicists. Pasolini's interest in Greek literature, however, dates back to his formative years and his first literary experiences. A rewriting of the myth of Oedipus, *Edipo all'alba* (1942)[98] and translations of Sappho's fragments into Italian and Friulian (1945–7)[99] are the most evident examples of his passion for Greek literature. The 'Friulian' years are also the ones characterized by his friendship with Giovanna Bemporad, who joined Pasolini's didactic experiment as a teacher of Greek and Latin in 1942, and by his didactic commitment.[100] In his *Diario di un insegnante* (1948), Pasolini annotated the importance of translation from the classical languages: 'La traduzione, in qualsiasi aspetto, è l'operazione più vitale dell'uomo' (Translation is, in every aspect, the most vital operation a man can undertake).[101] Pasolini charged with meaning the act of translation, and his work for INDA should be considered in light of such a statement.[102] When Pasolini began to translate Aeschylus, he was already undertaking a translation of Virgil's *Aeneid*. Soon after, precisely at the end of 1960, Pasolini also began to translate Sophocles' *Antigone*.[103]

In his *Lettera del traduttore*, a foreword to his translation of Aeschylus' trilogy, Pasolini outlined his poetics of translation as follows:

> Come tradurre? Io possedevo già un 'italiano' ed era naturalmente quello delle *Ceneri di Gramsci* [...] sapevo (per istinto) che avrei potuto farne uso. [...] La tendenza linguistica generale è stata a modificare continuamente i toni sublimi in toni civili: una disperata correzione di ogni tentazione classicista. Da ciò un avvicinamento alla prosa, alla locuzione bassa, ragionante. Il greco di Eschilo non mi pare una lingua né eletta né espressiva: è estremamente strumentale. Talvolta fino a una magrezza elementare e rigida: a una sintassi priva degli aloni e degli echi che il classicismo romantico ci ha abituati a percepire, quale continua allusività del testo classsico a una classicità paradigmatica, storicamente astratta.[104]
>
> How to translate? I already possessed an 'Italian' and it was naturally that of *Ashes of Gramsci* [...] I knew (by instinct) that I would be able to make use of it. [...] The general linguistic tendency has been to continually change elevated language into civil (popular/colloquial) language: a desperate correction of every classicist temptation. From which come an approach to prose, to low, rational locution. The Greek of Aeschylus does not seem to me to be either a superior or an expressive language. It is extremely functional, at times as far as an elemental and rigid leanness; to a syntax devoid of the auras and echoes which romantic classicism has taught us to perceive, that continual evocation of the classical text to a paradigmatic, historically abstract classicism.

According to Pasolini, Aeschylus' civil language reflects the themes of the trilogy, which have exclusively political significance.[105] Aeschylus' characters are understood as symbols: they express ideas on stage or, to use a term dear to Pasolini, an ideology. Yet, it is the foundation of democracy and the establishment of the suffrage that were to capture the poet's attention, thus stressing even more the socio-political approach informing his analysis and, therefore, his translation:

> Il momento più alto della trilogia è sicuramente l'acme delle Eumenidi, quando Atena istituisce la prima assemblea democratica della storia. Nessuna vicenda, nessuna morte, nessuna angoscia delle tragedie dà una commozione più profonda e assoluta di questa pagina. La trama delle tre tragedie di Eschilo è questa: in una società primitiva dominano dei sentimenti che sono primordiali, istintivi, oscuri (le Erinni), sempre pronte a travolgere le rozze istituzioni (la monarchia di Agamennone) [...] L'incertezza esistenziale della società primitiva permane come categoria dell'angoscia esistenziale o della fantasia nella società evoluta.[106]
>
> The high point of the Trilogy is certainly the climax of the Eumenides when Athena institutes the first democratic assembly in history. No incident, no death, no anguish of the tragedy gives a more profound and extreme emotion than this page. The drama of Aeschylus' three tragedies is this: in a primitive society primordial, instinctive, hidden emotions dominate (the Furies), always ready to crush the crude institutions (Agamemnon's kingship) [...] The existential uncertainty of the primitive society persists as a category of existential distress or fantasy in evolved society.

Pasolini's focus on the transhistorical nature of tragedy, to use the terminology of Vernant-Naquet, is evident from this excerpt.[107] Pasolini makes a silent comparison between the institution of the first democratic assembly in Athens and the creation of the Italian republic, fresh from civil war atrocities and having recently achieved universal suffrage. By insisting on the anthropological meaning of the Furies, Pasolini again alludes to the transhistorical level of the tragic conscience: from dark and primitive forces, the irrational aspects are transformed into the modern category of existential angst.

Pasolini's translation of Aeschylus' tragedy prompted a new phase in the poet's creative work.[108] A great deal of work for the theatre followed, including the *Manifesto del nuovo teatro*. His subsequent filmography drew extensively on Greek tragic material.[109] Pasolini's *Oresteia* also had a great impact on the media. Thanks to his exceptional communication skills, Pasolini drew new attention to the reception of Greek tragedy.[110]

Salvatore Quasimodo's translations of Greek tragedies, also completed for Syracuse, did not exert the same influence nor did it have a similar impact.[111] Quasimodo was involved with INDA at first as a theatre critic.[112] He translated Greek tragedy only later, between the 1940s and 1960s. Quasimodo took great pains to make the tragic text as intelligible as possible.[113] One must consider Quasimodo's incessant polemic with the classicists' translations, which he faulted as being hyper-literary.[114] His constant dialogue with theatre directors, the attention to their poetics and the use of everyday language were aimed at mastering a translation of Greek tragedy that everyone could access.[115]

A substantially different approach to the translation of Greek tragedy is that of Edoardo Sanguineti, another poet who translated for INDA and other Italian theatres.[116] Among the poets considered so far, Sanguineti is the one who most enthusiastically charged his translation with an ideological apparatus. According to Sanguineti, the historicity of language is responsible for the gap between historical ages.[117] Having thus acknowledged the unbridgeable division between languages of different periods, Sanguineti theorized translation as an accurate calque of the original. The calque allowed the closest proximity to the text and, at the same time, the greatest distance from it.[118] Sanguineti's idea of the calque for the translation of Greek tragedy interestingly recalls Vernant-Naquet's reflections on the role of Dionysus, as the protector god of the tragic genre, and on the function of his presence-absence.[119] The theory of the calque led to an extremely literal translation which challenged the formal elocution and the actors' dramatic skills. Such an alienating approach to translation served the purpose of increasing awareness of the historicity of language, which was further enhanced by the translator's own voice and Descartian quote *larvatus prodeo*.[120]

The three case studies here briefly discussed showcase some fundamental traits characterizing the poetic community approach to the translation of Greek tragedy towards the second half of the century, after poets were *called* to translate for the stage. The distance separating these versions to those of Sbarbaro's and Bemporad's is chronological and methodological. Pasolini, Quasimodo and Sanguineti, similarly to the classicists, articulated their reflection on the reception of Greek tragedy in conjunction with the theatrical medium. Their translations, conceived and completed for the stage, saw either the application of the anthropological perspective (Pasolini's case), the use of a normalizing and simplifying approach towards the text (and the script) to afford more readability (Quasimodo), or the use of a strong ideological filter based on the principle of alienation aimed at bringing to the fore the otherness embedded in the genre (Sanguineti). The application of critical categories is in evident dialogue with the staging context and the sets of issues the dramatic context poses to every translator. In light of this partnership between translation and staging, which characterized the reception of Greek tragedy in Italy throughout the entire century and involved different groups of cultural operators (namely academics, poets and theatre directors), Sbarbaro's and Bemporad's versions are a rarity. Their lack of involvement with the theatrical dimension of Greek tragedy and their focus on the question of rhythm make their translations novel achievements providing diverse instances of the reception of Greek tragedy in the Italian twentieth century, so far unexplored and in stark contrast with the most common trends. Their translations appear detached from ideological perspectives connected to the reception of Greek tragedy, critical categories of any kind (with specific references to the tragic as concept dislocated outside the genre) and theatrical purposes. In so doing, working from the margins of the Italian discourse on classical reception as well as from the partnership between the theatrical medium and other poets, Bemporad and Sbarbaro articulated a different kind of tragic rebirth. Mediating between classical scholarship and the spectacularization of Greek tragedy, Sbarbaro and Bemporad developed a rebirth of the genre based on the inherent theatricality of the tragic word as such and its ability to manifest itself only via a rhythmical translation.

2

Parole precise e ispirate

Camillo Sbarbaro and the Regenerative Function of Translating Greek Tragedy

Camillo Sbarbaro (1888–1967) was a poet, a teacher of Classics, a translator of Greek, Latin and French, and an expert on lichens.[1] Sbarbaro's relationship with the classical tradition is deeply rooted in his poetic discourse and intertwined with his lifelong didactic activities. The most substantial output of his interest in Graeco-Roman antiquity is to be found in his translations of Greek tragedy. Sbarbaro translated three Greek tragedies during the Second World War: Sophocles' *Antigone* (1943), Aeschylus' *Prometheus Bound* (1949) and Euripides' *Alcestis* (1952). In this chapter, I consider the role of the translation of Sophocles' *Antigone* in Sbarbaro's poetic opus. The translation of Sophocles is the author's first encounter with Greek tragedy and prompted him to translate Aeschylus' and Euripides' tragedies.

The translation of the *Antigone* had a multifaceted impact on Sbarbaro's poetic life. The first aspect to consider is the fact that the poet elaborated a wholly peculiar methodology for the translation of Sophocles. Through the analysis of selected passages of Sophocles' *Antigone*, this chapter shows how the poet puts into practice this method highlighting the interpretative framework behind it. Secondly, I argue that this translation methodology inspired in Sbarbaro a wider meditation on his own poetics and the metaphorical image of himself as a poet, translator and transcriber, which is fully expressed in his last book *Fuochi fatui* (1956).[2] In this regard, the material written during the translations of Greek tragedy, organized by the poet in the subsection titled '1940–1945', details the poet's thoughts on translation and poetics. Thirdly, I discuss the poet's stylistic choice of poetic prose for these translations connecting it to Sbarbaro's poetic discourse. The poetic prose and the aphorismatic nature of *Fuochi fatui* cannot be fully understood without the poet's intense rethinking of his first poetic achievement, *Pianissimo* (1914), which is constantly recalled in the translation of *Antigone*. The differences emerging from the comparison between translation of the Moderns and that of the Ancients help us to understand this connection between *Antigone* and *Pianissimo*. As we will see, when translating the Moderns Sbarbaro pairs the desire to write something new and to divert from the original, encompassing the experience in a playful dimension, but in translating the Ancients the poet embraces both a reverential attitude and a desire to restore the primary quality of the original. This desire of going backwards coincides with a rediscovery of Sbarbaro's own poetic past, the poetic vocation of *Pianissimo*. Through textual analysis, the chapter shows how the translation of Sophocles, his sober style and the moral themes investigated by his poetry, guided Sbarbaro in the rethinking of his first poetic experience. This mediation is fundamental to understand the poet's last book *Fuochi fatui*, where the metapoetic meditations intermingle with reflections on translation, and the bare style of *Pianissimo* is sought through the dryness of poetic prose.

Notwithstanding Sbarbaro's rich activity as a translator and the connection between his translation and poetics, scholarly debate on his translations of Greek tragedy is scarce. Gina Lagorio in her monograph *Sbarbaro: Un modo spoglio di esistere* was the first scholar to recognize the impact and the value of these translations by comparing the way in which Sbarbaro made the Modern meet the Ancient through his translations of Greek tragedy which were similar to the pivotal achievement of the *Lirici greci* by Salvatore Quasimodo.[3] This insightful, yet too concise, remark was not followed by a display of scholarly interest. The four bibliographies of secondary texts on Sbarbaro edited by Lorenzo Polato (1969, 1974[2]), Giorgio Bàrberi Squarotti (1971), Vanni Scheiwiller (1979) and Gina Lagorio (1981) record very few contributions to the critical discourse on his translations from the Classics as a whole, and the majority focus on his rewriting of Euripides' *Cyclops* (1952).[4] In the last fifty years, the studies devoting attention to this issue are Gina Lagorio's review of the *Cyclops*,[5] Anna Maria Mesturini's notes on the *Cyclops*[6] and the article on *Antigone*,[7] which first answered the call for attention expressed by Lagorio by drawing critical attention to the translation of Sophocles' *Antigone*. In her article, Mesturini offered a concise analysis of Sbarbaro's translation of *Antigone* recording the changes and interpolations made by the poet to the text. After the description of Sbarbaro's approach to the text, which was guided by linguistic and philological expertise, Mesturini proposed a reading of the translation as influenced by the historical period in which it was made. Based on the Hegelian interpretation of the tragedy as a conflict between private conscience and public laws, Mesturini suggests a reading of this translation as a mirror wherein Sbarbaro sees Italy's historical situation reflected. According to Mesturini, the poet's disagreement with the Fascist regime would then be expressed through the mask of this translation as a means to reflect on themes which were too painful to approach without the filter of literature. Paolo Zoboli's monograph *Sbarbaro e i tragici greci*, published in 2005,[8] followed on from Mesturini's first investigation on the *Antigone*, extending the enquiry to the other two translations of Greek tragedy, *Prometheus Bound* and *Alcestis*, and to Euripides' satyr play *Cyclops*. In his book, Zoboli identifies the editions and the commentaries used by Sbarbaro for the four translations aforementioned thus showing Sbarbaro's thorough work on the original texts and reasserting the poet's solid grasp of philology and linguistics highlighted by Mesturini's article. The analysis of the translations, and of their connection with the other Italian versions to which Sbarbaro had access, is a fundamental step towards contextualizing these translations. Zoboli's insightful analysis also demonstrates Sbarbaro's longstanding interest in classical literature by drawing connections with the poet's life. The major intellectual contribution of the book is to show the difference between the modes of the translations of Greek tragedy and those of the *Cyclops*, which can be defined a proper rewriting, thus suggesting different poetic agendas. According to Zoboli, Sbarbaro did not intend to make autonomous poetry with his translations of Greek tragedy, even if it is recognized that these are translations with many *pregi poetici* (poetic virtues).[9] Zoboli considers the *Cyclops* the translation where one can see Sbarbaro's most evident poetic engagement. The decision to write in verse and Sbarbaro's admission of having transformed the *Cyclops* into a work of his own have been taken as evidence for this.[10]

In this study I intend to demonstrate that the difference in terms of poetic engagement and interpretative effort between the *Cyclops* and Greek tragedy suggested by Zoboli is less clear-cut than the critic suggests. The translations of

Greek tragedy, as much as that of the *Cyclops*, can be considered as creative works reflecting the author's poetics and responding to a precise aim. The principle of faithfulness, wholly peculiar to these translations, and opposed to the *traduzione liberissima* (very free translation) of the *Cyclops*, to use Sbarbaro's own words, reveals an interpretive effort much deeper than one would expect at first. The choice of poetic prose for these translations should not be considered as evidence of a minor poetic involvement. On the contrary, it is Sbarbaro's most distinctive mark on his interpretation of Greek tragedy.

Zoboli's section on the tragedies and Mesturini's article on *Antigone* remain fundamental studies which first signalled the need for a critical debate on these translations and opened the path to further studies. Their findings highlighted the necessity to reflect on these translations as a means to show the poet's lifelong relationship with the Classics and to appreciate the poet's different agendas behind the texts translated, as in Zoboli's case, or to demonstrate Sbarbaro's use of the text as mask to protest against the political situation mediated by the voice of another author, as Mesturini argues.

The poetic silence during the years of the translations, the so-called *periodo delle frenetiche traduzioni* (period of frenetic translations),[11] motivated scholars to read Sbarbaro's translations as imperfect substitutes for his poetic voice. The latter approach obviously rests on the assumption that poetry is superior to translation, allowing the translations to enter the poet's canon only inasmuch as they appear to contain clues about Sbarbaro's own poetic voice.[12] As a result, scholars' interest in the *Cyclops* was driven primarily by its status as a rewriting. The history of the *Cyclops* editions, the use of the verse, and Sbarbaro's decision to include it in his final corpus (1967)[13] in the section *Versioni* (together with Pythagoras' *Golden Verses* and Pascoli's *Pomponia Grecina* and *Thallusa*) help to explain the difference of interest in terms of critical attention between this rewriting and the other translations of Greek tragedy.

Giuseppe De Robertis, in his review of Sbarbaro's *Fuochi fatui,* a *zibaldone* which was published in 1956 after the long period devoted to translations, highlighted the conceptual line of poetics emerging from this book of fragments. According to De Robertis, the conceptualization of Sbarbaro's poetics has no parallel compared with the other works in terms of poetic awareness. Among the variety of themes and forms present in the book, the propositions devoted to poetics are theoretical indications of Sbarbaro's modes of conceiving poetry. These remarks, while discussing the nature of the poetic act, are indeed poetry itself.[14]

The proximity of the translations of Greek tragedy to *Fuochi Fatui* is significant: they are chronologically and thematically continuous. *Fuochi fatui*, composed in the period when Sbarbaro was translating Greek tragedy, details his thoughts and meditations on the theme of translation. In the light of De Robertis' remarks, the intersection between Sbarbaro's poetics, reaching its maturity in this book, and his activity as a translator is charged with meaning.

Another important similarity between Sbarbaro's key motifs and the translation of Greek tragedy is to be found on a thematic level. In these translations, in fact, Sbarbaro develops his relentless interest in psychological and moral investigation, a constant feature of his work.[15] Starting from the analysis of *Fuochi Fatui*, the scholar Lorenzo Polato identified moral enquiry as a recurring feature in Sbarbaro's research as a poet:

> Ora assumendo la figura del saggio, mette a frutto la stessa esperienza dello scavo interiore, dell'autoanalisi che costituiscono la dimensione fondamentale della sua opera, al servizio degli altri, nella forma appunto dell'aforisma. La figura 'serena' di questo saggio, per la sua nitida intelligenza e per la sua cordialità, finisce con l'assomigliare a quella di uno stoico antico o di quei classici greci che tanto ha amato, e della cui struttura sintattica vi è più di qualche eco nel suo linguaggio poetico.[16]
>
> Now taking on the figure of the sage, the same experiences of interior excavation, of self-analysis which constitute the fundamental aspect of his work, he puts to good use in the service of others in the form of aphorism. The 'serene' figure of this sage, in his clear intelligence and cordiality, ends up resembling that of an ancient historian or one of those classical Greeks that he so loved, and of whose syntactical structures there are more than a few echoes in his poetic language.

This passage suggests how Sbarbaro's moral enquiry successfully mingles with the aphorismatic nature of *Fuochi fatui*. More importantly, according to Polato, Sbarbaro's passion for classical literature is traceable also in his syntax. The osmotic process between Sbarbaro being influenced by Greek syntax and actively taking advantage of sentence construction with which he was already familiar (the most obvious example is postposition of the verb) for stylistic reasons reflects his meditation on and familiarity with Greek literature.

The poetic prose has to be read as another common trait between Sbarbaro's own poetic work and his translations of Greek tragedy. Sbarbaro's stylistic alternation between poetry and poetic prose is visible in his collections of poems and prose, and it is the heart of a heated scholarly debate discussing Sbarbaro as a poet and as an artist.[17] Sergio Solmi showed that the oscillation between prose and poetry, together with the decision to rewrite certain texts, flags Sbarbaro's progression in his poetic research.[18] Similarly, Silvio Ramat pinpointed the importance of considering prose and lyrics as complementary aspects of the poet's discourse instead of separating the two categories and fuelling a sterile debate.[19] It would indeed be reductive to catalogue the translations into the 'prose phase' only on the basis of the choice of rhythmic prose to render his translations of Greek tragedy. On the contrary, Sbarbaro is inspired by the metric variety of tragedy, and his stylistic choices aim to reflect this quantitative diversity present in the Greek. Sbarbaro exploits the original oscillation of Greek tragedy between lyrical metres and dramatic sections. He alternates between a lyrical tone recalling his own way of making poetry, without encapsulating it into fixed metrical schemes, and a more prosaic form for the dialogues where we also find hendecasyllables, the verse of *Pianissimo*.[20]

Sbarbaro's oscillation, throughout his entire literary career, between his prosaic poetry, as Contini defined it,[21] especially visible in the use of the *endecasillabo libero*[22] (many of these are found in the translations of Greek tragedy), and the poetic prose of his fragments is clearly visible in his translations of Greek drama. They mirror his ideas on the relationship between poetry and prose and on their functions as well as offering the author the stylistic possibility of using the two modes within a single piece of work. A few passages from his translations of Greek tragedy actually became part of his *Trucioli dispersi*, *Fuochi Fatui* and *Cartoline in franchigia* thus showing the interchangeability between his translations and his creative work.[23] Key thematic words of Sbarbaro's poetic language appear with considerable frequency throughout his translations thus showing the use of his poetic memory when translating.[24] His translations of the *Antigone*, *Prometheus Bound* and *Alcestis* offered the poet the chance to reflect on themes dear to his poetic research filtered by some of the fundamental poetic archetypes of Western literature. Psychological and moral investigation, especially evident in the characters of the tragedy, is fully explored in Sbarbaro's translations. At the same time, he experiments with the balance between prose and poetry within the structure of Greek drama finally achieving the co-existence of two stylistic modes sought throughout his entire career. In addition to this, the methodology elaborated ad hoc to translate these texts (the literal translation) intermingled with Sbarbaro's pursuit of an equilibrium between prose and poetry, as well as serving interpretive purposes and offering him inspiration to shape the metaphor he uses for his own poetic identity, the *scrittura sotto dettatura*, a point which I will explain later.

The translations and their numerous editions have an intricate bibliographical timeline, reminiscent of the complicated textual history of Sbarbaro's poetic collections. This history has been studied in a specific section of *Bibliografia degli scritti di Camillo Sbarbaro*, edited by Angeleri and Costa. According to this catalogue, Sophocles' *Antigone* begins the list in 1943 and Jules Amedée Barbey d'Aurevilly's *Due storie diaboliche* ends it in 1977, ten years after Sbarbaro's death.[25] The translation of the *Antigone* was initially begun by Sbarbaro in 1928, but the *periodo delle traduzioni* begins in 1943 with the publication of the *Antigone* for Bompiani (2nd edition published in 1945).[26] Then, between 1942 and 1945 Sbarbaro translated Aeschylus' *Prometheus Bound*, Euripides' *Alcestis* and the satirical drama *The Cyclops*. However, *Prometheus Bound* was only published in 1949 by Bompiani,[27] and was then followed by *Alcestis* which was published together with *The Cyclops* in 1952 for Bompiani.[28] Sbarbaro then further explored the Classics by translating Pythagoras' *Golden Verses* (1958, 1960^2 and 1968^3)[29] and Giovanni Pascoli's Latin works *Pomponia Grecina* and *Thallusa* (translated by Sbarbaro in 1951–2, but posthumously published in 1984).[30] To this list we should also add his translation of book II of Herodotus' *Histories*, which is referred to in Sbarbaro's correspondence and can be dated to the same period as the *Antigone* translation. In a letter written by E. Vittorini to Sbarbaro, dated Milan, 11 March 1943 we read:

> Caro Sbarbaro, l'Antigone non è ancora pronta perché la tipografia che stampa i Corona rimase danneggiata il 24 Ottobre, e ha dovuto trasferirsi fuori Milano a Trevigli. Ora ha ripreso a lavorare, in questi giorni, ma io ho perduto quattro mesi. Cercherò di riguadagnarli. E anche per questo ti prego di mandare l'Erodoto più presto che puoi. L'Antigone uscirà verso maggio. Affettuosi saluti e scusa se ti rispondo con ritardo. Tuo, Vittorini.[31]

> Dear Sbarbaro, Antigone is not yet ready because the printing press that prints the Corona series was damaged on the 24 October and has had to be moved outside Milan to Trevigli. It's working again now but I've lost four months. I'll try to make them up. Because of this, please send me the Herodotus as soon as you can. Antigone will come out around May. With kind greetings and apologies for my late reply. Yours, Vittorini.

Based on the history of these editions, unanimously agreed upon by Sbarbaro scholars,[32] it has been possible to date the whole corpus of Sbarbaro's translations from Greek tragedy to his last poetic phase when he was composing *Fuochi fatui*. Through textual and stylistic analysis, archive research and examination of letter collections, this chapter focuses on the centrality of the translations of Greek tragedy in Sbarbaro's final work which completes his poetic trajectory by reconnecting with his poetic beginning.

'Camminare sulla corda' and 'scrivere sotto dettatura': Sbarbaro's Poetics of Literal Translation

The translations of *Antigone*, *Prometheus Bound* and *Alcestis* were commissioned by Valentino Bompiani for his series 'Pegaso teatrale. Teatro antico e moderno', as emerges from the letters exchanged between Sbarbaro and Bompiani (1942–5).[33] The letters inform us of the translation projects in which Sbarbaro was involved, confirming his expertise as a translator from Greek and Latin. A note kept in the folder lists the following titles as possible further works to be translated by Sbarbaro: The *Gothic War* by Procopio of Cesarea, the second book of Herodotus' *Histories*, Xenophon's *Anabasis* and Petrarch's *Familiar Letters*.[34] After being commissioned to translate *Antigone* and *Prometheus*, Sbarbaro became proactive towards this study of Greek theatre and expressed precise ideas about what he would like to translate. In a letter dated 26 October 1943, Sbarbaro suggests Euripides' *Alcestis* and *The Cyclops* and Aeschylus' *Persians*:

> Nell'eventualità che le comunicazioni si interrompessero, gradirei saperla d'accordo per i tragici greci; nel senso che, finito Barbey, mi metterei a: *Alcesti* di Euripide, *Il Ciclope* di Euripide, ed avanzando tempo, a: *I Persiani* di Eschilo.[35]

> In the event that our communications are interrupted, I would like to be in agreement about the Greek tragedies: in the sense that, Barbey being finished, I would work on Euripides' *Alcestis* and *The Cyclops*, and later, Aeschylus' *Persians*.

His commitment to translate *Prometheus Bound* and *Antigone* prompted him to reread the whole corpus of Greek tragedy, as emerges from another letter sent by Sbarbaro to Bompiani on 3 May 1944:

> Caro Bompiani, La ringrazio della Sua cortesia e del desiderio che mi manifesta che per la Sua Casa io traduca qualche altra cosa del teatro greco. A mia volta La assicuro che divido anch'io questo desiderio. Solo la prego di volermi concedere dell'altro tempo per farle proposte concrete: sto rileggendomi a questo scopo quel che rimane della tragedia greca per fissare la mia scelta. Ho del resto, come Lei sa, ancora due di queste versioni da consegnarLe: l'*Alcesti* e il *Ciclope* di Euripide.[36]
>
> Dear Bompiani, thank you for your kindness and for the desire you have shown for me to translate some more Greek theatre for your publishing house. In turn I assure you that I too share this desire. I only ask that you give me further time to make a concrete proposal: to that end I am re-reading what remains of the Greek tragedies to fix on my choice. As you know moreover, I still have two translations to submit to you: Euripides' *Alcestis* and *Cyclops*.

A cross-analysis of two other collections of letters – that between Sbarbaro and Lucia Rodocanachi, and Enrico Falqui – offers valuable information for analysing Sbarbaro's approach to the translation of the Greek tragedians. In a letter dated Genova, 25 May 1942 Sbarbaro writes to Rodocanachi about his first impression of Sophocles' poetry:

> Ora mi sono messo a Sofocle; che subito mi ha *atterrito*. Ma placherò in qualche modo anche questo mostro.[37]
>
> Now I've started on Sophocles which immediately terrified me. But somehow, I'll appease this monster too.

Despite being concerned about the difficult task posed by this text, Sbarbaro is confident of his skills. Another letter written to Rodocanachi a month later (Genova, 22 June 1942) restates the poet's self-confidence to tackle the task:

> Sto lavorando all'*Antigone* e, al solito, comincia a parermi che il camminare sulla corda sia meno difficile di quel che credevo.[38]

> I'm working on *Antigone* and, as usual, walking on the tight rope starts to seem less difficult than I thought.

The metaphorical expression *camminare sulla corda* is a key phrase to encapsulate Sbarbaro's idea of his role as a translator. The difficult mediation between the original and the translated is expressed through the idiomatic expression of a person's challenging balance when walking on a tight rope. The rope also alludes to the very restricted space for personal intervention, an idea consistently elaborated by Sbarbaro himself as we can infer from two letters from Sbarbaro addressed to Bompiani. Sbarbaro writes to the publisher twice (24 November 1944 and 14 January 1945) to express his dissatisfaction with the the *Cyclops* and the other translations of Greek tragedy being published in the same series. Sbarbaro states that his translation of Greek tragedies aimed at adherence to the original (*aspirano soprattutto ad essere quanto possibile aderenti al testo*: they aspire above all to be as close to the text as possible) as opposed to that of the *Cyclops* which Sbarbaro defines a *riscrittura* (rewriting).[39] Sbarbaro's choice of a literal translation seems to allow very little room for original changes, and this should probably be the message to read in the aforementioned expression (*camminare sulla corda*, walking on the rope). However, Sbarbaro's desire to stick closely to the original and his understanding of the translation of the Greek tragedy as a matter of subtle equilibrium, with small room for personal intervention, should not induce us to read these undertakings as free from interpretative effort.

The desire to adhere to the original and how to achieve this goal stylistically is expressed by Sbarbaro in another letter (Genova, 19 July 1942) written to Rodocanachi:

> Ho consegnato l'*Antigone*; io non ne sono (o: non ne ero) scontento; viceversa quello *stile legato* [my emphasis] che m'illudo renda qualcosa del testo, dev'essere dispiaciuto a Vittorini che fu qui un momento, diretto a Bocca di Magra (con un bel bambino. Demetrio). Peccato (oppure: fortuna) perchè con Sofocle non saprei comportarmi diversamente.[40]
>
> I've delivered *Antigone*; I'm not unhappy with it (or I wasn't): instead that *stile legato* (a style in which there is limited freedom) which I deceive myself renders something of the text must have displeased Vittorini who was here a moment, heading to Bocca di Magra (with a beautiful boy. Demetrio). Shame (or rather: luck) because I wouldn't know how to behave differently with Sophocles.

The *stile legato* relates to Sbarbaro's stylistic work on the text translated, a work mainly based on a wholly peculiar use of punctuation and on word ordering, which I will take into account in the section of this chapter devoted to textual and stylistic analysis of the tragedies. But the *stile legato* also hints at Sbarbaro's adherence to the text translated and to the metaphorical image of the poet walking on a thread elaborated by Sbarbaro.

However, Sbarbaro's fear of Vittorini's dissatisfaction turned out to be unnecessary as we can see again from another letter to Rodocanachi (Spotorno, September, 1943):

> Ho una notizia sola, buona, da darti; voglio dire: consolante per me. Come sai ero convinto che, a Vittorini almeno, la mia tragedia dal greco fosse dispiaciuta. Invece Bompiani mi manda una lettera unicamente per dirmi che ha letto *l'Antigone con un grande godimento*; che devo tradurre delle altre tragedie per lui ecc. Meno male. Mi ha fatto molto piacere.[41]
>
> I've got one piece of news, good news, to give you; I should say, comforting for me. As you know I was convinced that Vittorini didn't like my Greek tragedy translation. Instead, Bompiani sends me a letter just to tell me that he read *Antigone with great enjoyment*; that I must translate some of the other tragedies for him, etc. Thank goodness. I was really pleased.

From the letters we can see how Sbarbaro alternates between satisfaction and concern for the task of translating Greek tragedies as part of his publishing commitments. The only way he felt he could translate Sophocles was the *traduzione letterale*, as another letter to Enrico Falqui also confirms:

> Mi imbarazza il fatto che chiede [i.e. Vittorini] delle versioni 'moderne'. Non saprei, con Eschilo o Sofocle, permettermi degli svolazzi. L'unica traduzione possibile mi pare quella letterale.[42]
>
> I'm embarrassed that he [Vittorini] asks for the 'modern' version. I don't know, with Aeschylus and Sophocles, if I could permit myself embellishments. It seems to me that the only translation possible is a literal one.

The letter draws again attention to the adherence to the original, to the literal translation as the only possible way for Sbarbaro to translate the text. The *versioni moderne* (modern versions) hints at the common practice in translation according to which the translator transforms passages which would sound obscure to a modern public and attempts to offer a valid equivalent in a modern context. Sbarbaro's consideration of this practice is quite frank: '*non saprei permettermi degli svolazzi*' (I could not permit myself embellishments). He identifies the modernizing approach to an ancient text with superficial and unnecessary rhetorical flourishes (*svolazzi*), and such rhetorical 'flights' are the opposite of his walking along the 'tightrope' of literal translation. The translation of Greek tragedians is no easy task: it inspired Sbarbaro but also produced a sense of inhibition. Another letter addressed to Enrico Falqui (Genova, May 1942) clearly shows Sbarbaro's ambivalence towards these translations:

> Ora mi sono messo a Sofocle! Vita di lusso! Niente da Longanesi, per ora; nè da quell'altro che mi scrivesti pel Greco. Ma trovo più divertimento a tradurre dei moderni. Troppa soggezione, gli Antichi![43]
>
> Now I've got to Sophocles! Life of luxury! Nothing from Longanesi for now; nor from that other one who wrote to me for the Greek. But I find translating the moderns more fun. Too much subjugation from the Ancients.

From this letter, we first derive the image that Sbarbaro supremely enjoys translating Sophocles. The image is then immediately dismantled by the poet himself who confesses to his friend and literary critic his preference for the translation of modern authors. The *soggezione* (subjugation) exerted by the Ancients was also an active force which oriented Sbarbaro towards a literal translation and the interpretative side connected to it. The *divertimento* (fun) experienced when translating modern authors surely alludes to a fun dimension, but we cannot ignore, given Sbarbaro's typical ambiguity, the etymological root of the word *divertere* which means to divert. And it is this aspect indeed which discloses the different agenda behind the translation of the Moderns and of the Ancients. With the Ancients the desire is that of adherence, going deep to the core of the message while keeping the structure of the text as much as possible. With the Moderns the desire is that of escaping, transforming the text into something else and interpreting the original as only an occasion to develop, at times, a completely different content.

Notwithstanding the supposed *soggezione* (subjugation) exerted by the Ancients, Sbarbaro expressed his desire to translate more tragedies after he had translated Aeschylus and Sophocles, as revealed in a letter addressed to Bompiani where he confessed to the publisher that he was re-reading the entire canon of Greek tragedy in order to make a choice on what he would like to translate. The letters are therefore a valuable source of information to record

Sbarbaro's fluctuating thoughts on the texts translated, but most importantly to monitor the shaping of a method employed while he was working on these texts: the metaphorical image of *camminare sulla corda* (walking on the rope) is then made explicit in the *traduzione letterale* (literal translation) and put into practice through a *stile legato*.

These remarks on translation extrapolated from the letters are to be integrated with Sbarbaro's thoughts on poetics and translations scattered in *Fuochi Fatui*. A key passage from *Fuochi fatui 1940–1945* is illuminating in helping us to interpret Sbarbaro's *stile legato* and his stylistic interpolations in the text translated:

> Al lavoro di tradurre il compenso che non può mancare è il diletto che vi trovo; diletto, forse perché traducendo esaudisco le possibilità che mi restano di scrittore in proprio: modeste, se le appaga il giro dato a un periodo, una cadenza, la scelta d' un aggettivo.[44]

> In the work of translation, the absolutely essential recompense is the pleasure that I find in it; pleasure, perhaps because in translating I satisfy the possibilities that remain to me as writer in my own right: modest, if one is satisfied by the turn given to a sentence, a cadence, the choice of an adjective.

The *diletto* (pleasure) Sbarbaro derives from translating is connected with his personal intervention in the text translated. The modesty of the pleasure taken from translation is determined by the supposedly limited ways in which Sbarbaro acts upon the text. The sentence shape, the adjective choice and the rhythm are where the poet-translator identifies his sphere of action. The overlapping figures of translator and poet are evident from this passage. The two figures mingle as Sbarbaro explicitly states that he expresses unexplored poetic ideas and formal solutions when translating. The *stile legato* mentioned by Sbarbaro in a letter to Rodocanachi (previously quoted), according to which the poet hopes to have rendered the original in the best way possible, is outlined here by the three stylistic devices. This passage shows Sbarbaro's awareness of the strong identity between himself as a poet and a translator, especially when it comes to making stylistic choices. The passage itself is indeed one of those fragments in the book where theoretical indications about his poetics, here deeply intertwined with translation, are expressed with such accuracy and density of meaning that it is poetry itself, as De Robertis pointed out. The verb *appaga* (to get sastisfaction) links to the initial statement of pleasure (*diletto*) thus bringing the linguistic and stylistic remarks (*il giro dato a un periodo, una cadenza, la scelta di un aggettivo*) into a sensorial dimension.

Sbarbaro's awareness of his translation activity and the poetic inspiration involved in it enrich the scope of translation in his work as a whole. The possibility ('*esaudisco le possibilità* [...] *modeste che mi restano di scrittore in proprio*') of unveiling hidden concepts or ideas is restated in his 'Nota del traduttore' to the translation of Joris-Karl Huysmans' *À rebours* (*Controcorrente*).[45] The preface[46] offers another point of comparison between Sbarbaro's different agendas when he translates the Ancients and when he deals with the Moderns:

> Traducevo allora a rottadicollo e accettai come accettavo qualunque proposta di traduzione, un po' per necessità familiari e più per *illudermi di scrivere ancora* [my emphasis]. Il testo che non conoscevo mi entusiasmò e scartai *Volupté* che pure in gran parte avevo tradotto, rispondendo che non mi sentivo all'altezza del compito. Era vero ma in realtà *smaniavo di provarmi col nuovo*.[47]
>
> I was translating like mad then and I accepted just like I accepted any translation proposal, partly from personal necessity and more *to deceive myself that I was still writing*. Text that I didn't know excited me and I rejected *Volupté* which I'd already translated most of, replying that I didn't feel up to the work. It was true but really *I was craving to test myself with something new*.

The author describes this period as incredibly intense as he was accepting every job offer he received. But this recollection should be taken with some caution. From the exchange of letters it has been possible to demonstrate that the authors to be translated were objects of intense discussion and that Sbarbaro refused to translate several works. Sbarbaro only translated what he felt he could do well, to use his own words.[48] However, from this passage we can draw two important points, namely his hope for a new creativity ('*e più per illudermi di scrivere ancora*') and the desire to deal with new poetic ideas ('*smaniavo di provarmi col nuovo*'). When translating the Moderns, the novelty represented by the *Other* fuels the illusion of an enrichment coming from an unknown, unexplored source. By contrast, the solemnity of the Ancient guides Sbarbaro towards a literal translation and at the same time inspires him, as we will see from the analysis of his translation of Greek tragedy, to revisit his poetic past, the essentiality of *Pianissimo*. In the light of the author's views on the scarcity of his poetic voice, which also becomes a recurrent theme in poetry, as Polato has noted,[49] this enrichment connected with translation activity is particularly meaningful and appeared to have brought solace and satisfaction to the poet. The vital role of poetic expression in Sbarbaro's life and the comparison between his creative writing and translation is further reinforced in a late letter (Spotorno, Gennaio-Maggio, 1967) to Enrico Falqui:

> Sono grato al poco che ho scritto in proprio, perché m'ha aiutato a vivere; ma chi sa che il mio meglio non sia nelle traduzioni.[50]
> I am grateful for the little I've written myself because it's helped me to live; but who knows whether the best I have written has not been translations.

Sbarbaro's approach to translation of Greek tragedy, especially the expression of *camminare sulla corda* as a symbol of an equilibrium between the co-existence of two poetic voices, has to be read in light of another image of the poetic Self elaborated by the poet in *Fuochi fatui*, from where it is possible to gather some useful information on Sbarbaro's ideas about poetics and his method as a translator.

The preface to the book, where the poet expresses the reasons behind writing it, devotes a significant passage to the role of translation as something connected to his poetic silence. Starting from the title of the preface and the epigraph, the book connects with the classical tradition. The title of the preface '*Ars (iners) poetica*' and the epigraph '*Absens ades / m'ardi velata lampada vicino*' starts an intricate web of classical references. The preface title '*Ars (iners) poetica*' immediately recalls Horace's *Ars poetica* but undermines the sense of an official declaration of poetics with the adjective *iners*, and perhaps it is linked to the idea of the poet as 'transcriber' and to the dimension '*sotto dettatura*' which will be discussed later. As Zoboli demonstrated, the direct source of the epigraph is Ovid's *Epistula ex Ponto* (2, 10, 49) written to his friend Pompeius Macer from his exile in Pontus ('*hic es et ignoras et ades celeberrimus absens*' – you are here, even if you don't know; even if you are absent, you are constantly present).[51] Pontani, who has devoted some attention to Sbarbaro's translation of Pascoli's Latin works, further problematizes the epigraph by interpreting the use of the adjective *absens* as a debt towards Pascoli. Pontani's reading of this passage as debt to Pascoli is supported by the fact that *absens* has been identified by Traina and Garboli as a thematic adjective in the Latin works of Pascoli, which were translated by Sbarbaro. In the light of this, Pontani quotes Pascoli's *Poesia* from *Canti di Castelvecchio* to further strengthen his point (I, ll. 1–5): '*Io sono una lampada ch'arda / soave!*' (I am a lamp that burns / sweet!) and (IV, ll. 55–9): '*o quella [scil. lampada] velata, che al fianco / t'addita*' (Oh that veiled one (the lamp) which at your side points to you).[52] Pontani interprets this nexus of references and echoes within the crucial theme of Sbarbaro's poetry, which is '*il santuario della famiglia*' (the sanctuary of family) to use a line from *Antigone* translated by Sbarbaro.[53] In Pascoli's poem quoted by Pontani, *lampada* refers to the poet's mother. At this point, the issue of Sbarbaro's dedications enriches the network of references. Pontani agrees with Zoboli's conjecture regarding the dedicatee of the book: Sbarbaro's dear friend Elena De Bosis Vivante. Pontani, also on the basis of Lagorio's study of Sbarbaro's lifelong relationship with Elena Vivante, interprets the rapport between the two friends as being similar to that of a mother and a son. The meaning of the *lampada* then is fully contextualized in a family dimension thanks to this web of hidden references and reasserts the centrality of the theme to Sbarbaro's poetics. The family theme expressed by this epigraph is not the only connection with the myth of Antigone. The term *lampada* in fact was used by Sbarbaro long before he had translated Pascoli's Latin poems, and it appears in Sbarbaro's translation of the *Antigone* as almost a perfect transliteration of the Greek term λαμπάδος (torch). It is in the fourth episode where Antigone dialogues with the chorus and she is preparing herself to be buried alive in the cave (ll. 877–82). The passage contains the key theme of the Eros denied to Antigone and her subsequent marginalization and creation of a parallel universe in the underworld where she will rebuild her family nest and her funereal wedding will take place. With this choice, Sbarbaro colours the epigraph with all the nuances mentioned above and anticipates one of the main themes of the book, the memory of the beloved family members.[54] The preface to *Fuochi fatui* can therefore be considered a manifesto where Sbarbaro invites the reader to consider the entire trajectory of his poetic quest and to read the various books as connected by his ultimate objective, the '*ritratto*' (portait). The book, presented after some years of silence, institutes a connection between the poet's translations and his last book, and the poet comments on his fragmentary ideas which he refers to as asterisks:

Il giorno che mi trovai in capo il primo di questi asterischi (per gratitudine accolto tra gli altri), nel trasferirlo a buon conto sulla carta, non mi immaginavo che m' era venuto in mano il bandolo di una matassina che, cinque anni dopo, ancora non avrei finito di dipanare. [...] Ma questa volta uscivo da un silenzio durato tre lustri (il periodo delle frenetiche traduzioni): inevitabile il sospetto di aver per strada perduto la voce e il bisogno d'una riprova fuor di me.[55]

The day when I found the first of these asterisks (out of gratitude collected with the others) in my head, in transferring it in any case to paper, I did not imagine that there had come into my hands the end of a skein which, five years later, I would not yet have finished unravelling. [...] But this time I was coming out of a silence that had lasted three *lustri* (the period of frenetic translations): the suspicion of having lost my voice on the way and the need for a confirmation from outside of myself was inevitable.

Sbarbaro's suspicion of having lost his personal voice during his translation activity is further complicated by his comparison between himself as a poet and a transcriber:

Capii allora che come a scrivere non m'ero rimesso di proposito, era illusione credere che di proposito potessi smettere; nato da sé, *senza mio intervento altro che quello di decifrare e trascrivere*, anche questa volta il libretto da sé si sarebbe fatto a mio scapito o vantaggio non importa se era necessario. Ancora una volta obbedivo: [...] al bisogno [...] di compiere insomma il ritratto, spero non solo mio, al quale chiamato mi misi da quando fui in grado di esprimermi.[56]

I understood then that just as I had not started writing on purpose, it was delusion to believe that I could, on purpose, stop; born by itself without any intervention from me other than that of deciphering and transcribing, this time also the little book would be done by itself to my detriment or advantage, no matter if it was necessary. Again, I obeyed [...] the need [...] to complete the portrait, I hope not only my own, to which I have been called ever since I was able to express myself.

The dimension of *scrivere sotto dettatura* is expressed again in the pages immediately following the preface of *Fuochi fatui*:

Scrittore, lavorai sempre a intermittenza; [...] Di non avvertire alcuna sollecitazione a scrivere, accettavo con la stessa passività con cui, avvertendola, vi avevo ubbidito. Non mi misi mai di proposito davanti a un foglio bianco;

per aver pubblicato, non sentii mai d'aver contratto impegni, neppure con me stesso. *Lavorai* non è quindi la parola giusta; se la frase non si prestasse a interpretazioni metafisiche, direi che scrissi sempre sotto dettatura.[57]

As a writer, I always worked intermittently; [...] Not feeling any insistence to write, I accepted with the same passivity with which, having felt it, I would have obeyed. I never purposefully put myself in front of a blank page; not having published, I never felt that I had made any commitments, not even to myself. I *worked* is therefore not the right word; if the phrase did not lend itself to metaphysical interpretation, I would say that I always wrote under dictation.

The dimension of writing *sotto dettatura*, or as simply 'transcribing', recalls the image of the translator *che cammina sulla corda* and connects the two figures more strongly if we think that the book was written during the period when Sbarbaro's activity as a translator was particularly intense. Both images allude to a limited space for intervention. The comparison becomes meaningful because the metaphor of *camminare sulla corda* was elaborated by Sbarbaro when he was translating Sophocles' *Antigone*. The image of writing *sotto dettatura*, used by Sbarbaro in relation to his own poetry, stresses the poet's limited freedom and connects with the translator's role. As we have seen before, the direct contact with the text and the mediation between his voice and that of the author translated was expressed in his stylistic development which Sbarbaro identified in the pace of the phrase, the rhythm and the lexical choices. Furthermore, his translating experience and the exegetic contact with the ancient texts prompted to him poetic reflections expressed in his last book. Another example of how Sbarbaro connects the possible evolution of the links between words and images to the activity of translations can be found again in the *Fuochi fatui* 1940–5 sections:

> Dopo anni di silenzio, capita che le parole più prendano in bocca un sapore, uno spicco insoliti. Lievitano, si direbbe; aggallano da sé, precise e insieme ispirate. È il vocabolario che si rivergina come alla sua stagione l'albero rinverdisce. Capisco allora che sarebbe tornato il tempo di esprimermi, ma esito ad approfittarne come a entrare in acqua chi teme dopo tanto tempo d'aver disappreso a nuotare.[58]

After years of silence it happens that the words take on a flavour in the mouth, an unusual relevance. They grow, one could say; they fertilise on their own, both precise and inspired. It is the vocabulary that becomes new like the tree that becomes green again with the new season. I understand then that the time to express myself will return, but I hesitate in taking advantage of it, like entering water after so much time that one fears one's forgotten how to swim.

Lexical choice is here deeply connected to the regenerative function which is implicitly attributed to translation. The temporal indication *dopo anni di silenzio* (after years of silence) hints at the period devoted to translation which can be read as an incubator for words, for the re-creation of the fleshly bond described by Sbarbaro between the word and his poetic Self. The *parole precise e ispirate* are the result of a process of rejuvenation of Sbarbaro's poetic vocabulary produced by silence and translation. The novelty, the refreshment here alluded to is the benefit coming from translation where Sbarbaro experiences the word of the *other* (deriving from it a new colour), feeds his hope for new poetic inspiration (*illudermi di scrivere ancora*) and prompts him to rethink his poetic past. Translation of Greek tragedy, on account of the thematic consistency with Sbarbaro's poetic ideas and the formal equilibrium between prose and poetry, offered him a major opportunity to rejuvenate his poetic vocabulary and to find the poetic inspiration necessary to write his last book.

Sbarbaro's Interlinear Translation

The *poetica dell' aderenza* (poetics of adherence) was outlined by Sbarbaro himself in an exchange of letters between the poet and Valentino Bompiani.[59] The letters revolve around the complicated editorial history of *The Cyclops*, which Sbarbaro translated first in prose and then in verse.[60] His translations of Greek tragedies aimed at adherence to the original ('*aspirano soprattutto ad essere quanto possibile aderenti al testo*'),[61] but *The Cyclops* was translated with different criteria, mostly that of complete reinvention, and this translation was considered a proper rewriting rather than a faithful rendition. This is the reason behind Sbarbaro's decision to withdraw *The Cyclops* from the series where *Antigone* and *Prometheus Bound* had already been published. The *poetica dell' aderenza* is also the differentiating element in his translation of the Classics from that of French authors. As emerges from a letter addressed to Giovanna Bemporad, Sbarbaro describes his method of translating Zola's *Germinal* as '*infedelissimo*':

> Cara Giovanna, (il foglietto è macchiato di caffè. Non farci caso). Ho letto subito la tua *Elettra* e si è rinnovata la mia ammirazione per il tuo modo di tradurre; questa volta, non conosco e non potrei leggere il testo; ma sento che come per Omero la traduzione è insieme aderentissima eppure un'opera d'arte a sé. Ben diverso il mio modo di tradurre perché sono infedelissimo (*Germinal*, per esempio, l'ho tradito; da romanzo terreo, tetro è diventato quasi... giocoso).[62]
>
> Dear Giovanna (the page is stained with coffee. Take no notice). I read your *Electra* immediately and it renewed my admiration for your style of translating: this time I don't know and couldn't read the text; but I feel that, like for Homer, the translation is both extremely close and a work of art in its own right. Very different from my way of translating because I am unfaithful (for example, I've betrayed *Germinal*; from an earthy, gloomy novel it's become almost... playful).

It is evident from this letter that the translation process is very different from what is previously found in his exchange of letters with Rodocanachi, Falqui and Bompiani. In this passage the author even puns with the topos *tradurre-tradire*. Literal translation is thus not a consistent approach to all translation by Sbarbaro but, I argue, specific to his versions of Greek tragedy. The aim of literal translation can be better understood in the light of a significant incident recalled by critic Carlo Bo who happened to be in a class taught by Sbarbaro for a few months. His memory confirms Sbarbaro's use of the literal approach while stressing the poet's originality in the learning process:

> Io sono in grado di portare [...] una testimonianza diretta perché ho avuto la fortuna di avere Sbarbaro come insegnante di greco, sia pure per pochi mesi: comunque quel breve periodo è stato sufficiente per fornirmi dei dati che hanno poi soccorso la mia natura di lettore. Tanto per cominciare Sbarbaro non era un professore né insegnava come un professore: era piuttosto un innovatore senza dirlo ma sicuro del proprio metodo che era poi quello della partecipazione, della comunicazione fra discente e docente. Leggeva in quell'anno 1928 che facevo la seconda liceo l'*Antigone* e la leggeva come si legge una notizia di cronaca su un giornale: parola per parola, quasi si trattasse di una traduzione interlineare, senza commenti estetici, senza riferimenti storici, ma con appena qualche rapida e marginale notazione che doveva aiutare lo studente a non perdere il punto centrale della tragedia. Era un modo di lavorare umilissimo e che a qualche spettatore o uomo del mestiere avrebbe anche potuto apparire pedestre ma l'impegno del professor

Sbarbaro era proprio quello di non aggiungere nulla che potesse distorcere il senso originale del testo, nulla che suonasse come inutile amplificazione retorica. Anche da questo punto di vista per Sbarbaro contava soltanto il testo: non faceva sfoggio di scienza filologica che pure possedeva né – tanto meno – si richiamava alle estetiche di moda di quel tempo.[63]

I am in a position to offer [...] a direct testimony because I was fortunate to have Sbarbaro as a teacher of Greek, though only for a few months: in any case that short period was sufficient to supply me with information that then aided my nature as a reader. To begin with, Sbarbaro was not a professor and did not teach like a professor: he was rather an innovator without saying so but sure of his own method which was that of participation, of communication between teacher and student. In 1928, when I was in the second year of college, he was reading *Antigone* and he read it as one reads a report in the newspaper: word for word, it was almost an interlinear translation, without aesthetic comments, without historical references but with just a few brief and marginal notes to help the student to not lose the core of the tragedy. It was a very humble way of working and which to some spectators or men of the trade could even have appeared uninspiring, but Professor Sbarbaro's task was precisely that of not adding anything that could distort the original meaning of the text, nothing that would sound like useless rhetorical flourishes. From this point of view too, only the text counted for Sbarbaro: he didn't flaunt philology which of course he possessed, let alone refer to the fashionable aesthetics of the time.

Sbarbaro's attention to the single word ('*parola per parola*') is part of a pedagogic discourse, which I will discuss in Chapter 4 of this book. Philological and aesthetic expertise, though present, is muted to maintain focus on the text itself. Sbarbaro's didactic methodology coincides with his translation approach. The scant remarks made by the poet were understood by Bo as Sbarbaro's way of helping the student to better understand the core of the tragedy. The passage confirms the poet's rejection of rhetorical amplification, the *svolazzi* mentioned in the letters quoted previously. The literal translation, here described by Bo as almost interlinear, however, is not disconnected from a structured interpretative effort.

Between 1900 and 1928 there had been fundamental works by philosophers and scholars on translation issues. The debate brought to the fore the importance of translation as a linguistic practice and generated a broad theoretical debate which laid the foundations for the future of translation studies. Walter Benjamin's seminal essay 'The Task of the Translator' was published in 1923, five years before Sbarbaro's first encounter with the translation of the *Antigone*. It is very unlikely that Sbarbaro could have read the essay. However, Benjamin's argument can help to illuminate Sbarbaro's methodology. Benjamin ends his essay with a comparison between the translation of Sophocles and that of the Holy Scriptures. Benjamin points to a difference between a text in which there is a risk of the sense being lost in the depths of language, referring to Sophocles, and a text where there is no need for a mediation on meaning as it is immediately apparent, as in the case of the Holy Scriptures. The dimension of the revelation, in its Judaic meaning, and the rationale connected to it are absent from Sophocles and from tragedy as a whole, as Steiner demonstrated.[64] Yet Greek tragedy is the place where the concept of revelation and unveiling of truth worked not only as a narrative engine but also as the interpretative key to the ultimate meaning of ethics and morality. The consequences that such truths unveiled generated a vigorous debate on morality and ethics for which tragedy has become, especially for the modern audience, the archetype. Going back to Benjamin's question at the end of his essay, it is worth asking what kind of consequences the dimension of revelation produces in translation. For Benjamin the whole issue becomes a matter of trust since 'just as language and revelation must be united in text, literalness and freedom must be united in the form of interlinear translation. For to some degree all great writings, but above all the Holy Scriptures, contain their virtual translations between the lines. The interlinear version of the Holy Scriptures is the prototype or ideal of all translation.'[65]

Benjamin's argument can be applied to Sbarbaro's translation of Greek tragedy. His literal translation pursues the objective of re-creating a text, which naturally reveals itself through the word ordering. In the light of this interpretation Sbarbaro's use of literal translation and his fondness for a word order that reflects the original as well as the re-creation of rhetorical devices when possible acquire a profounder meaning.[66] After having examined the overlap between the figure of the translator and that of the writer as both oriented by the voice of the *Other* as we saw in the cross-analysis of the collection of letters and *Fuochi fatui*, the choice of literal translation reveals an ideological intention. Sbarbaro builds his translation of Greek tragedy from an understanding of the text, which can be defined as almost 'biblical'. The reverential attitude towards the text and the idea that only a literal translation would be suitable are implicitly informed by Sbarbaro's conviction that by reproducing the Greek word ordering the revelation aspect in the original would become available to the modern reader as well. Aesthetic interpretation or other rhetorical devices should not obscure the core of the tragedy, which was the ultimate goal of Sbarbaro's translation. In this essentialist interpretation, which is, however, not deprived of ideology and can indeed be read for interpretative clues as well, lies Sbarbaro's method and understanding of Greek tragedy. Uprooted from its religious and political context, Greek tragedy becomes for Sbarbaro the occasion to rethink his own poetic images and to augment his poetic vocabulary. Translating word for word meant for Sbarbaro a *journey* through his own personal poetic vocabulary which led him to a rethinking of his first poetic experience of *Pianissimo*.

The quest for what Bo called 'the core of tragedy' ('*il punto centrale della tragedia*') was indeed the quest for his poetic awareness stimulated by the grand themes of humankind as contained in the poetic archetype of Greek tragedy. Benjamin's reference to Hölderlin's *Antigone* helps us to interpret what Sbarbaro meant by the core of the tragedy: it is similar to Hölderlin's quest for the *Grundton*, the general colour of the text sought by the German poet in his *Antigone*. Antoine Berman in his essay *Hölderlin: le national et l'étranger* described how the poet-translator fostered a methodology in which literal translation merged with the interest in etymology, producing what we can call an *etymologizing literalness*.[67] The example used by Berman to demonstrate this mechanism is *Antigone*'s line 20, in the prologue, when Ismene asks Antigone the reason for her troubled mood: 'Τί δ' ἔστι; δηλοῖς γάρ τι καλχαίνουσ' ἔπος.' It is worthwhile comparing Sbarbaro's translation of this line with that of Hölderlin. The German poet translates the line as '*Was ist's, du scheinst ein rottes Wort zu färben*', which translated into English would be: 'What's the matter? You seem to paint a red/purple word.' Sbarbaro's translation reads: '*Che è? Sento che ribolli d'una parola che t'urge dentro*.'[68] What we can see here is the fact that both translations pursue the same desire to go to the primary meaning of the word καλχαίνω which literally means 'to make purple'. The difference is that Sbarbaro aims at maintaining meaning rather than pursuing a literality that would almost confine with the absurd, as it is in Hölderlin's case. Sbarbaro therefore avoids what Benjamin denounced as one of the dangers of the literal translation: 'Hölderlin's translations are subject to an enormous danger inherent in all translation: the gates of a language thus expanded and modified may slam shut and enclose the translator with silence.'[69]

Using the word 'ribolle' Sbarbaro in fact activates the Italian native speaker link between the verb *ribollire* (to boil) and the noun *sangue* (blood) thus re-creating the etymological meaning of καλχαίνω through the expression 'ti ribolle il sangue'. Sbarbaro does not get lost in the depths of language: he pursues meaning while maintaining the etymological meaning of καλχαίνω. In addition to this, Sbarbaro colours the line with a concept very dear to his poetics: the urgency of the word ('una parola che t'urge dentro'). The interest in literality as a means to access the core of the tragedy, the etymological research and the respect for the word ordering are indicative of Sbarbaro's meditation on the text of Greek tragedy as guided by a precise desire to make the text reveal itself through the original collocation of words without depriving it of its meaning.

The Translation of Sophocles' *Antigones*: Lyric and Dramatic Solutions

Sbarbaro's poetic oeuvre contains two passages that come from the translation of Greek tragedy, where lines of the text translated become part of his poetic memory and surface in his writings. It is not a systematic operation but much more a free associative mental mechanism. However, the insertion is interesting as it unveils the interiorization of a portion of text and its place in the author's poetic memory. The quotation of the first line of *Antigone*'s stasimon is found in *Cartoline in franchigia: Lettere a Angelo Barile* (1966):[70]

> Con pezzi di carbon fossile perduti da qualche carro ho scritto sugli scogli tra Varigotti e Noli *l'eros anicate machan* ... E' Marzo, c'è il sole e presto a capo Matapan fiorirà la *Lavatera maritima*. È come già sentissi cantare le campane di Pasqua e m'accorgo ogni giorno più di amare la vita...[71]
>
> With pieces of fossilized carbon fallen from some cart, I wrote on the rocks between Varigotti and Noli *l'eros anicate machan* ... It is March, it is sunny and soon *Lavatera maritima* will bloom at Cape Matapan. It is as if I already heard ringing the bells of Easter and I notice every day that I love life more.

The line, quoted by Sbarbaro as a transliteration, is extrapolated from the third stasimon of *Antigone* (ll.781–805) where the chorus sings a hymn to Aphrodite and Eros. The stasimon employs the vocabulary of war, which is consistent with the previous argument between Haemon and Kreon, and describes the power of Eros who can reduce into slavery even the wisest people or Gods. The tragic wedding between Antigone and Haemon which will follow, and the morbid identification between eros and death represented by the wedding in the underworld, is anticipated by this ode to the invincible power of Eros:

Χορός
Ἔρως ἀνίκατε μάχαν,
Ἔρως, ὃς ἐν κτήμασι πίπ-
τεις, ὃς ἐν μαλακαῖς παρει-
αῖς νεάνιδος ἐννυχεύεις,
φοιτᾷς δ' ὑπερπόντιος ἔν τ'
ἀγρονόμοις αὐλαῖς·
καί σ' οὔτ' ἀθανάτων φύξιμος οὐδεὶς
οὔθ' ἁμερίων σέ γ' ἀνθρώ-
πων. ὁ δ' ἔχων μέμηνεν.
Σὺ καὶ δικαίων ἀδίκους
φρένας παρασπᾷς ἐπὶ λώ-
βαι, σὺ καὶ τόδε νεῖκος ἀνδρῶν ξύναιμον ἔχεις ταράξασ·
νικᾷ δ' ἐναργὴς βλεφάρων
ἵμερος εὐλέκτρου
νύμφας, τῶν μεγάλων πάρεδρος ἐν ἀρχαῖς
θεσμῶν. ἄμαχος γὰρ ἐμπαί-
ζει θεὸς, Ἀφροδίτα.

Coro
Amore invincibile in battaglia,
amore che su chi piombi lo fai schiavo;
che sulle morbide gote
della fanciulla stai in agguato
e t'aggiri sul mare e nelle agresti capanne;
da te né degli Eterni alcuno può scampare
né degli uomini effimeri; e chi ti ha è fuor
                              [di senno.
Tu anche dei giusti, rendendoli ingiusti,

travii con un urto da nulla la ragione e li
    [avvii a rovina;
tu anche questa contesa
tra consanguinei hai suscitato.
Ma trionfa, lampeggiando dalle ciglia, l'u-
    [mido sguardo dell'amabile
fanciulla, pari in comando alle grandi
leggi: senza combattere si piglia gioco di noi
    [la dea Afrodite.[72]

Love, the unconquered in battle, Love, you who descend upon riches, and watch the night through on a girl's soft cheek, you roam over the sea and among the homes of men in the wilds. Neither can any immortal escape you, nor any man whose life lasts for a day. He who has known you is driven to madness. You seize the minds of just men and drag them to injustice, to their ruin. You it is who have incited this conflict of men whose flesh and blood are one. But victory belongs to radiant Desire swelling from the eyes of the sweet-bedded bride. Desire sits enthroned in power beside the mighty laws. For in all this divine Aphrodite plays her irresistible game.[73]

The passage exemplifies the translator's attention to the respect for word order, the predilection of maintaining the position of the verb at the end of the sentence in order to colour the passage with a lyrical tone. Sbarbaro's interpretative effort is particularly evident in the lexical choices and in the creation of a metaphor which will become a constant in the other tragedies translated and it will inform a variant of a poem from *Pianissimo*. In the original Greek, the passage is built circularly: the end of the ode reconnects with the first line and reasserts the lack of logic in the situation and the weakness of human beings. Eros is invincible while Aphrodite mocks everyone without even fighting. The playful dimension of the last line links with the light tone and the remark on youth ('che sulle morbide gote / della fanciulla stai in agguato'; desire swelling from the eyes of the sweet-bedded bride) which had previously introduced a series of contrasts annihilated by the power of Eros. The element of youth is also the occasion for the poet to translate ἵμερος, the term for erotic desire, with a striking image: 'l'umido sguardo dell'amabile fanciulla'. To fully understand the reason for this change we need to consider that tears are, in Sbarbaro's poetry, the final springs of life against the dryness of the alienated

Self, represented by the correlative objective of the stone (a natural element very present in *Pianissimo*). Erotic desire is always paired with a sense of guilt in the poet's perceptions but is also the engine which prompts self-consciousness and awareness of a state of marginalization, especially in *Pianissimo*.[74] In this passage, Sbarbaro creates an identification between eros and tears, absent in the original, on the basis of his reading of Antigone's destiny. Through the negation of eros, explicitly lamented by Antigone in the fourth episode (l. 877, ἀνυμέναιος, unwedded) when she is preparing to be buried alive and to reconnect with her family already in the underworld, the heroine perceives her marginalization from society which condemns her to death. The use of this image is guided by the reading of the power of Eros made by Sbarbaro. This pair of eros and death becomes a common thread uniting the translations of *Antigone* and *Alcestis*. The metaphor of 'ciglia umide' is consistently elaborated in the two tragedies and appears to have informed the variant 'ciglio asciutto' in the poem *Padre che muori tutti giorni un poco* (Father you who are every day dying a little) from *Pianissimo*. The evolution from the 'occhio asciutto' (in the 1914 edtion) to the 'ciglio asciutto' (in the 1960 edition) is probably inspired by the passages translated. The correction should be read in the light of Sbarbaro's translation of the epilogue of *Alcestis* at ll. 1046–8:

Ἄδμητος
    οὐκ ἂν δυναίμην τήνδ᾽ ὁρῶν ἐν δώμασιν
    ἄδακρυς εἶναι: μὴ νοσοῦντί μοι νόσον
    προσθῇς: ἅλις γὰρ συμφορᾷ βαρύνομαι

Admeto
Non richiamarmi a mente con quest'incarico la mia sciagura. A vedere questa donna aggirarsi per la reggia restare a ciglio asciutto non potrei.[75]

Do not remind me of my troubles. For if I were to see this woman in my house, I could not hold back my tears.[76]

Sbarbaro derives inspiration from the translations of these passages and inserts the metonymy as a variant in *Padre che muori tutti giorni un poco*, one of the most important within the collection for it brings together the conflictual relationship with the father. Faced with his father, the poet has the *ciglio asciutto* (dry eye) and throughout the poem he restates his inability to cry in front of him thus stressing the state of erotic paralysis and inhibition created by the father. The paralysis has a profounder meaning: in Sbarbaro erotic desire is the mechanism that arouses awareness of man's alienation just like the poetic word does. The inhibition of erotic desire therefore implicitly suggests the poet's incapability of performing the poetic act, conceived as a moral duty.

The metonymy of 'ciglio' used for the eyes is employed again to describe Admetus mourning Alcestis' death at ll. 597–605:

Χορός
καὶ νῦν δόμον ἀμπετάσας
δέξατο ξεῖνον νοτερῷ βλεφάρῳ,
τᾶς φίλας κλαίων ἀλόχου νέκυν ἐν
δώμασιν ἀρτιθανῆ:

Coro
Pur oggi la casa spalancandogli,
accolse, sebbene avesse umido il ciglio, lo straniero;
sebbene la cara moglie piangesse
da poco morta in casa.[77]

And now, throwing open the gates of his house, he has received a guest though his own eyes were wet, weeping for the loss of his dear wife so recently perished in his house.[78]

The intersection of the theme of tears and eros is further expanded and enriched by Sbarbaro in his translation of the *Antigone* and *Alcestis* where the pair intermingles with a family context. The centrality of the theme of family in Sbarbaro's poetry is restated in the figures of the two Greek heroines who are deeply entangled with a dark destiny. If Sbarbaro reaffirms the importance of family in these tragedies, it is always in a funereal dimension. His identification with Antigone is at its strongest when the heroine longs for the underworld metaphorically expressed by the pair sleep-death, two personifications very present in Sbarbaro's collection of poems *Pianissimo*. Squarotti[79] has demonstrated how Sbarbaro annihilated the superiority of the 'nido pascoliano' as the ultimate shelter for the preservation of the human element, by asserting the co-existence of family affection and its dissolution into alienation, especially evident in the poem *Esco dalla lussuria* (I leave lust).[80] The funereal dimension of Antigone and Alcestis, with the re-creation of a parallel life in the underworld after being rejected by their own family affection, reinforces Sbarbaro's mythopoietic act. Through these translations what is openly reasserted is the poet's awareness of the absurdity of human existence and the total alienation of the human being who can find no solace in family, love, friendship or any other human relationship. On the basis of this conception of poetry the relationship between the pair sleep and death becomes a fundamental one and it is the main theme orienting Sbarbaro's translation of *Antigone* and *Alcestis*, heroines who respond to the marginalization and cruelty imposed by society by choosing a life amongst the dead. This theme finds a perfect fit in Antigone's re-creation of her family nest in the underworld, a passage which Sbarbaro intensively reworks. This is a passage where Antigone is comparing her destiny to that of another heroine, Niobe, and in this way she anticipates her own future, that of being imprisoned alive in a cave by Kreon. In the fourth episode, Antigone is having a dialogue with the chorus who are lamenting her miserable fate. The theme of wandering and walking towards the last light introduces Antigone's speech (ll. 823–33) which unveils the major topics of Sbarbaro's poetics:

Ἀντιγόνη
 τὰν κισσὸς ὡς ἀτενὴς
 πετραία βλάστα δάμασεν,
 καί νιν ὄμβροι τακομέναν,
 ὡς φάτις ἀνδρῶν,
 χιών τ᾽ οὐδαμὰ λείπει,
 τέγγει δ᾽ ὑπ᾽ ὀφρύσι παγκλαύτοις
 δειράδας: ᾇ με
 δαίμων ὁμοιοτάταν κατευνάζει.

Antigone
 A guisa d'edera tenace
 una vegetazione di pietra
 la imprigionò. Lei che si strugge, piogge
 – è fama –
 e neve mai lasciano;
 e bagna dalle ciglia sempre in pianto i fian-
  [chi. Ad essa, me
 somigliantissima il destino mette a dormire.[81]

How, like clinging ivy, the sprouting stone subdued her. And the rains, as men tell, do not leave her melting form, nor does the snow, but beneath her weeping lids she dampens her collar. Most like hers is the god-sent fate that leads me to my rest.[82]

The stone is the correlative objective recalling the poet's condition of aridity. The vegetation, usually a positive element in Sbarbaro's poetry, in the form of ivy creates a prison where the Self is caged and alienated. Then the natural elements of the snow and rain anticipate the theme of tears again expressed by the 'ciglia' metonymy and introduce the allegory of death. The translation of the syntagm δαίμων κατευνάζω with 'il destino mette a dormire' while being a literal and faithful translation is also resonant of one of Sbarbaro's main poetic themes: the intersection between the personification of sleep and death as an inescapable destiny. In the poem *Sonno, dolce fratello della Morte* this connection is evident:

> Sonno dolce fratello della Morte,
> che dalla vita per un po' ci affranchi
> ma ci rilasci tosto in sua balia
> come gatto che gioca con il gomitolo;
> di te, finché la mia vita giustifichi
> la vita della mia sorella e un segno
> che son vissuto anch'io finché non lasci,
> io mi contenterò e del tuo inganno.[83]

> Sleep, sweet brother of death
> you who free us for a little from life
> but soon release us into its mercy
> like a cat that plays with a ball of wool;
> as long as my life justifies
> the life of my sister and a sign
> that I too lived as long as you allow,
> I will be glad of you and your deception.

Sbarbaro's characteristic stylistic features such as the postposition of the verb and the use of punctuation to achieve a paratactic pace of the phrase recur in the translations while mingling with the principle of respecting word ordering and the interest in morphological calques. But if the punctuation in his original poetry was used to create an oscillating rhythm, in the translations Sbarbaro exploits this tool to intervene in the text in two directions: to isolate nuclei dear to his poetics and to enlarge rhythmical units in Italian which would re-create the original length of the Greek metre. Especially in the lyric sections the literal translation and the desire to adhere to the original, conveyed by the respect for word order, intermingle with the poet's interpretative effort and stylistic goals.

An example of the use of punctuation which helps the poet to problematize a passage where one of Sbarbaro's main themes is encapsulated at the very beginning of the prologue of *Antigone*, at ll. 1–10:

Ἀντιγόνη
ὦ κοινὸν αὐτάδελφον Ἰσμήνης κάρα,
ἆρ' οἶσθ' ὅ τι Ζεὺς τῶν ἀπ' Οἰδίπου κακῶν
ὁποῖον οὐχὶ νῷν ἔτι ζώσαιν τελεῖ;

Antigone
Mia compagna di destino, sorella cara,
Ismene, del retaggio di Edipo sai un male,
sai quale, Zeus non avvererà mentre noi
due siamo ancora in vita?[84]

Ismene, my sister, true child of my own mother, do you know any evil out of all the evils bequeathed by Oedipus that Zeus will not fulfil for the two of us in our lifetime?[85]

Sbarbaro's interpretative effort is subtle yet evident. The poet isolates the sister within the first sentence: he stresses its grammatical function (apposition) through the insertion of two commas, separates it from 'Ismene', which is moved to the beginning of the second verse, and refers 'κάρα' (head) directly to the sister ('sorella cara' – beloved sister). The poet maintains the phonetic similarity between 'κάρα' and 'cara' as well as the position within the sentence. The lexical choices are also indicative of Sbarbaro's revealing work on the text. Translating κοινὸν (common) with 'compagna' (companion) is ambiguous if we consider the use of the term in Sbarbaro's poetry. The term is in fact often paired with the word 'perdizione' as we can see from at least three occurrences in *Pianissimo*. Sbarbaro by choosing the word 'compagna' in this translation is also evoking this link with perdition and proposing the co-existence of myth of family affection in an erotic context thanks to a lexical choice. This aspect has been identified by George Steiner as one of the key factors determining the huge success enjoyed by *Antigone* for the entire nineteenth century. In the first part of his book *Antigones*, Steiner traces the reasons which consecrated Sophocles' *Antigone* as the most perfect work of art ever produced according to Idealist and Romantic criteria. One of the reasons he offers is that in the relationship between brother and sister the issue of sexuality, and the estrangement inherent in it, are present yet sublimated in the element of φιλία.[86] Sbarbaro's translation and his lexical choice do not achieve the positive synthesis proposed by Steiner in the element of sisterliness as a means to defy alienation. On the contrary the author maintains the tension between the erotic and family spheres by creating ambiguity. This aspect is further enriched by another connotation of the term *compagna* in the poem *Ora che non mi dici niente* (Now that you say nothing to me). The text is a hymn to *Dolore* as the only feeling perceived as possible by the alienated poetic Self. The numb condition ('mi tocco per sentire se sono': I touch myself to feel if I exist) depicted in the middle of the poem introduces the description of a life which cannot be lived, but is always seen from the outside, from the detached condition of the poet. In this passage, Sbarbaro uses the term *compagna*, which refers to this usual condition of not feeling anything, and it prepares for the invocation of *Dolore* which pairs with the personification of life (*Vita*):

> [T]'odio, compagna assidua dei miei giorni,
> che alla vita non mi sottrai, facendomi
> come il sonno una cosa inanimata,
> ma me la lasci solo rasentare.
> [...]
> Voglio il Dolore che m'abbranchi forte
> e collochi nel centro della Vita.[87]

> I hate you, constant companion of my days,
> you who do not steal me from life, like sleep
> making me an inanimate thing,
> but let me only skirt it.
> [...]
> I want the Pain that grips me strongly
> and sits in the centre of Life.

The term *compagna* is also more explicitly referred to another personification in Sbarbaro's poetry. This is in the poem *Nel mio povero sangue qualche volta* (In my poor blood sometimes), from *Pianissimo*, where the poetic Self is now experiencing the other condition of his double situation. Alienation, the numb condition and dryness alternate with a stark desire to live, identified by Sbarbaro with the pair of pleasure and pain which are always connected with the presence of death ('Mi cresce l'ansia dentro di morire / senza avere il godibile goduto / senza aver il soffribile sofferto': within me grows the anxiety of dying / without having enjoyed the enjoyable / without having suffered the sufferable). In the same poem the personification of perdition, *Perdizione*, is paired with *compagna*:

> [C]on per compagna la Perdizione
> a cuor leggero andarmene pel mondo.[88]

> With Perdition as companion
> with a light heart I go through the world

The term 'compagna', however, maintains an ambivalent vestige in the light of another poem where Sbarbaro explicitly mentions his sister and their journey through life. It is the poem *Forse un giorno, sorella, noi potremo* (One day perhaps, sister, we will be able to), from *Pianissimo*:

> Forse un giorno, sorella, noi potremo
> ritirarci sui monti, in una casa,
> dove passare il resto della vita.
> Sarà il padre con noi anche se morto.
> Noi lo vedremo muoversi per casa.
> E allora capirà tutto il dolore
> che traversammo uniti per la mano,
> tu, la vita, sorella, senza amore,
> io la vita, sorella, senza inganni.
> [...]
> E vivremo così in compagnia
> dei maggior fratelli, i fiumi e i boschi,
> pacificati con la nostra sorte.
> Perché ciò sia, sorella, io faccio patto
> che il mio dolore duri quanto me,
> anzi di giorno in giorno mi s'accresca.[89]

> Perhaps one day, sister, we will be able to
> retire to the mountains, to a house
> in which to spend the rest of our lives.

Father will be with us even if he is dead.
We will see him move about the house.
And then he will understand all the pain
That we passed through hand in hand,
you, sister, a life without love,
I, sister, a life without deception.
[…]
And we will live thus in the company
of our older siblings, the rivers and the woods,
at peace with our fate.
For this to be, sister, I make a pact
that my pain lasts as long as myself,
indeed from day to day it grows in me.

The poem is significant inasmuch as the father's presence hovers over the siblings just as in *Antigone*'s prologue. The poem daydreams about the creation of a family nest, just as Antigone does in the fourth episode (ll. 891–902). The heroine connects death, eros and family: she identifies her graveyard with the wedding chamber and the only joys she can derive from this identification is that of seeing in the underworld the rest of her family:

Ἀντιγόνη
ὦ τύμβος, ὦ νυμφεῖον, ὦ κατασκαφὴς
οἴκησις ἀείφρουρος, οἷ πορεύομαι
πρὸς τοὺς ἐμαυτῆς, ὧν ἀριθμὸν ἐν νεκροῖς
πλεῖστον δέδεκται Φερσέφασσ᾽ ὀλωλότων:
[…]
ἐλθοῦσα μέντοι κάρτ᾽ ἐν ἐλπίσιν τρέφω
φίλη μὲν ἥξειν πατρί, προσφιλὴς δὲ σοί,
μῆτερ, φίλη δὲ σοί, κασίγνητον κάρα:
ἐπεὶ θανόντας αὐτόχειρ ὑμᾶς ἐγὼ
ἔλουσα κἀκόσμησα κἀπιτυμβίους
χοὰς ἔδωκα.

Antigone
O tomba, stanza nuziale, sotterranea dimora che per sempre mi guarderai, dove i miei raggiungerò che quasi tutti già Persefone ha accolto tra i morti!

[...]
Là tuttavia ho ferma speranza che il mio
arrivo sarà gradito a te, padre; a te, madre; caro a te, mio fratello beneamato, se,
morti di mia mano vi lavai e composi e
versai libagioni sulla vostra tomba.[90]

> Tomb, bridal-chamber, deep-dug eternal prison where I go to find my own, whom in the greatest numbers destruction has seized and Persephone has welcomed among the dead! Last of them all and in by far the most shameful circumstances, I will descend, even before the fated term of my life is spent. But I cherish strong hopes that I will arrive welcome to my father, and pleasant to you, Mother, and welcome, dear brother, to you. For, when each of you died, with my own hands I washed and dressed you and poured drink-offerings at your graves.[91]

Going back to the poem it is interesting to see how the poet and his sister are together in the dimension of pain which differs for both of them: in a life without love, in the sister's case, and in a life without deception, in the poet's as he refers to his ruthless and fierce self-consciousness expressed by his poetic word. The pain (*dolore*) is personified in this poem (as it is in several other poems from *Pianissimo*), but it is described as a shared dimension which bonds the poet to his sister, just like Antigone to Ismene. The dimension of 'being together' is here rendered through the periphrasis 'uniti per la mano' whereas the semantic field of 'compagno, compagnia' is here used for the spiritual connection felt by Sbarbaro with the element of nature encapsulating the idea of a pre-established path of life thanks to the use of the word *sorte*: 'E vivremo così in compagnia / dei maggior fratelli, i fiumi e i boschi, / pacificati con la nostra sorte.' (and we will live like this in the company / of our elder brothers, the rivers and the woods, / at peace with our fate).

The translation of the beginning of the *Antigone* activates Sbarbaro's poetic memory and inspires him to make a few changes which are evident in the lexical choices and in the use of punctuation. The sister is identified as the interlocutor and is syntactically isolated by the use of commas. The choice of the word *compagna* (companion) recalls the two poles around which Sbarbaro's poetic experience is built: the alienated, cynical and dry condition of the poetic Self and the morbid desire for physical pleasure inextricably connected with death and sense of guilt. The syntagm *compagna di destino* unveils another intervention by Sbarbaro's poetic voice in the text and recalls a key notion of Greek tragedy: the belief that life is a pre-assigned condition of pain. Such a condition is always invoked and treasured by Sbarbaro as it represents the only link left with a non-alienated reality. The sister partakes of this condition of pain and this shared dimension temporarily bonds the poet to his family nucleus.

Another intervention in punctuation made by Sbarbaro in order to strengthen the images and to expand the rhythmical unit of verses, while keeping the word order, is found in the parodos of *Antigone*. The entrance at l. 100 of the chorus, composed of fifteen old men who are serving the city as a Council of Elders, introduces the setting of Thebes to the audience. The narrative of the parodos is encapsulated within the long descriptive and celebrative song. The chorus reminds us of the horrors of the wars, the threats of Polynices and finally exhorts the city to forget about the past war ll. 150-1 (ἐκ μὲν δὴ πολέμων / τῶν νῦν θέσθε λησμοσύναν; Finita la guerra, / di essa ora scordiamoci), to join Dionysus' dances and to celebrate all the gods. The beginning of the parodos was also a song in honour of the gods of Thebes.[92] The first lines are devoted to the light of the Sun, then the ode moves to celebrate Ares, Zeus, Victory and Dionysos:

Χορός

    ἀκτὶς ἀελίου, τὸ κάλ-
    λιστον ἑπταπύλωι φανὲν
    Θήβᾳ τῶν προτέρων φάος,
    ἐφάνθης ποτ' ὦ χρυσέας
    ἁμέρας βλέφαρον, Διρκαί-
    ων ὑπὲρ ῥεέθρων μολοῦσα,
    τὸν λεύκασπιν Ἀργόθεν ἐκβάντα φῶτα πανσαγίαι
    φυγάδα πρόδρομον ὀξυτέρωι χαλινῷ.

Coro

    Raggio del sole, la più bella – che sia spun –
      [tata su Tebe
    dalle sette porte – luce sino ad oggi,
    sei apparso finalmente, o dell'aureo
    giorno pupilla,
    sulle correnti dircee;

> e il biancoscudato guerriero venuto tutto
> [armato da Argo
> in fuga hai cacciato, e pianta ora, per te,
> [con più furia lo sprone nel cavallo.[93]

> Shaft of the sun, fairest light of all that have dawned on Thebes of the seven gates, you have shone forth at last, eye of golden day, advancing over Dirce's streams! You have goaded with a sharper bit the warrior of the white shield, who came from Argos in full armor, driving him to headlong retreat.[94]

Sbarbaro stretches the length of the opening lines by inserting a parenthetic clause. Through the use of punctuation, he introduces a pause that is not in the original. The image of sunlight (*raggio del sole*) begins the first line and expands to the end of the second one (*luce*). The city of Thebes sits between these images of light. The commas in the original are rendered with two dashes thus imposing a longer pause and yet respecting the original versification of the text and word order. In terms of imagery Sbarbaro maintains the two metaphors at the beginning of the parodos, the sun's ray and the 'pupil of the day'. He makes small changes aimed at enhancing the strength of the images. For instance, at ll. 108–9, the metaphor of the sun which makes the horse of Argos' king run faster is slightly reworked. In the original we have the image of the horse being urged with a sharper bit. Sbarbaro's translation 'pianta con più furia lo sprone nel cavallo' stresses the dynamism of the scene. Instead of keeping the image of the bit (χαλινός) which conjures up the change of direction rather than the speed of the action, Sbarbaro uses the word 'sprone' (spur). Together with the added complement 'con più furia' he continues the image of flight from the previous line 'in fuga hai cacciato' (φυγάδα) while creating an assonance and an alliteration ('in fuga … con più furia').

From these examples it appears that Sbarbaro's translation of the choral sections enhances the lyric quality of the original. This is done by reproducing the disposition of the lines of the original and by respecting the word order. At the same time, he introduces new pauses to the text thus stretching the rhythmical units of the single lines. The syntax is often more contorted than in the original and the verse often lingers on the reader's ear until it finds the verb, usually placed at the end of the sentence. Rhetorical devices also often enrich the lyric sections. The most used is alliteration, mainly employed in the same places where the original Greek also has it. When translating these tragedies Sbarbaro produces echoes of his main poetic themes, all expressed in *Pianissimo*. The lyric parts are where the grand themes of *dolore, pietrificazione* (pain, petrification, alienation of the Self) and *alienazione dell'io* intermingle with the tragedy's themes. Sbarbaro's need for tears, as a metaphor for the constant quest for life in an alienated Self, is given full freedom of expression in these tragedies where family issues and mourning intertwine with a desire for death. However, his awareness of his status as a poet often generated irony and sarcasm in his poetry. The dramatic parts of the translation are where this satirical vein is given more space. The prose is less dense and supports the change of register. In the alternation between the choruses and the dramatic parts we can see the quest for balance between the verticality of the lyric sections which evoke universalising moral reflections, and the horizontality of the prose which has found the object of meditation outside the Self. The translation of Greek tragedy represents the ideal place where this formal equilibrium may be practised. We can see this tension, the alternation between prose and poetry, put into practice within these translations which therefore offer a synthesis never fully achieved by Sbarbaro in his other books.

Sbarbaro's translation also offers a key change of register which reflects a similar change in the original. The first episode in *Antigone* stages the presence of Kreon who shares his political views with the Chorus regarding the traitors to the city. The tone is solemn. Kreon asks the Elders to watch over his orders and Polynices' corpse, for someone might disobey his laws and be corrupted by money. Before the chorus has the chance to reply to Kreon's speech, the entrance of the guard interrupts the dialogue. His appearance (ll. 223 ff.) introduces the second part of the stasimon and it immediately lightens the tone with his almost comical words:

Φύλαξ
    Ἄναξ, ἐρῶ μὲν οὐχ τάχους ὕπο
    δύσπνους ἱκανω κοῦφον ἐξάρας πόδα.
    Πολλὰς γὰρ ἔσχον φροντίδον ἐπιστασεις,
    ὁδοῖς κυκλῶν ἐμαυτὸν εἰς ἀναστροφήν·
    ψυχὴ γὰρ ηὔδα πολλά μοι μυθουμένη·
    Τάλας, τί χῶρεις οἷ μολὼν δώσεις δίκην;
    τλήμων, μενεῖς αὖ; κεἰ τάδ' εἴσεται Κρέων

ἄλλου παρ' ἀνδρός, πῶς σὺ δῆτ' οὐκ ἀλγυνῇ';
Τοιαῦθ' ἑλίσσων ἤνυτον σχολῇ βραδύς.
χοὔτως ὁδὸς βραχεῖα γίγνεται μακρά.
[…]
Φράσαι θέλω σοι πρῶτα τἀμαυτοῦ· τὸ γὰρ
πρᾶγμ' οὔτ' ἔδρασ' οὔτ' εἶδον ὅστις ἦν ὁ δρῶν,
οὐδ' ἂν δικαίως ἐς κακὸν πέσοιμί τι.
[…]
Καὶ δὴ λέγω σοι· τὸν νεκρόν τις ἀρτίως
θάψας βέβηκε κἀπὶ χρωτὶ διψίαν
κόνιν παλύνας κἀφαγιστεύσας ἃ χρή.

Guardia
>Re, non ti dirò che arrivo senza fiato da tanto ho corso lesto. Al contrario! Quante volte i pensieri m'han fermato per via e fatto voltare per tornarmene! Il cuore mi diceva: 'Infelice! Perchè vai dove appena giunto verrai punito!' – 'Ah ti fermi, insensato? E se Creonte viene a sapere da altri, come puoi sperare di non pagarla cara?' In questi pensieri m'indugiavo: e ci ho messo a far la strada! Anche corta diventa lunga a questo modo una strada! […] Lascia che dica prima di me. Né ho fatto la cosa io né ho visto chi l'ha fatta. Per cui sarebbe brutta che toccasse un guaio a me. […] Le notizie, se son brutte, ce ne vuole a buttarle fuori. […] Ecco, dico. Qualcuno, poco fa, seppellito il morto, si è squagliato; dopo avergli gettato sopra terra asciutta e compiuto riti d'uso.[95]

My king, I will not say that I arrive breathless because of speed, or from the action of a swift foot. For often I brought myself to a stop because of my thoughts, and wheeled round in my path to return. My mind was telling me many things: 'Fool, why do you go to where your arrival will mean your punishment?' 'Idiot, are you dallying again? If Kreon learns it from another, must you not suffer for it?' So debating, I made my way unhurriedly, slow, and thus a short road was made long. At last, however, the view prevailed that I should come here—to you. Even if my report brings no good, still will I tell you, since I come with a good grip on one hope, that I can suffer nothing except what is my fate.[96]

Griffith described this character as 'one of the more colourful characters in Greek tragedy'.[97] Sbarbaro does not fail to represent this character with an appropriate change of register and an accurate vocabulary choice. Colloquial expressions such as 'tanto ho corso lesto', 'pagarla cara', 'ce ne vuole a buttarle fuori' and 'si è squagliato' characterize the sentry's speech. He is very much responsible for driving the plot and his constant fear creates an ironic and sarcastic point of view on the situation. At the same time, the sentry is no monolithic character incapable of other tones. It is on these occasions where Sbarbaro takes advantage of the choice of poetic prose in order to descend to a more comical and ironic tone, also typical of some of his late poetry (especially the *Fuochi fatui*). The translation again is not free from interpretation despite being faithful to the original. For instance at ll. 256 ff. the sentry describes a fight scene which could be a comical scene, but Sbarbaro here inserts some verses also reminiscent of his own poetry:

Φύλαξ
Οὐκ οἶδα. ἐκεῖ γὰρ οὔτε του γενῇδος ἦν
πλῆγμ', οὐ δικέλλης ἐκβολή. στυφλὸς δέ γῆ
καὶ χέρσος, ἀρρὼξ οὐδ' ἐπημαξευμένη
τροχοῖσιν, ἀλλ' ἄσημος οὑργάτης τίς ἦν. [...]
Λόγοι δ' ἐν ἀλλήλοισιν ἐρρόθουν κακοί,
Φύλαξ ἐλέγχων φύλακα, κἄν ἐγίγνετο
πληγὴ τελευτῶσ', οὐδ ὁ κωλύσων παρῆν.

Guardia
Non so. Sul posto non si notava scasso di vanga né palata di terra: il suolo era sodo e asciutto, non rotto né solcato da ruote. [...] Scoppiarono tra noi male parole. Una guardia incolpava l'altra; e minacciava di finire in botte né c'era chi lo impedisse.[98]

'Scoppiarono tra noi male parole' is one of those perfect *endecasillabi* scattered throughout his translation. The line is also another intersection with Sbarbaro's poetry and the use of the verb *scoppiare* probably activated Sbarbaro's poetic memory and therefore the use of the metre. For instance, in the poem *Lacrime, sotto sguardi curiosi* the poet asserts the frailty of his emotional condition and connects it to the vain nature of his words:

Lacrime sotto sguardi curiosi
non mi scoppiate a un tratto mentre parlo
di vane cose (mi sovviene a un tratto
del mio cammino sotto cieli bui,
non avendo una mano che m'incuori;

e l'inutilità di ciò che dico
di ciò che faccio mi fa grave il cuore).[99]

Tears under curious gazes,
do not suddenly burst from me while I speak
of empty things (to my mind there suddenly comes
my path under dark skies,
having no hand to comfort me;
and the uselessness of what I say,
of what I do makes my heart heavy.

The poetic memory of *Pianissimo* surfaces and creates a connection between tears and words, thus colouring the translation of the passage with a lyrical tone. The comic character of the sentry, and the dramatic part generally, are often nuanced through poetic echoes of Sbarbaro's original writing thus showing the poet's consistent use of his poetic memory when dealing with both the dramatic and the lyric parts of the translation.

The Freedom of Writing under Constraints: Sbarbaro's Poetic Prose in Sophocles' Translation

Sbarbaro wrote only one preface to his translations of Greek drama, for Euripides' *Alcestis* and *The Cyclops*. This introduction is the most extended and articulated piece written by the author on Greek theatre. Here he outlines his thoughts on Greek tragedy through a comparison between Aeschylus, Sophocles and Euripides:

> Con Euripide si verifica nella tragedia greca una violenta frattura. Se precise indicazioni di tempo mancassero, chi crederebbe l'autore di *Alcesti* contemporaneo di Sofocle? Questi non era meno acuto psicologo di Euripide; ma mentre l'amore del vero porta Sofocle a tratteggiare al più qualche macchietta (vedi nell'*Antigone* quella così efficace della guardia) che, relegata al posto di comparsa, serve con la sua presenza ad accrescere la verisimiglianza e con la sua ombra a dare risalto ai grandi caratteri dominanti nel suo teatro; il verismo apertamente malevolo di Euripide inquina tutti i personaggi e li abbassa a uomini e pegpeggio [sic], siano essi, re eroi o numi. [...] L'intreccio, assente si può dire in Eschilo, e lineare in Sofocle, si complica

in Euripide, da far nascere la necessità di un prologo che illumini il pubblico sull'antefatto [...]. A turbare definitivamente la severa linea classica, fa la sua comparsa un acceso romanticismo e la cavillosa discussione sofistica; e s'inaugura l'uso e l'abuso di tutti gli espedienti teatrali (colpi di scena e riconoscimenti eccetera) che passeranno poi in eredità alla commedia nuova. Il coro preponderante in Eschilo, si impoverisce, perde contatto con l'azione [...] lo stile eloquente in Eschilo e intenso in Sofocle, si fa discorsivo sino a rasentare la sciatteria.[100]

With Euripides, a violent rift happens in Greek tragedy. If precise indications of time were lacking, who would believe that the author of Alcestis was a contemporary of Sophocles? He was not a less acute psychologist than Euripides; but while love of the truth led Sophocles to sketch to the utmost some caricatures (see in *Antigone* that incisive rendering of the guard) who, relegated to the position of background, with their presence serve to increase the verisimilitude and with their shadows put into relief the great dominating characters of his drama, the openly malevolent realism of Euripides tarnishes all the characters and debases men and worsens them, whether they be kings, heroes or divinities. [...] The plot, absent one might say in Aeschylus and linear in Sophocles, is complicated in Euripides, giving rise to the need for a prologue which enlightens the public regarding the backstory [...]. To definitively disturb the severe classical line, he makes his background intense romanticism and complex sophistic discussions; and he inaugurates the use and abuse of all the theatrical expedients (plot twists and recognition scenes, etcetera) which are handed down to New Comedy. The prevalent chorus in Aeschylus is depleted, loses contact with the action [...] style, which is eloquent in Aeschylus and intense in Sophocles, becomes colloquial even bordering on sloppy.

From this passage it is evident that Sbarbaro understands how Sophocles' 'amore del vero' results in 'grandi caratteri dominanti' and also 'qualche macchietta'. To re-create this aspect, and the contrast between an elevated tone and a lower one, the poet-translator makes a stylistic choice: the use of poetic prose, which allows a change of register and a more wide-ranging representation of the characters. However, this choice is also an important intersection between Sbarbaro's translations of Greek tragedy and his poetics. The poet's oscillation between prose and poetry is a constant feature in his creative work. In these translations Sbarbaro has the chance to mix his lyric voice together with his prosaic fragments. This stylistic solution signals the elaboration of one of the most important turning points in his poetic life: the declaration of his poetics which becomes poetry itself in *Fuochi fatui*. Eugenio Montale, in an article written in memory of the poet, described what poetry was for Sbarbaro: 'Scrivere era per lui attendere il momento in cui maturasse la dettatura...da parte di chi?' (For him, writing was waiting for the moment when dictation came to fruition ... from whom?)[101]. Montale here refers to the image of the transcriber used by Sbarbaro himself in the preface to *Fuochi fatui*. The interconnection between the image of Sbarbaro writing 'sotto dettatura' and the metaphor of himself 'che cammina sulla corda' when translating Greek tragedy offers a comprehensive image of how the poet felt he could experience the poetic word. The literal translation of Greek tragedy and the metaphorical image used by Sbarbaro himself for this activity helps us understand the poet's evolution in shaping a distinct poetics, as it emerges in the preface to *Fuochi fatui*, that of a transcriber writing under dictation.

Fuochi fatui is also a book that looks backward to Sbarbaro's poetic origins, which is to say to *Pianissimo*.[102] The author himself pointed to this inward perspective at the end of his preface:

> Rimasto nelle cose che dico fedele a me stesso, se poi anche nel modo di dirle è vero che mi sono per naturale decantazione spogliato fin dove possible di letteratura, riaccostandomi alla povertà di *Pianissimo*, avrei assolto il mio compito. Dice il poeta: Soltanto ciò che torna al suo principio / ciò che si chiude in circolo, è perfetto. / Perfetto, cioè etimologicamente, compiuto.[103]
>
> Having remained faithful to myself in the things I say, if then it is also true that in the way of saying them, through natural decantation, I have stripped myself of literature as far as possible, returning to the poverty of *Pianissimo*, I would have discharged my task. So says the poet: Only that which returns to its beginning / that which closes the circle, is perfect. / Perfect, that is, etymologically, completed.

The desire to return to the beginnings thus bringing his poetic trajectory full circle, appears to be fundamentally mediated by translation. This analysis of Sbarbaro's collections of letters, archive documents, poetic oeuvre and his translations of Greek tragedy has revealed a relationship with the classical tradition which finds its expression on several levels. Pedagogy and translation commitments were the occasions through which the poet was able to develop his fondness for Greek tragedy and to make it relevant to his thought. The translation of the *Antigone* does not only symbolically begin the translation period nor is just the result of publishing commitments, but it also shaped Sbarbaro's awareness of himself as a poet. The difficult task posed by this text, the methodology elaborated ad hoc to tackle the assignment and the sense of reverence towards these texts are aspects deeply consonant with his conception of poetry and of the necessity of his poetic word.

The most illuminating aspect arising from the experience of translating Greek tragedy is to be found in the development of the metaphor elaborated by Sbarbaro for his relationship with poetry as a whole. The metaphor of the translator 'che cammina sulla corda', elaborated by Sbarbaro in the context of his translations of the tragedians, anticipates that of the poet who writes 'sotto dettatura' expressed in *Fuochi fatui* and the metapoetic meditation mixed with the remarks on translation present in the book.

The choice of poetic prose for the translations of Greek tragedy conveys Sbarbaro's interpretative effort, his desire to preserve the word order in his translation without sacrificing meaning. This aspect is mostly evident in the lyrical sections where we also find phenomena such as etymological calques (especially evident in the use and creation of compounds) and rhetorical devices aiming at the re-creation of sounds present in the original.[104] Dramatic parts are where the prose is given more freedom and where the poet's sarcastic vein is explored. These sections are also intertwined with Sbarbaro's way of making poetry as we can find several hendecasyllables scattered throughout these parts re-creating connections with the prosaic hendecasyllables of *Pianissimo*. This oscillation, which found full expression in *Fuochi fatui*, begins in these translations where the moral investigation offered by the themes of the original tragedy successfully mingles with Sbarbaro's fundamental lines of poetic development. Poetic prose is also the means through which Sbarbaro achieves this goal: the prose allows the poet to be more in command of collocation of words and lexical choices as well as making syntactic alterations to isolate passages dear to his poetics (visible in the use of punctuation and parenthetical clauses). Considering the metapoetic meditation and its interconnection with translation, expressed in the form of poetic fragments, present in *Fuochi fatui*, we should understand these translations of Greek tragedy as the achievement of equilibrium between a lyrical and prosaic mode inspired and mediated by his practical experience of translation.

Sbarbaro's ultimate goal is to produce a harmonious translation where stylistic flourishes do not affect his principal aim: namely a translation that would preserve meaning rather than create obscurity and opacity, despite these being present in the original. The poet-translator avoids the risk of getting lost in the depths of language, as often happens when choosing a literal approach. Sbarbaro's translations of Greek tragedy might fall into that category of translations that George Steiner would include in his first periodization where he places translation theories which stemmed from direct and practical work on translations.[105] However, Sbarbaro's versions are also to be read beyond this category, as from this practice he was able to refine a meditation on translation deeply intertwined with his own quest for the poetic word.

The necessity of writing under the constraints of another voice expressed by Sbarbaro in the preface of *Fuochi fatui*, and reminiscent of his limited freedom of action when translating Greek tragedy, is a turning point overlapping with his constant concern with the dryness of his poetic voice. It is indeed from this apparently disabling condition that Sbarbaro derives his poetic strength and inspiration. Sbarbaro's translations are not merely stylistic exercises, even if the inspiration coming from Greek syntax is strong and evident, but they were the occasions for the poet to rethink his own poetry. It is no coincidence that translations of Greek tragedy are all read through the filter of *Pianissimo*. Sbarbaro revisited through these translations themes and tropes expressed in his first collection, which remains the pivotal achievement of his poetry.[106] It was after the rethinking of these themes through the translations of Greek tragedy that Sbarbaro was able to state with no uncertainty, as is evident from the *Fuochi fatui* preface, what he had pursued since *Pianissimo*. His desire to reconnect with that first experience, thus reasserting its importance, is encompassed in the final part of his poetic trajectory through the meditation inspired by the translation of Greek tragedy. These translations were not carried out just to respect his publishing commitments or as a mere stylistic experiment, but are an integral part of Sbarbaro's poetic *iter*, linking its opening and concluding phases.

3

Giovanna Bemporad's Early Translations of Greek Tragedy

Giovanna Bemporad (1923–2013) was an Italian poet of Jewish origins and a translator of classical and modern languages who contributed to the field of poetic translation from Graeco-Roman literature in a way that has few parallels in twentieth-century Italian literature. The uniqueness of her work as a translator is twofold. First, Bemporad only translated poetry, covering a large part of the Western literary canon.[1] Second, and this is peculiar to some of her translations of the classical literature, Bemporad retranslated the same text(s) many times. This demonstrates that she thought of her work as never quite finished but always in progress.

Her relationship with classical literature is deeply rooted in her own poetic discourse. In an interview, Bemporad compared her activity as a translator of poetry to a journey into the canon of Western literature, a journey in which her fascination with literary archetypes was her guiding star:

> Il mio percorso, pur così accidentato, pieno di dubbi, di smarrimenti, di incertezze su quello che doveva essere il metro, il ritmo, il linguaggio, i contenuti della poesia del secondo Novecento, ha avuto uno svolgimento tutto sommato abbastanza coerente. Sono partita dalla poesia pura dei lirici greci e da Leopardi, che si può considerare l'ultimo dei greci, e dopo aver attraversato – considerando Virgilio il primo dei poeti decadenti – tutti gli istmi della poesia europea (anche il barocco e il liberty) sono approdata e ritornata come in un cerchio che si chiude, alla poesia più assoluta, primigenia, che è all'origine di tutta la letteratura occidentale, al libro dei libri: l'*Odissea* di Omero.[2]
>
> My path, though bumpy, filled with doubt, confusion, uncertainties over what should be the metre, the rhythm, the tone, the subject matter of poetry of the second half of the twentieth century, has all in all had a fairly coherent

progression. I started from the pure poetry of Greek lyric and Leopardi (who can be considered the last of the Greeks); then, considering Virgil the first of the decadent poets, after having passed through all the isthmuses of European poetry (even Baroque and Liberty), I arrived and returned, like a circle that closes, to the most absolute, primigenial, that which is at the source of all Western literature, the book of books: Homer's *Odyssey*.

Her 'literary' journey began with Greek lyrical poetry and ended with the *Odyssey*.[3] The fact that Greek literature marks the beginning and end of her 'circular' quest suggests the prominence of the classical legacy in her poetic thought. The affinity between her translations of the classical languages (especially her anthologies of the *Aeneid* and of the *Odyssey*) and her book of poems *Esercizi* is all the more significant considering the determined effort she put into the numerous new editions of these texts.[4] Bemporad's kinship with classical antiquity extends further than the horizon sketched so far. Bemporad's personal archive contains an unpublished corpus of translations from the three Greek tragedians, Aeschylus, Sophocles and Euripides, thus confirming the centrality of Greek literature and its legacy in her literary journey. Over the course of four months (from July to October 1940), as the dates on the manuscripts indicate, Bemporad translated several Greek tragedies.[5]

This chapter focuses on her translation of Sophocles' *Electra*, a tragedy that, together with Aeschylus' *The Libation Bearers* and Euripides' *Electra*, forms a virtual triad about the Argos dynasty. The drama occupies a unique place in the canon of classical literature as it allows us to see how the mythical cycle of Electra was developed by the three tragedians.[6] Bemporad's fascination with Electra's character began with Sophocles' tragedy, but she continued to explore the psychology of the tragic heroine in her translation of Aeschylus' *The Libation Bearers*. It is worth noting that Bemporad translated the only play of the *Oresteia* trilogy that focuses entirely on the character of Electra, signalling indirectly her interest in the character. Her research into the Greek heroine was further developed in her translation of Hofmannsthal's *Electra* (1981), which is based on Sophocles' version of the myth.[7] These translation choices demonstrate an explicit interest in and fascination with this mythical figure which then had an impact on Bemporad's own poetic discourse. Chronologically speaking, her translation of Sophocles' *Electra* is one of her first encounters with Greek literature, making Bemporad's poetic engagement with this text one of the earliest examples of that inextricable dyad of poetry and translation which is the essence of her work and the fundamental cornerstone of her poetics.

The collection of letters (1940-3) between Carlo Izzo and Bemporad provides a useful historical contextualization for these translations of the tragedians which remain, to this day, unpublished. The correspondence directly refers to the translations of Greek tragedies whilst offering insights into Bemporad's poetic workshop. One of the most prominent themes emerging from this exchange is metrical experimentation and the idea of poetic translation as the creation of a new *melos*. Remarks and thoughts on prosodical issues feature heavily throughout the letters. More than once we read Izzo's comments on Bemporad's confidence in the use of hendecasyllable, allusions to different metrical experiments (for instance the *esperimento barbaro*) and forms (such as her use of the *quinario* – five-syllable line – and the *settenario* – seven-syllable line).[8] Their remarks on the technical aspects of their translation practice, with a specific focus on the musical element of versification, is a constant object of discussion between Izzo and Bemporad. Her version of Sophocles' *Electra* in hendecasyllables is a pristine sample where one can see how these ideas on metrics and rhythmics are applied to translation practice.

Bemporad's choice and devotion to the hendecasyllable raises the issue of the kind of dialogue the young poet-translator sought to establish with the Italian poetic tradition. At the heart of the matter is how Bemporad drew on this tradition in her translation of Sophocles' tragedy. It is perhaps no coincidence that the poetic echoes traceable in Bemporad's version belong to poets who greatly contributed to the metrical debate and to the field of translation from the classics. For example, Giacomo Leopardi's influence on Bemporad's poetics of translation is prominent and it inflects upon different aspects. Leopardi's presence can be felt in Bemporad's tendency for Leopardian vocabulary in the translation itself, in digressions in which she introduces Leopardian motifs, and in the fact that her approach to translation is indebted to his translation theories. The very nature of Bemporad's translation of Sophocles' *Electra* is dependent on Leopardi's ideas on the poetic function of translating Greek poetry. Bemporad attempts 'to initiate a poetic moment' by means of translation, or as Leopardi puts it, to create that moment in which 'la mente tumultua' (the mind riots).[9] Bemporad's translation of Sophocles' *Electra* goes beyond a stylistic exercise; her poetic version of the drama is instead an attempt to create the conditions that would trigger a moment of poetic inspiration and allow poetic creation to take form.

Apart from Leopardi, other voices are clearly discernible in her poetic engagement with Sophocles' *Electra*. Giuseppe Ungaretti's defence of the hendecasyllable resonates in Bemporad's ideological choice of the metre, unveiling her poetic agenda behind this translation.[10] Giovanni Pascoli's monumental contribution to the translation of the Classics left a complex legacy in Bemporad's work and has been understood in diverse ways by scholars who have devoted their attention to Bemporad's poetic translations.[11] As far as the poetic translation of Sophocles' *Electra* is concerned, Pascoli's influence echoes in the prosodic solutions aimed at expanding of the rhythm beyond the metrical unit thanks to a significant use of vowel encounters between words.[12] In the *Electra*, Bemporad focuses her attention on the elastic potential of the hendecasyllable as a verse capable of hosting a variety of rhythmical units.

The translation of *Electra* played a significant role in the early stage of Bemporad's poetic journey. The chronological proximity between Bemporad's translations of Greek tragedies and her original poetry invites to think about the osmotic links between these undertakings. A comparative reading of the opening section of the *Esercizi* (entitled 'Diari') and Bemporad's translation of *Electra* unearths recurring tropes that shed light on the impact of translating Greek tragedy on her poetic imagination. Bemporad's interpretation of the Greek heroine becomes a model for her poetic self: Electra's existential condition and her quest can be read as an allegory for Bemporad's own poetic condition and her journey, thus making the experience of translating Sophocles a pivotal step in the shaping of her poetic discourse as a whole.

'In una musica che è subito tua': Carlo Izzo and Giovanna Bemporad's Letters

A recently published collection of Carlo Izzo's letters to Bemporad (covering the years 1940–3) details Bemporad's life and work in the months during which she was translating Greek tragedies.[13] A letter dated 24 June 1940 offers a telling glimpse into the relationship between the student and the teacher at the time:

> Mandami pure qualche frutto dei tuoi troppo notturni sudori; mi farà sempre piacere; sebbene più me ne farebbe di sapere che nascono non di lunare tormento ma di solare sanità, i tuoi frutti canori. [...] Sto rileggendo Platone. [...]. Mentre il mondo mi sta crollando intorno – sai nulla tu della guerra? Del mondo che si sfascia e si rinnova? – io mi rifugio nella divina serenità, nella immutata serenità di Platone. Nella tua penultima hai trascritto: 'e quando in cielo rosseggiò l'aurora e si spensero i lumi delle stelle, scorgemmo di lontano i colli oscuri, l'umile Italia. E primo 'Italia' grida Acatae, Italia la salutano festosi i miei compagni...' troverai da te un errore metrico che è certamente un errore di copiatura. E quei tre versi che mi citi nell'ultima sono del tuo 'Edipo re'? o di dove? Me li potresti ritrascrivere? Io leggo: 'servo d'un altro – d'un uomo privo di beni', ma non sono certo e poi: 'la tomba dei morti'? O Sbaglio? Non fare troppa stima del tuo corrispondente, mi raccomando![14]
>
> Send me some fruits of your excessive nocturnal labours; they always please me; even though it would please me even more to know that your singing fruits were born of sunlit sanity rather than moonlit torment. [...] I'm reading Plato again. [...] While the world is collapsing around me – do you know nothing of the war? Of the world that is falling apart and renewing? – I find refuge in the divine serenity, the unchanged serenity of Plato. In your last you transcribed: 'and when in the sky the dawn turns red and the lights of the stars go out, in the distance we glimpsed the dark hills, humble Italy. And Acatae first cries 'Italy' and my joyful companions greet Italy', you will find by yourself a metrical error that's surely a copying error. And those three verses that you cite in your last letter are from your *Oedipus Rex*? Or where? Could you send me them again? I read: 'servant of another – of a man without riches', but I'm not sure and then: 'the tomb of the dead'? Or am I wrong? Please don't overestimate your correspondent!

The final part of the letter tells us of an interesting practice of Bemporad and Izzo – a practice confirmed by the rest of the letters – namely their mutual exchange of translations. Moreover, the reference to the 'errore metrico' (metrical mistake) introduces a recurrent theme in these letters.[15] Metrical and prosodic rules are often a subject of discussion in Izzo and Bemporad's correspondence, which testifies to their attention to rhythmic aspects. Izzo's keen interest in metrics emerges again from another letter dated Venice, 1 July

1940. Izzo begins the letter by once again venting his disapproval of Bemporad's anti-conformist behaviour. Having advised his young pupil to try to have a more 'normal' life, Izzo turns his attention to Bemporad's metrical experiments:

> Naturalmente che tu ti esprimi in endecasillabi. Ma supponevo che le tue recenti esercitazioni in esametri latini ti avessero indotta a tentare un esperimento 'barbaro'. Quanto ai branetti dal greco mi sembra, francamente, non valgano le traduzioni dal latino; i brani stessi delle *Georgiche* mi sembrano assai migliori. Forse non sei ancora matura per la suprema semplicità dei greci. Abbi pazienza: e non dimenticare che le culture intensive danno frutti insapori. Tempo al tempo, Giovanna, tempo al tempo. [...] Ti prometto solennissimamente che riprenderò a trascrivere e commentare i tuoi versi appena saprò che hai normalizzato la tua vita entro limiti compatibili con le necessità del tuo corpo, con le esigenze del mondo pratico e, soprattutto, con la sanità della tua mente, preziosamente dotata, se non vorrai bruciarla malamente in un falò insensato.[16]
>
> Naturally you express yourself in hendecasyllables. But I supposed that your recent exercises in Latin hexameters would have induced you to try a 'barbaric' experiment. As for the little Greek passages, it seems to me honestly that they're not of the same worth as the Latin translations; the passages from the Georgics themselves seem to me rather better. Perhaps you're not yet mature enough for the supreme simplicity of the Greeks. Have patience: and do not forget that haste in growing gives flavourless fruit. Give it time, Giovanna, give it time. [...] I solemnly promise you that I will start transcribing and commenting on your verses as soon as I find that you've organised your life within boundaries that are compatible with the needs of your body, with the demands of the practical world and, above all, with the sanity of your mind, so preciously equipped, if you don't want to badly burn it in a senseless bonfire.

Here, the first line 'naturalmente che tu ti esprimi in endecasillibi' alludes to Bemporad's metrics for her own poetry and it echoes Ungaretti's ideas on the hendecasyllable as the most 'natural' verse for Italian poets.[17] The recent 'esercitazioni' (exercises) in Latin hexameters probably refer to Bemporad's translation of Virgil's *Georgics* that immediately follows in the letter, whereas the 'esperimento barbaro' (barbaric experiment) recalls Giosuè Carducci's *metrica barbara* (barbaric metrics), giving the reader an insight into Bemporad's broad interest in metrics.[18]

A letter dated 12 January 1941 confirms that Bemporad translated Sophocles' *Antigone*,[19] which is then cited again in another letter, dated 29 January 1941:

> L'Antigone: trovo fiacche le battute iniziali: 'E dunque ucciderai – e l'una e l'altra'? 'No; tu dici bene ...' etc. Forse hai anche copiato male un verso che non mi pare torni: 'l'altra no perchè non ha sepolto'. (Appunto a lato: forse manca un 'ma') Correggi, o rettifica. Appena puoi spaziare di più, prosegui invece benissimo e i cori sono stupendi: 'verdeggianti di grappoli in rigoglio' è uno dei tuoi bei versi, voglio dire di quelli che io amo di più: tuoi. Anche: 'un germoglio di pietra come foglia'. Ed è quanto mai evocativo il tono delle narrazioni: 'Ho udito raccontare etc.' 'Anche la bella Danae sofferse ...' Sei ricca a milioni: bada solo di non spenderli con troppo sfarzo, alla D'Annunzio, ma non mi sembra che tu corra quel pericolo: anzi, la cosa che più mi piace in te è la sobrietà: non tradirla mai.[20]

> Antigone: I find the opening lines dull: 'And so you will kill them both'? 'No; you say well ...' etc. Perhaps you've also copied a verse wrongly: 'the other no because she did not bury'. (Note: perhaps a 'but' is missing). Correct or adjust. As soon as you can range further, however, you get on very well and the choruses are marvellous: 'lush with blooming bunches' is one of your beautiful lines, I mean of those that I love the most: yours. Also: 'a sprout of stone like a leaf'. And the tone of the narration is as evocative as ever: 'I have heard tell etc.' 'Beautiful Danae also suffered ...' You are rich in the millions: just be careful not to spend them with too much pomp, like D'Annunzio, but it doesn't seem to me that you run that risk: rather, what I like best is your moderation: never betray it.

From this description we understand that Bemporad must have sent long excerpts of her *Antigone* to Izzo, if not the entire text. Izzo's precise feedback identifies strengths and areas for development: the young student achieves her best results when she can operate in longer, lyrical units ('Appena puoi spaziare di più, prosegui invece benissimo e i cori sono stupendi') as opposed to short exchanges between the characters. It is in the lyrical sections that the teacher recognizes the student's talent by going as far as describing her translation as guided by her own music ('è uno dei tuoi bei versi, voglio dire di quelli che io amo di più: tuoi'). The line quoted by Izzo as an example of Bemporad's evocative translation is from the fifth chorus song of the *Antigone* (ll. 1130–5):

καί σε Νυσαίων ὀρέων
κισσήρεις ὄχθαι χλωρά τ' ἀκτὰ

πολυστάφυλος πέμπει,
ἀμβρότων ἐπέων
εὐαζόντων Θηβαΐας ἐπισκοποῦντ᾽ ἀγυιάς

The ivy-mantled slopes of Nysa's hills and the shore green with many-clustered vines send you, when accompanied by the cries of your divine words, you visit the avenues of Thebes.[21]

The line quoted ('verdeggianti di grappoli in rigoglio') is a standard hendecasyllable, in which a musical effect is achieved through the alliteration of the guttural sound (g) (in the original Greek we had the alliteration of the letter π). The line shows a tendency to stretch the verse beyond the syllabic constraints thanks to a repetitive rhythm created by the insertion of similar sounding prepositions (*di*; *in*) after long and resonant words. These pauses freeze the verse in minuscule suspensions thus enlarging the rhythmical unit of the line. Izzo appreciates the evocative tone of the narrative sections and again quotes the beginnings of two verses: 'Ho udito raccontare etc.' and 'Anche la bella Danae sofferse …'. The finest quality the teacher seems to appreciate in his pupil's work is sobriety ('la cosa che più mi piace in te è la sobrietà: non tradirla mai') and her poetic engagement. The translation of *Antigone* is mentioned again in another letter dated Venice, 13 May 1941, where Izzo reiterates his admiration for Bemporad's ability to express her poetic voice at her best when translating Greek tragedy:

> Ho dimenticato l'Antigone [*sic*], e se ne faccio più che in fretta tu mi pensi di sicuro a un pietoso silenzio. Come se io fossi capace di pietosi silenzi! Dunque: il principio, tutto quello che mi trascrivi, intendo, mi sembra bellissimo: ci sono versi fra i tuoi più belli. Copia pure tranquillamente.[22]
>
> I forgot *Antigone* and if I just do it quickly you will surely think me pitifully silent. As if I were capable of pitiful silences! Therefore: the beginning, everything you've sent me I mean, is beautiful: there are some of your most beautiful verses. So feel free to carry on.

In another letter dated 24 March 1941, Izzo compares her translation of Sophocles' *Oedipus at Colonus* with that of Shakespeare's *Macbeth*. The teacher's comments shed light on the pupil's stylistic sensitivity towards different authors and literary traditions in translation:

> Il coro dell'Edipo a Colono è forse anche più bello [i.e. del *Macbeth*], ma la tua voce, come, in tutt'altro senso, la mia è sempre la stessa: più melodiosa

quando traduci dai classici, più aspra quando da Shakespeare: ma così dev'essere. Credo – vuoi fare l'esperimento – che se tu mi mandassi dieci brani di traduzione da qualsiasi lingua in italiano, e tra quelli uno soltanto tuo, lo scoverei fuori con assoluta sicurezza alla seconda lettura: non credo io possa farti lode migliore, nè più sincera.[23]

The chorus of Oedipus at Colonus is perhaps even more beautiful [than *Macbeth*] but your voice, like in another sense mine, is always the same: more melodious when you translate from the classics, harsher when translating Shakespeare: but that's how it should be. I believe – you could experiment – that if you sent me ten translation extracts from any language into Italian, and amongst them only one of yours, I would discover it with absolute certainty on the second reading: I don't believe I can give you better or more sincere praise.

The letter draws attention to Bemporad's change of timbre and voice in translation according to the nature of the original. The voice is more melodious ('più melodiosa') when translating from the Classics, specifically from Greek tragedy, and harsher ('più aspra') when translating from modern tragedy (Shakespeare). The passage highlights Bemporad's poetic maturity, picturing a scenario in which the young student has developed a voice of her own in translation, a voice that her master boasts he would recognize among many others without hesitation. Bemporad's distinctive style as a translator, in connection with her translations from Greek tragedy, is referenced again in another letter dated Venice, 3 April 1941:

> E c'è musica, e musica tua, nei brani di Euripide. I tuoi commenti al solito catastrofici e piagnoni, sono assolutamente ingiustificati: come un riccone che passasse la vita a meditare sulla inenarrabile tristezza di non essere anche più ricco. Ma via! Ti prendo un po' in giro? Un po' forse, ma è la primavera a mettermi di buon umore. Scusami.[24]
>
> And there's music, your music, in the Euripides passages. Your usual dire and whining comments are absolutely unjustified: like a rich man going through life meditating on the unspeakable sadness of not being richer. Come on! Am I making fun of you a little? A little perhaps, but Spring has put me in a good mood. My apologies.

Another letter dated Venice, 23 January 1942, in which Izzo mentions Bemporad's attempted translations of *Medea*, further corroborates Bemporad's engagement with Greek tragedy in conjunction with her metrical experiments:

> Per la Medea, invece, andiamo male. Ho guardato tra i tuoi scritti, ho guardato una per una anche le tue centotrentasei lettere: niente. Ho il principio, ma non quel punto lì in endecasillabi; lo ho nella seconda stesura in versi rotti. Credo che tu non me l'abbia restituito, quel pezzo, dopo che te lo detti per rivederlo. È possibile?[25]
>
> For Medea, instead, it's going badly. I've looked through your writings, I've looked through your 136 letters one by one: nothing. I've got the beginning, but not that point in hendecasyllables; I've got it in the second draft in shorter verses. I don't think you've given it to me, that bit, after I gave it to you to look at again. Is that possible?

Clearly alluding to the existence of two metrical versions of the tragedy: one in hendecasyllables and one, which he has, in shorter verses ('versi rotti'),[26] the remark reaffirms Bemporad's attentiveness to metrical and rhythmical experimentation with regards to her versions of Greek tragedy.

These letters track Bemporad's learning journey from her early beginnings as a translator and child prodigy to a stage where, thanks to Izzo and her own obstinate stamina, she obtained recognition from such critics as Leone Traverso, Mario Praz and Vincenzo Errante, who are very present in these letters and provide contact with publishing houses. The letters describe the struggle of a young poet seeking accomplishment through the activity of poetic translation, fully aware of the fact that writing poetry and translating poetry are two paths that often meet and will be the defining feature of her literary career. The exchange is also a powerful reminder of the tragic historical period that witnessed the birth of these letters. The letters where Izzo invites Bemporad to think of a different *nom de plume* (Giovanna della Bianca and Giovanna Bembo) in order to be able to continue with her publication commitments draw our attention to the humiliation of the racial laws that the young poet endured because of her Jewish origins.[27] The letters, however, contain few direct references to the events that marked the historical period. Worries about the *hic et nunc* of Italy and Europe, the outbreak of war and the deteriorating living conditions are barely acknowledged, if we exclude the very few passages where Izzo mentions the cold and the lack of paper. The focus is on literature, poetic translation, metrics, the two friends' numerous literary projects, the literary network they were part of and their hope for the future, which is definitely a future of more poetry. The letters testify to the variety of down should not be underestimated. It is an impact which could be described, in Freudian terms, as *uncanny*: the appearance of something familiar that comes back in a strange and thus terrifying form. This something is the classical world and, more specifically, the Greek world.

The perceived otherness of the ancient Greeks as a perturbing experience thus created a long- standing though fruitful paradox in Leopardi's poetics: for him, the impossibility of translating literally and faithfully leads to the 're-creation of the Ancient voice' starting with the re-creation (or discovery) of one's own voice. In order to establish a relationship with Greek poetry, therefore, one has to achieve that 'strato profondo e naturale che accomuna al di qua del linguaggio, il poeta antico e quello modern'[32] ('that deep and natural layer beyond language that links the ancient and modern poet'). Bemporad's extensive, and intensive, engagement with Greek tragedy appears guided by this kind of quest, using Sophocles' poetry as a spur to discover her own voice. The shock and the creative energy described by the young Leopardi after reading Greek poetry is somewhat re-proposed by the young Bemporad after translating Greek tragedy. The paratext in her translations, mostly in the form of annotations and marginalia at the beginning and end of the manuscripts, shows the state of euphoria and excitement she experienced after translating Greek tragedy. By reproposing this kind of disruptive experience, Bemporad's encounter with the tragedians reads as the internalization of the Leopardian lesson on poetic education through translation of the Classics, especially of Greek literature. The creative energy liberated by the process of translating Greek poetry naturally draws attention to the idea of poetic inspiration, an overarching theme and object of research in Bemporad's poetic practice. Inspiration and translation are inextricably linked in her thought: according to her own words, poetic translation is the only activity during which the poet can open herself to inspiration and create poetry.[33] Bemporad goes even further by comparing inspiration to a devotional call, fulfilling a cogent need experienced from within:

> Io non ho paura di usare la parola 'ispirazione' per chi si sente chiamato a scrivere da un'invincibile necessità, come per vivere bisogna respirare. Scrivere – diceva Rilke – è come respirare attraverso la penna. E io aggiungerei che se esiste una 'santità' laica, il poeta dovrebbe a pieno titolo esservi iscritto. È quasi un luogo comune che la vita o la si vive o la si scrive, e io posso ben

dire che è stata la letteratura nel bene come nel male, nel giusto come nell'ingiusto, a condurre per mano la mia vita, e non viceversa. Dunque, poeti prima si nasce e poi si diventa.[34]

I'm not afraid of using the word 'inspiration' for one who feels themselves called to write by an invincible need, like the need to breath to live. Rilke said that to write is to breathe through the pen. And I would add that if a secular 'sanctity' exists, the poet should be enrolled with full privileges. It is almost a common place that life is either lived or written, and I can well say that literature, for better or worse, rightly or wrongly, has led my life by the hand, and not vice versa. Therefore, poets are first born and then become.

The identification between writing and life, and the prioritization of literature as the driving force determining life choices, together with the key word 'inspiration', are further reminders of Leopardi's influence on her work and thought. However, it is Leopardi's belief in the impossibility of a faithful translation and the need for the re-creation of the Greek text via the creation of one's own poetic voice that exerted the strongest influence on Bemporad's theoretical ideas on translation.[35] Bemporad, like Leopardi, believed that poetry was untranslatable.[36] Notwithstanding this deep conviction, she made poetic translation the core of her literary activity. The creative potential of this contradiction has been pinpointed by another poet-translator (Yves Bonnefoy) who reflected on the meaning of this paradox:

> Ce témoin d'un autre poète serait incité à en devenir un et puissamment aidé à y parvenir, les difficultés de sa tâche ne pouvant que l'ancrer toujours plus dans ce projet. Un paradoxe? Le paradoxe du traducteur? Ce qui rend impossible la traduction de la poésie, c'est cela même qui suscite ou renforce en son traducteur qui en souffre une vocation de poète. Et la compensation, la voici. Le traducteur apprend à s'aventurer au profond de soi; ou, s'il le fait déjà, comprend qu'il a le pouvoir de le faire encore plus.[37]

This witness of another poet would be spurred on to become one and powerfully aided to succeed, the difficulties of their task would only anchor them ever more in the project. A paradox? The paradox of the translator? What makes the translation of poetry impossible is the very thing that arouses or compels the translator who suffers from it the vocation of being a poet. And here is the compensation. The translator learns to venture into the depths of themself; or, if they are already there, they understand that they can go even further.

According to Bonnefoy, the impossibility of translation awakens the poet to his or her poetic vocation encouraging them to venture into the depths of their own poetic awareness. Bonnefoy's sentence 'Le traducteur apprend à s'aventurer au profond de soi' echoes Leopardi's quest for that 'strato profondo e naturale che accomuna al di qua del linguaggio, il poeta antico e quello moderno', in D'Intino's words. The creative effects of the paradox are therefore directly connected with the issue of poetic inspiration. In his collection of essays *L'autre langue à portée de voix*, Bonnefoy offers an insightful perspective on this problem:

> Pourquoi une traduction ne pourrait-elle pas faire fleurir l'écrit qu'elle sollicite, en effet, fleur restée parfois en bouton? Sans trahir davantage que le rosier porté d'un sol à un autre n'est trahi pas ses roses alors quelquefois plus belles? La traduction de la poésie a pouvoir d'être un dialogue, mais même aussi une collaboration. [...] En bref, si le traducteur est poète la traduction est possible, et ni plus ni moins difficile que la création poétique directement pratiquée.[38]
>
> Why can not a translation make blossom the writing that it solicits, a blossom that occasionally stays in bud? Does it betray more than the rose bush, taken from one soil to another, is betrayed by its roses which are then sometimes more beautiful? The translation of poetry has the power to be a dialogue but also a collaboration. [...] In brief, if the translator is a poet, translation is possible and neither more nor less difficult than directly undertaking poetic creation.

In this passage we can see how Bonnefoy overcomes the logical paradox pertaining to the differences between languages. If the translator is a poet, Bonnefoy suggests that one must understand that the activity of poetic translation is as complex as that of creating poetry. In addition to this, Bonnefoy argues that the poet translator has the possibility to disclose hidden presences in the text. The poet who translates can develop the poetic text and make explicit poetic concepts that were silent in the original. Bonnefoy's blossoms metaphor helps us to understand Bemporad's translation of the *Electra*. As we will see in the following section, her translation methodology is heavily informed by the principle of *amplificatio*. Bemporad often adds new elements and takes the liberty to rearrange and develop certain themes by adding new words or even lines.

Bemporad's Translation Methodology

Bemporad translated Sophocles' *Electra* in 1940 as part of a wider exploration of the tragic genre. As a result, in between the summer and the autumn of 1940 she translated almost the entire dramatic corpus.[39] Her manuscript of *Electra*, which remains unpublished to this day, does not indicate the reference edition used for this translation.[40] Similarly, dictionaries, commentaries or any other aids (such as reference translations) are not mentioned throughout the pages of this juvenile exercise. A closer look at the fabric of text, however, together with an analysis of the Italian translations of Sophocles' *Electra* available at the time,[41] points in the direction of Enrico Turolla's translation, the pocket-slender format of the series *Biblioteche di letteratura*.[42] Lexical borrowings and syntactical similarities reveal that Bemporad, in all probability, had this translation before her eyes, and treated it both as a model, when she used the same or similar words, and as an anti-model, when she changed Turolla's generally archaizing word order.[43] Apart from having dissimilar poetic colours, the most striking difference between the two translations is that Turolla opts for a version in prose, whereas Bemporad – remaining faithful (even when working not for publication) to her principle to translate only poetry into poetry – uses blank hendecasyllables. This difference draws the attention to the trends in those years regarding the translation of Greek tragedy. Versified versions of Greek tragedy before and after the 1940s are the exception to the rule. As mentioned in Chapter 1, the intellectual influence of Benedetto Croce and of his positions on the nature of translation, and by proxy of the entire academic establishment of classical scholars, loomed large on the Italian cultural scene and on the publishing industry. Paolo Zoboli's bibliographical catalogue of Italian translations of Greek tragedy (covering the years 1900–60), from 1900 to 1940 lists only two translators out of a total of eight who produced metrical renditions of Sophocles' *Electra*.[44] Prose also remains the prevalent choice after 1940:[45] out of a total of five translations of Sophocles' *Electra* produced in 1940–60, none is metrical, with only the notable exception of Salvatore Quasimodo's rhythmical version of *Electra*.[46] The novelty of Bemporad's hendecasyllabic *Electra* appears all the more cogently against this ideological background. Her choice of the hendecasyllable, the most canonical verse of the Italian poetic tradition, is, however, a poetics of sorts, and one which was a defining feature of her literary career. The epistolary exchange with Carlo Izzo sheds light on her preference for this metre and on her metrical experimentation. In later years (1989), Bemporad herself reflected upon her choice of the hendecasyllable as the chosen metre for her translations and her poetry:

> Usare l'endecasillabo non significa applicare la misura di un verso stereotipo eguale in chiunque lo adoperi. C'è l'endecasillabo di Dante e quello del Petrarca, l'endecasillabo di Foscolo e quello del Leopardi e poi via via quello di Ungaretti (di *Sentimento del tempo*) quello di Saba e perfino quello del primo Pasolini. Non è certo mai in nessun caso lo stesso endecasillabo: ognuno opera al suo interno una sua propria personale e inconfondibile invenzione.[47]
>
> Using the hendecasyllable does not mean adopting the metre of a stereotypical verse that is the same in whoever employs it. There is Dante's hendecasyllable, Petrarch's one, Foscolo's hendecasyllable and Leopardi's one and little by little that of Ungaretti (in *Sentimento del tempo*), that of Saba and even that of early Pasolini. It is certainly not the same hendecasyllable in each case: each makes within it their own personal and unique creation.

This excerpt, taken from an essay discussing Bemporad's own translation of Homer's *Odyssey*, unravels her ideas on metrics, translation and originality. The choice of translating Homeric hexameters into hendecasyllables leads to a more general reflection upon the versatility of this metre. The 'personal' list of hendecasyllabic poets offered by Bemporad reads as a declaration of intellectual debt towards her poetic models. Most importantly, by comparing her hendecasyllabic translation of Homer to the ways in which the same verse was used by Petrarch, Dante, Foscolo, Ungaretti, Saba and Pasolini for their poetry, Bemporad discards the difference between translation and composition. The identity between poetic translation and original poetry – expounded by a reflection on the use of the metre – is evident from this passage. According to Bemporad, the poet's distinctive contribution lies in the personal use of the metre and on the creative modifications that can be made.[48] Such emphasis on the rhythmical design of the verse is further corroborated by another extract where Bemporad compares translation to reading a musical script:

> Ho cominciato a tradurre poesia quando ero appena una adolescente: i classici greci e latini soprattutto, ma anche Shakespeare, Goethe, Novalis,

> Hofmannsthal, Byron, Shelley, Keats. Poi i simbolisti francesi e i moderni lirici tedeschi (Hölderlin, Rilke, George): una specie di lettura o di interpretazione a prima vista di qualunque testo letterario come fosse uno spartito musicale.[49]
>
> I started translating poetry when I was just a teenager: the Greek and Latin classics especially, but also Shakespeare, Goethe, Novalis, Hofmannsthal, Byron, Shelley, Keats. Then the French Symbolists and the modern German Lyricists (Hölderlin, Rilke, George): a type of reading or sight-reading of whichever literary text as though it were a musical score.

The passage firstly draws attention to the prominent role that her poetic translations of Graeco-Roman literature had in her early years. The key idea of this excerpt, however, is the comparison between a musical score ('spartito musicale') and a text. Translation is described as a distinctive interpretative reading inspired by the music of the text. The analogy between words and musical notes further confirms her idea of poetry as music and showcases her belief in poetic translation as a practice aimed at creating a new *melos*, a concept that is continuously reiterated in Izzo's letters. The poetic version of *Electra* dates back to these formative years in which Bemporad was exploring her authorial voice whilst translating poetry. Bemporad's ideas on the use of the hendecasyllable as a metre capable of embracing a variety of voices and her reflection on the use of prosodic solutions (such as the iato, synaloepha, dieresis) that lend the line a desired rhythm are evident in her translation of *Electra*. This early translation of Sophocles demonstrates some of Bemporad's 'personale invenzione' (personal invention) using the metre, to use her own words. The *Electra*, like other tragedies, employs a variety of metres and rhythms in compliance with the genre's structural divisions into lyrical and recited sections.[50] The first thing to notice is that, although Bemporad respects these divisions (in the manuscript one reads the classical labels of parodos, stasimon, epeisodion, for example), in her translation, she reduces the metrical variety of the original by translating every line in hendecasyllables. In so doing, she tests the hendecasyllable prosodic possibilities in her effort to reproduce a variety of rhythmical designs in the original. Although it is obvious that to use the same metrical unit does not mean to reproduce the same rhythm over and over again, there is a tendency, in this translation, to expand the rhythmic length of the original. In addition to this, thanks to an extensive use of vocalic syllables placed in strategic positions within the verse (to facilitate as many vocalic encounters as possible) and in conjunction with a widespread use of enjambment, words within a single line, and verses within a given stanza, connect in a sort of 'waterfall' structure.[51] The result is an amplification of the vocalic timbres of the lines, a sense of openness and an occasional overlapping in terms of sound between the verses. This kind of reworking is paired with a tendency to hyper-translate. By reducing the metric and rhythmic variety of the original Greek to the hendecasyllable, Bemporad substantially lengthens the word count. The additions, ranging from single words to minor rewritings, often entail a syntactical restructuring of the line(s). If one reads Bemporad's translation in parallel with the original, the structural change between the place of thematic words and what we define as sensitive positions of the verse is immediately noticeable. The translator's attention to this repositioning of words within the verse is revealing of her awareness of how much the intricate design of the internal rhythm of the line rests on word order. It is precisely in these changes that one can see Bemporad's authorial hand. At the heart of this methodology is the poet-artisan's careful reflection on the process of creating a new syntax for the line, both from a content and rhythm viewpoint. The syntactical restructuring of the verse is informed by the desire to draw attention to certain thematic words and, at the same time, Bemporad uses the rearrangement to enhance key musical features of the line. Electra's θρῆνος / threnos (ll. 86–120) is a telling example of this way of working where Bemporad's translation methodology appears very much informed by a rhythmical design that emphasizes a specific feature of the Greek heroine:

Ἠλέκτρα
ὦ φάος ἁγνὸν
καὶ γῆς ἰσόμοιρ' ἀήρ, ὥς μοι
πολλὰς μὲν θρήνων ᾠδάς,
πολλὰς δ' ἀντήρεις ᾔσθου
στέρνων πληγὰς αἱμασσομένων,
ὁπόταν δνοφερὰ νὺξ ὑπολειφθῇ·
τὰ δὲ παννυχίδων ἤδη στυγεραὶ
ξυνίσασ' εὐναὶ μογερῶν οἴκων,
ὅσα τὸν δύστηνον ἐμὸν θρηνῶ
πατέρ', ὃν κατὰ μὲν βάρβαρον αἶαν

Elettra
O luce pura, tu etere che forte
la terra avvolgi, o miei infiniti canti
lamentosi; infinite, pur sul petto
sanguinante, ricevi le percosse
quando la notte lunga si disperde
nel chiarore dell'alba e il mio giaciglio
odiosa l'angoscia dei miei canti
delle veglie che celebro festosa
nelle mie case! Quanto, o padre mio
infelice, oh quanto ahimé, ti piango!

O you pure sunlight, and you air, light's equal partner over earth, how often have you heard the chords of my laments and the thudding blows against this bloodied breast at the time of gloomy night's leaving off! My accursed bed in that house of suffering there knows well already how I observe my night-long rites – how often I bewail my miserable father.[52]

Before this point in the play, Orestes and the pedagogue occupy the stage. Electra interrupts the dialogue, coming out from the palace to sing her mournful song. In the morning light (the time of action) Electra laments the fact that no light shines upon her cruel destiny and her endless sorrow. Bemporad adds the adjective 'forte' (strong), absent in the Greek,[53] at the end of the first hendecasyllable *a minore* 'O luce pura, tu etere che forte' with caesura after the fifth foot. The adjective 'forte' answers the evident metrical necessity of having an additional disyllabic word to finish the hendecasyllable. However, strength, together with endurance, is a crucial trait of Electra's psychology and one of the tragic questions raised by the play.[54] Bemporad's insertion of the adjective 'forte' in Electra's first words shows the translator's desire to enhance the element of strength. The adjective 'forte' is also placed at a critical point: it occupies the clausola of the first and second line and it is in enjambment, the first of a long list (twenty in total) in the space of this monody. This enjambment creates a pause on the syntactic function of the adjective (predicative of the subject) and stresses the intensity of the sorrow, which is a prominent theme of the tragedy and aspect of Electra's personality. Electra invokes pure light and strong ether, the highest part of sky, to introduce her endless sorrow, thus suggesting identification with the cosmos. Bemporad's lexical choice for ἁγνὸν is also striking. The adjective literally means chaste and according to LSJ (Liddell-Scott-Jones) it is said of things and places dedicated to the gods. The reference to Electra's chaste life and the holiness of her mourning for her father's impious death, soon to be confirmed by the Erinyes' appearance, are indeed projected in this φάος ἁγνὸν invoked by Electra. However, the rendering of ἁγνὸν with 'pura' (pure) might respond more to Bemporad's rhythmic interest rather than expressing the holiness conveyed by this term. The initial invocation 'o', in anacrusis, is followed by the trochaic rhythm of the words 'lúce púra', which also offer an internal assonance in their first syllables. These elements give a descending pace to the first hemistich in contrast with the second hemistich where the semantic presence of 'strength' influences the rhythm. In fact, after the syntactic pause of the comma, the second hemistich has a strong beginning, with the personal pronoun 'tu' followed by the *sdrucciola* 'étere' creating a rhythmic pause before the final 'fórte'. This example shows how Bemporad works to create a correspondence between the content of the verse and its rhythm: a parallel between the semantic climax of Electra's first line and its metric structure.

In the subsequent lines, Bemporad continues to make translation choices that, on the one hand, expand the wordcount of the text and, on the other, illuminate her interpretation of some of the key features of the Greek heroine.[55] For example, the decision to translate the line 'ὁπόταν δνοφερὰ νὺξ ὑπολειφθῇ' with 'quando la notte lunga si disperde / nel chiarore dell'alba' (at the time of gloomy night's leaving off) creates a correspondence between Electra's sorrowful songs and the time when she performs her *threnos*, namely 'la notte lunga' (the long night) which is absent in the Greek. The adjective 'δνοφερός' (l. 91), referring to night, means dark, or musky, and Bemporad's choice to render it as 'lunga' (long) has the effect of drawing attention to the element of the length, linking Electra's laments to that of a long night. By lengthening the night-time in her translation, Bemporad also draws attention to the Night, the metaphorical significance of which is an essential stage for Electra as a tragic heroine. Georges Méautis pinpointed how Electra's tragic initiation begins and develops when she experiences 'la nuit obscure', (the dark night) a state of absolute desperation. Yet, within a tragic context, the experience of darkness is only to discover the light, often metaphorically speaking.[56] Bemporad here expounds this connection thanks to the introduction, in her translation, of the light ('al chiararore dell'alba') that is found by the tragic hero at the end of his journey, anticipating what the play has not revealed yet. The insertion of the element of light in connection to the extension of the night-time is significant because it intersects with one of Bemporad's most vital poetic nuclei. As Pagnanelli subtly observed, Bemporad's poetic space is identifiable with the Night:[57] Night conceived as the privileged space for concentration and meditation, the time when appearances dissolve and a truer dialogue with the world and the Self can be established. Night as a symbol of Death (together with the 'ombra': shadow) is a structural presence in Bemporad's *Esercizi*, and specifically in the section 'Diari' (which was composed at the time she was translating Greek tragedy). But there is more to it. Bemporad's introduction, in her translation of the *Electra*, of the couple Light–Night metaphorically describes the heroine's desire to reunite with her brother Orestes, who she perceives as a part of her Self that is sadly lost. In a specular way, in her original poetry Bemporad longs for a reunion with a Self that she perceives as lost and her mourning, just like Electra's, focuses on the ways in which she can reunite with the object of her desire. If we consider this together with Pagnanelli's observation on Bemporad's belief in the exercise of poetry as giving access to a pre-natal reunion,[58] we can better identify the vestiges of Electra's condition in Bemporad's poetic imagination, and in particular in her dedication of her *Esercizi*: 'a una forma sorella' (to a sister figure):

> L'epigrafe di *Esercizi* (*a una forma sorella*) rende bene lo sforzo per ri-trovare la parte mancante di sè, la fede nella poesia come modalità della reunione prenatale; il sintagma va letto in una duplice direzione, fecondamente ambivalente: la 'forma sorella' è *in primis* la parola, poi, per chi fa poesia, la traduzione e viceversa, in seguito anche la consolatrice Natura. A mio giudizio, è ineliminabile la simmetria psichica con la desinenza 'femminile' del vocabolo.
>
> The epigraph of *Esercizi* (to a sister figure) clearly expresses the effort to find again the missing part of the self, the faith in poetry as a path to prenatal reunion; the fruitfully ambivalent phrase can be read in two ways: the 'sister figure' is firstly the word then, for one who makes poetry, the translation and vice versa, later also Nature the comforter. I think the psychic symmetry with the 'feminine' ending of the word is ineradicable.

According to Pagnanelli, Bemporad's poetic exercise is dedicated to poetry itself and to her poetic persona, perceived as a sister with whom she desires to reunite. The elements of Night and Light are symbolic spaces which are interconnected and allow for a narrative of pain and relief. Just like Electra who through her nightly suffering hopes to reconnect with her 'other half', her brother Oreste, so Bemporad explores the Night in its metaphorical stance, together with its analogues, in order to reconnect with the missing part of herself, the 'forma sorella', the poetic word.

Lines 105–10 are another example in which we can see how Bemporad takes the opportunity in her translation to develop the theme of light in connection with the length of desperation and sorrow. In the original, Electra uses the light of the stars and the image of the nightingale deprived of its own babies as terms of comparison for the length of her lament. Bemporad's insertion of the possessive adjective 'mia' (my) (absent in the Greek) in the first hemistich ('questa mia luce': this light of mine) stresses the personal connection with the dimension of light. Bemporad again enhances the length by introducing 'lungo' (long), which is absent in the original. In addition to this, she chooses a verb with more vowels ('echeggiare': to echo) and places the word in enjambment.[59] Overall, Bemporad seeks longer verses that aim to reproduce the lyrical dimension of Electra's monody. The high number of vocatives and the exclamations of grief (five in the original Greek and eighteen in Bemporad's translation) serve to highlight Electra's nature: she is pure lament.[60] Bemporad then further enhances this feature thanks to the position of these vocatives next to a word beginning or ending with a vowel. The verse thus stretches in length as the accumulation of vowels produces longer sounds. These long vocalic sounds can be read as the musical correspondence of Electra's grief. At the beginning of the parodos (ll. 121–8) is another example of Bemporad's tendency to expand the original and rework the text starting from key words that trigger her literary imagination:

Χορός
ὦ παῖ, παῖ δυστανοτάτας
Ἠλέκτρα ματρός, τίν' ἀεὶ
τάκεις ὧδ' ἀκόρεστον οἰμωγὰν
τὸν πάλαι ἐκ δολερᾶς ἀθεώτατα
ματρὸς ἁλόντ' ἀπάταις Ἀγαμέμνονα
κακᾷ τε χειρὶ πρόδοτον; ὡς ὁ τάδε πορὼν
ὄλοιτ', εἴ μοι θέμις τάδ' αὐδᾶν.

Coro
Figliuola mia, o Elettra, tu figliuola
di madre sciagurata, perché spargi
inutilmente sempre il tuo insaziato
gemito? Il padre tuo che da lunghi anni
fu empiamente tradito dalla mano
malvagia di tua madre ingannatrice
Agamennone, piangi. Oh possa presto
morire lei che ha osato profanare
con la morte il suo talamo, se pure
io posso dirlo!

Ah, Electra, child of a most wretched mother, why are you always wasting away in this unsated mourning for Agamemnon, who long ago was godlessly ensnared in your false mother's wiles and betrayed by her corrupt hand? May the one who did that perish, if I may speak such a curse without breaking the gods' laws.[61]

Here the chorus is sympathizing with Electra. The horrible crimes that have been committed are again the object of discussion, together with Electra's endless weeping. Bemporad inserts a small rewriting that summarizes Clytemnestra's crime: 'Oh possa presto / morire lei che ha osato profanare / con la morte il suo talamo, se pure / io posso dirlo!' The original Greek 'ὡς ὁ τάδε πορὼν / ὄλοιτ᾽ εἴ μοι θέμις τάδ᾽ αὐδᾶν' is more reticent (literally: May the one who did that perish, if I may speak such a curse without breaking the gods' laws). Death and *thalamus* are combined in the same line, providing a powerful image of Clytemnestra's impious sin as well as revisiting the literary topos of eros and *thanatos*. Bemporad makes explicit what was left intentionally implicit in the original, creating hendecasyllables that are thoroughly interlaced in terms of rhythm and content.[62] The first is a hendecasyllable *a minore* with the stress on the fourth syllable. The metrical pause of caesura *femminile* after 'tuo' does not coincide with a syntactical pause. The effect is that of creating a sighing moment of suspension after the name of the father. The second hemistich ends with synaloepha in the metrical syllable (-ghián-). A longer vocalic sound conveys the semantic meaning of the final part of the verse ('lunghi anni'). The intimate tone of the line is then followed by two hendecasyllables (twelve syllables) developing Clytemnestra's murder. A chiastic structure is also visible between the first and the third line: 'padre' and 'madre', and 'tuo' and 'tua' are in a crossed disposition, which works as a container for the thematic heart of the central line: the impious betrayal committed by the murderer's hand. In this way, both the father and mother figure are left out from direct connection to the crime, which is associated with the impiety of the hand. The first and the third verse are also structured similarly: the possessive adjectives 'tuo/tua' follow or precede the caesura creating a metrical pause. The possessives, whether they follow or precede the noun, create a sort of internal enjambment, which impacts the whole length of the passage. The first verse insists on the length thanks to the number of words used to compose the verse (eight in total) and the abundance of vocalic sounds. The third verse uses assonance ('malvagia tua / madre ingannatrice') and the alliteration of strong patterns of mute and voiced dental fricative in conjunction with the liquid sound of the 'r' (dr/tr) to highlight the harshness of Clytemnestra's lies. The analysis of these three hendecasyllables gives us an idea of the rhythmic movement created by Bemporad within the verse. An oscillation of longer sounds, internal fractures and suspended pauses produces an unstable rhythm that aims to reproduce the emotional distress in Electra's lament. Later in the tragedy (third epeisodion, ll. 1127–170), Electra is given her brother's ashes. The cinerary urn is the symbol of her brother's memory and the only physical remnant left of him:

ὦ φιλτάτου μνημεῖον ἀνθρώπων ἐμοὶ
ψυχῆς Ὀρέστου λοιπόν, ὥς σ' ἀπ' ἐλπίδων
οὐχ ὧνπερ ἐξέπεμπον εἰσεδεξάμην.

O tu ricordo
dell'uomo a me più caro, tu che solo
rimani della vita del mio Oreste!
Come diversamente ti rivedo
dopo tante speranze ahimè da quelle
che t'avevo affidate!

Memorial of him whom I loved best on earth, sole remnant of Orestes' vitality! How contrary to the hopes with which I sent you away do I receive you back![63]

The initial *quinario* presents three key features of Bemporad's interpretation of Electra: the vocative, recalling the heroine's constant invocation, the personal pronoun 'tu', hinting at the dialogical dimension of Electra's lament, and the element of memory ('ricordo'). 'Ricordo' is a key concept in this tragedy. The entire play revolves around past actions: mourning Agamemnon's death, bringing justice to the father's memory and repeating Orestes' past promises. Now that Orestes is dead the dimension of memory encompasses everything. The original concision of the Greek (three lines) is expanded by Bemporad's translation (six lines). The insertion of the personal pronoun 'mio', absent in the original, in synalœpha with the name of Orestes, recalls the symbolic sound 'o' of her lament, as well as reinforcing the brotherhood between Electra and Orestes. The personal pronoun 'tu' (in its direct and indirect forms) is repeated five times overall and highlights the dialogic nature of this monody. The μνημεῖον ('ricordo', a memory), the key word of this passage, leads Bemporad to develop an excursus on lost youth, vanished hope and a wished-for death in the following lines:

> (Oh fossi morta prima
> prima di abbandonarti in una terra
> straniera e sola prima di mandarti
> in questa terra a conquistarti il regno
> della tua fanciullezza e ritornando
> la più nera compagna che fingendo
> la tua città non potrà più mostrare i lumi
> delle stelle il mio pianto salirà
> con più dolore ad ascendere il cielo
> se ti mando).

> (Oh if I died earlier
> before abandoning you in a foreign
> land, and alone, before sending you
> to this land to conquer your
> childhood kingdom, and with the blackest
> companion returning, she pretended
> your city would no longer be able to show the lights
> of the stars, my tears will rise
> with more pain to ascend to heaven
> if I send you).

The passage is an addition, as signalled by the brackets in the manuscripts. Solitude, tears and pain are also very Leopardian themes. Had she died before abandoning Orestes, Electra would not feel so much pain. The presence of two gerunds ('ritornando', 'fingendo', characteristically Leopardian verbs) create a syntactically complex construction that enhances the impossible hypothesis, which echoes through the entire passage by means of the extensive enjambments. The subject of the first gerund is 'La più nera compagna', the Night. The theme of return, which has a positive connotation for Electra until this moment, is now paired with that of the Night and Death. Yet the Night, on this occasion, does not lead to light and brings a broken promise to Electra. In the following lines, Electra weeps over Orestes' shadow ('ombra'), another personification of the Night. This identification of Death and the word 'compagna' also surfaces in Bemporad's original poem 'Mia compagna implacabile la morte' ('Death my relentless companion').[64] In this poem, the personification of Death introduces the element of long and silent vigils ('la morte / persuade a lunghe veglie taciturne') recalling Electra's sleepless nights spent mourning. In the following lines of the translation we see that Electra, after this journey into impossibility, steps again into the realm of remembrance 'Eri fanciullo ancora / e io ti allontanai dalle mie case / figliuolo luminoso'; You were still a boy / and I sent you away from my house / golden boy). Desperation now leaves space for the desire of death as a way to emptiness, for the detachment from sensorial perception. The desire to be nothing but emptiness is where Electra finds the two halves reuniting ('la sorella / che non è ormai più nulla / e tu sei nulla:' the sister / who is no longer anything / and you are nothing). At the peak of her desperation Electra again finds a new vital impulse. The void in which she and her brother reunite for eternity is pure joy for Electra ('Così vivrò per sempre accanto a te!': So I will always live close to you). The motif of a new life in death also emerges in Bemporad's poetry, in the poem *Intarsio* (*Inlay*) ('O morte nella vita / la certezza che usurpa in noi da vivi/ tutto il senso di esistere': Oh death in life / the certainty that usurps in we who are living / all the meaning of existence).[65] The desire for emptiness and death is also the last reference of a series of Leopardian echoes in this passage. The Leopardian themes of lost youth, memory, solitude and broken hope are closely interconnected in this excerpt. However, Electra's joy that results from a lack of desire and suffering is probably the most resonant theme. Orestes is dead and, after desperation, Electra embraces death as the cessation of suffering, as Bemporad eloquently puts in her translation of ll. 1165–70:

καὶ γὰρ ἡνίκ᾽ ἦσθ᾽ ἄνω,
ξὺν σοὶ μετεῖχον τῶν ἴσων, καὶ νῦν ποθῶ
τοῦ σοῦ θανοῦσα μὴ ἀπολείπεσθαι τάφου.
τοὺς γὰρ θανόντας οὐχ ὁρῶ λυπουμένους.

ed ora voglio morta riposare
accanto a te, fratelllo! Oh è vero, i morti
non soffrono più nulla.
And now I want to lie down, dead,
close to you, brother! Oh, how true,
the dead do not suffer any longer.

In this passage, Death becomes the new light, the place and time where she can, at last, rest and reunite with her beloved brother. The prominence of Death and Night in Electra's discourse resurfaces in Bemporad's own poetic universe and conception of poetry. Night and its analogues shape Bemporad's poetic discourse and constitute a recurring trope in her work, as Pagnanelli outlined in an essay discussing Bemporad's poetry:

> Per mezzo di paramenti velari e di soavi paesaggi, la Notte lenisce il dolore con l'efficacia della contemplazione, il cui orizzonte è quello del riposo non violento. Al margine della visione si spalanca quell'altra notte (della letteratura e del libro) di cui discorre Blanchot, identificandone gli specifici orfici e metafisici nelle poetiche di Rilke e Mallarmé. In questi termini si realizza un' esperienza al contempo cognitiva e di abreazione. *Analogon* semantico e fonico della Morte e del Sonno, nella Notte si avvera, si rende possibile l'astensione del e dal desiderio (che Leopardi giudica nello *Zibaldone* stato della massima gioia, dell'infinito piacere che si prova nell'epochizzazione degli stimoli), con emergenza d'una rêverie nella fantasia della fine felice, nel rientro nel reame rassicurante della Natura.[66]

> By means of veiled vestments and pleasing landscapes, Night soothes pain with the efficacy of contemplation, whose horizon is that of non-violent rest. On the edge of vision opens wide that other night (of literature and the book) which Blanchot speaks of, identifying in it the Orphic and metaphysical characteristics of Rilke and Mallarmé's poetry. In these terms, an experience that is simultaneously cognitive and emotional takes place. The semantic and phonic *analogon* of Death and Sleep is brought about in Night, making possible the forbearance of and from desire (which Leopardi in the *Zibaldone* judges to be the state of maximum joy, of infinite pleasure that is felt in the

suspension of desires), with the emergence of a daydream in the fantasy of a happy ending, in the return to the reassuring realm of Nature.

The desire for emptiness and detachment from desires invoked by Electra is here contaminated, in Pagnanelli's reading, by the Leopardian view on what would be the state of supreme joy: the removal of any kind of feeling. The state of emptiness, paired with a morbid desire to be in the Night, to be accompanied by Death, to sink into a timeless Sleep and to be haunted by a Shadow are states of being that are more than once invoked by Bemporad's poetic Self in her work. Bemporad's poetics of Death, which finds full expression in her 'Diari', is deeply intertwined with the figure of Electra and informed by her vocabulary. Another example showing Bemporad's tendency to reinforce the presence of Night, also on the level of the signifier, can be found in her translation of the dialogue between Electra and Orestes (ll. 1203–29). The negative tones of the dialogue, which in its content continues to stress the emptiness felt by Electra after Orestes' death, are boosted in Bemporad's translation by means of placing numerous vocatives ('oh') next to the negative particles. The negation 'non' and 'no' together with the 'oh' achieves the double goal of lingering on vocalic sounds and recalling, on the level of the signifier, the metaphorical presence of the 'Notte' as the deepest moment of Electra's desperation. In defiance with classicistic and archaicizing tendencies, Bemporad's translation focuses instead on solutions that bring out the endless lament of the Greek heroine by designing hendecasyllables that often lengthen the rhythm thanks to the choice of words and sounds that defy the syllabic constraints of the metres. By emphasizing, when possible, the presence of the Night (and its analogues) as the defining feature of Electra's psychological profile, Bemporad shapes her interpretation of the heroine as a nocturnal being or agent whose existence is defined by her desire to embrace a state of absence of being (represented by her morbid attraction to Death) and by her vocalization of this desire in a relentless, nightly lament.

Electra's Translation in the Context of the *Esercizi*: Thematic Nuclei and Poetic Archetypes

The translations of the Greek tragedies were completed in 1940, when Bemporad was finalizing the first edition of her only book of poems, the

Esercizi, which was then published for the first time in 1948.[67] The chronological proximity between these two projects is not the only element that hints at the intersectionality between Bemporad's engagement with Sophocles' tragedy and her poetry. On a macrolevel, the structure of the *Esercizi*, composed of the sections *Poesie* and *Traduzioni*,[68] and its understated title, foreground Bemporad's viewpoint on the relationship between translation practice and original oeuvre. The *Esercizi* is an editorial project that defies the conventional conception of translation by which the translation is to be measured against an original. Within the enclosed space of the book, translations – printed without the parallel text – and poems are organically arranged, deploying a narrative that develops around a well-defined set of themes. As a result, the book becomes a porous site in which authorship and translatorship feature as *equals* (also in terms of wordcount), working in partnership to piece together the fragments of one poetic voice. This form of collaboration between translation and authorial voice, which is one of Bemporad's most distinctive trademarks, is best appreciated if read through the category of plasticity applied to translation.[69] According to the plastic model, translation is a place wherein the text continues to develop and morph reclaiming a life of its own.[70] Bemporad's translations – those in the *Esercizi* as well as those published as independent editions – fit this *continuation model*. Her translations respond to the stimuli of the original, often enriching and expanding the text. These extensions, or continuations, are the result of a dialogue between her own voice and those emanating from the source text. In other words, Bemporad's translations are a response of her own, an experience in which Bemporad performs an execution of her inner Self (*'esecuzione dell'intimo'*).[71] As mentioned before, the interconnectedness between the two sections of the *Esercizi* is most evident on the recurrence of certain tropes. On the one hand, the thematic links between her translations and the original poetry further strengthen the connections between the two practices whilst drawing the reader's attention to Bemporad's object of poetic contemplation. On the other, Bemporad's themes have a structural importance. According to Andrea Zanzotto, Bemporad's poetic creation happens in a cyclic movement where a concise set of themes (and stylistic lines) establishes and defines her voice:

> Giovanna Bemporad aveva già fin da allora fissati i termini di un suo movimento ciclico, da 'eterno ritorno', quasi al di fuori del flusso della storia

con i suoi eventi ma anche con le sue mode spesso effimere. La 'classicità' della Bemporad vive dunque di un compatto nucleo di temi e linee stilistiche, destinati non a variare ma ad approfondirsi, ad arricchirsi quasi sotterraneamente nel tempo.⁷²

Since then Giovanna Bemporad had fixed the terms of her cyclic movement, from 'the eternal return', almost outside the flux of history with its events but also with its often fleeting fashions. The 'classicity' of Bemporad thus lives in a compact nucleus of themes and stylistic features which are destined not to change but to deepen, to become richer over time in an almost clandestine way.

Bemporad's unremitting investigation of selected topics becomes an opportunity to reassert the necessity of these very topics. As a result, her poetic quest is grounded in a state of endless interrogation of her themes, almost in an attempt to defy the temporal dimension. In light of this, unearthing the origin of her poetic themes is not just a stylistic exercise but is revealing of her poetics and can illuminate the nature of her lyrical discourse.

Among her numerous translations, the versions of Greek tragedy and, specifically, the case study of Sophocles' *Electra* are of particular interest because they shed light on the origin of these thematic nuclei whilst offering the opportunity to witness the plastic model at work. Bemporad's poetics of Death, which substantiates the opening section of the *Esercizi*, together with the recurring presence of the Night, often invoked as metaphor and accompanied by a set of analogues, bears a striking kinship with the looming atmosphere of the Sophoclean tragedy. Electra's overpowering mourning experience is further accentuated by Bemporad's translation: the heroine's lexicon and agency speak of an extreme, marginalized condition from where she seems only able to lament the loss of her loved ones, herself included. These elements, transfigured and disguised, resurface in the majority of Bemporad's poems. Vestiges of Electra's condition, of her vocabulary and actions, are interspersed in the *Esercizi* either in the form of thematic references or recurring tropes. The appropriation of these traits, together with an emphasis on the themes of strength and of everlasting sorrowful song – which are contaminated by Bemporad with key Leopardian imagery – are at the heart of Bemporad's metapoetic reflections on her persona. Whereas the idea of an enduring lament prompted a number of intellectuals to interpret the heroine as a symbol of the rightful claim for justice overwhelmed by the oppression of an unjust power,[73] as we have seen from the close reading of Bemporad's translation, she appears to be interested in expanding the length of Electra's lament by means of hyper-translations, displaying an overall tendency to elongate the sound of her lines. In so doing, she reclaims the necessity of Electra's lyrical lament and, by extension, that of poetry. Electra becomes the symbol of an enduring devotion to a mourning *melos*. The necessity of her lament finding its reason for being in a void that needs to be filled is constantly described as a compensation for a life half-lived. Bemporad's poetic persona, as it appears in the *Esercizi*, and her metapoetic reflections bear a striking similarity with Electra's existential condition and her identification with pure lament. Pier Paolo Pasolini, in his review of the *Esercizi*, was the first to pinpoint this feature, describing Bemporad's poetic quest as a response generated by an emotional void, using Cocteau's image of the tightrope walker ('Potrei citare Cocteau: "I gesti dell'equilibrista devono sembrare assurdi a coloro che non sanno che egli cammina sul vuoto e sulla morte"' / I could quote Cocteau: 'The gestures of the tightrope walker must look absurd to those who are unaware that he is walking over the void and over death').[74] Remo Pagnanelli further expanded on this observation highlighting how the experience of alterity follows from the void, thus bringing together two key elements of Electra's personaltity: her isolated and different status and the emotional deprivations she experiences as a result of the tragic events of her family.[75] The combination of the elements of void and difference (connected by a relationship of causality) as the catalysing elements of poetic song are evidently reminiscent of Electra's condition. Electra is not only hated by her mother Clytemnestra and her lover Aegisthus, but she is also despised by her sister and, at times, by the chorus as well which explicitly reproaches her at the beginning of the play for her overly intense mourning. In Sophocles' play, Electra starts her song, a lament for lost love, a call for justice, a desire for death, from this condition of void and difference. The only affirmative thoughts are those in which Electra longs to reconnect with her beloved brother Orestes, whom she also describes as a part of herself that has been lost. Similarly, Bemporad's poetic self in the section 'Diari' of the *Esercizi* is staged on the repetition of this condition of loss and isolation, making death the protagonist of the majority of the poems. By a variety of means, the poems express the desire to reunite with her 'forma sorella', which Pagnanelli acutely identified with poetry itself.[76] The enactment of this pattern results in poems in which death is celebrated.[77] The opening poem of the 'Diari' section, 'Preludio', already contains the majority of Bemporad's key themes and it opens a series of ten poems revolving around the concept of death.[78] The poem begins by sketching a situation of eternal repetition ('Per mille e mille autunni sia guanciale / la terra alle mie palpebre socchiuse': For thousands and thousands of autumns / earth be a pillow to my half-closed eyes) in which we find the presence of a shadow ('presagio d' ombra': portent of shadow) set in a space confined by eternity and ambiguous laughter ('spasimi e sorrisi': agonies and smiles). This introductory image, metaphorically suggesting a condition resembling death, contributes to defy the dimension of time, lending to the poem an overall atmosphere of atemporal immobility of the poetic Self, which is introduced at the end of the poem by the image of a mask. Words like 'ombra' (shadow), 'smorta' (lifeless), 'assorta' (absorbed), 'sepolcro' (tomb) and 'immortalmente' (immortally) are scattered throughout the poem, effectively enacting Bemporad's poetics of Death which is also further explored in the text via analogues of Death, such as Night and Sleep (embedded in vocabulary like 'guanciale' and 'palpebre socchiuse'). The mask of the poetic Self and the litotic construction expressing the desire for death ('e non scolpita immortalmente vegli/ la mia maschera, chiusa in un cristallo': and not immortally sculpted may keep watch / my mask, enclosed in a crystal) contained in the final hendecasyllables end the composition, recalling at once the atemporal condition of the poetic Self and the Death-dominated lexicon of the piece.[79] After this initial poem, the theme of death continues to dominate the entire section, along with the themes of nostalgia and lost youth. In the second poem, the Self asks and appears astonished at the fact the end has come ('Veramente io dovrò dunque morire / come un insetto effimero del Maggio / e sentirò nell'aria calda e piena / gelare a poco a poco la mia guancia?': Must I really die therefore / like a fleeting insect of May / and will I feel in the warm, full air / my cheek, little by little, freeze?). Death is pictured as leading to silence and intimacy through the passing of a shadow in the third poem of the 'Diari': 'Mia compagna implacabile la morte / persuade a taciturne intimità / per un tramite d'ombra e di silenzi': Death my relentless companion / cajoles me into a silent intimacy / along a path of shadow and silences.[80] The theme of memory and silence as the two entities in which human existence is finally encompassed ('prima che ogni gesto si traduca in memoria e che ogni voce si impligli nel silenzio': before every gesture translates itself into memory and every voice gets caught in silence) further extend the nexus of metaphorical references exploring the idea of finitude. The poem 'Variazione su tasto obbligato' (Variations over an obliged fingerboard)[81] apparently breaks from the death theme to delve into the issue of 'dolore' ('quando non amerò che il mio dolore': when I will love nothing but my pain) in conjunction with the poetic Self's dream of light ('come il sogno di un'alba': like the dream of dawn). In particular, the words 'orma' and 'inganni' can be read – I argue – as a reference to Electra's recognition scene with her brother Orestes. The 'orma' (footprint) could recall the unknown footprint in Electra's father's burial place, which puzzles the Greek heroine. The word 'inganni' (deceits) could allude to the series of devices (in Bemporad's words, 'per inganni è morto e per inganni è tornato': through deception he died and through deception he returned) devised by Orestes to be able to return home. Together with these thematic words alluding to Electra's story, the dreamy desire of seeing the light at the end of the tunnel and the poetic Self's emotional attachment to grief could be read as references to Electra's painful condition. In the fifth poem ('Già comincia a segnare luci e ombre': Already beginning to mark lights and shadows), the poetic Self wishes to die ('In così dolce sera / non altro si vorrebbe che morire': In such a sweet evening / it wants nothing but to die).[82] The sixth ('Non soccorre all'eclissi vespertina': Do not aid the evening eclipse) pictures death through the metaphor of a ship sailing from riverbank to riverbank in a crowd of shadows ('E un poco risentita va la bianca / vela a smarrirsi in una selva d'ombre/malcerta di approdare a un'altra riva': And a little resentful goes the white / ship to lose itself in a forest of shadows / uncertain of reaching the other bank).[83] The seventh poem ('Dolore, che mi seguiti immortale': Pain, that follows me immortal) depicts pain as the eternal companion of humankind until death brings liberation ('Dolore, che mi seguiti immortale/ e indomabile fino al limitare / della morte, avrò gioia dagli spazi?': Pain which follows me immortal / and indomitable until the border / of death, / will I have joy from the gaps?).[84] The eighth piece ('Non farmi così sola come il vento': Do not make me as alone as the wind) depicts a personification of death coming to establish a physical contact with the poetic persona ('E avrò più cara / la morte se in un attimo, decisa, / piano verrà, toccandomi una spalla': And I will hold death more dear if in an instant, determined, / it will come gently to touch me on the shoulder).[85] The ninth poem ('Vorrei gettare ciecamente al nulla': I want to throw myself blindly into nothingness) uses a simile to create an identification between sleep and death and closes the thematic section on death ('l'intima oppressione / si converte in sopore e cede all'afa / che il mio pensiero dominante annulla / nel sonno non dissimile alla morte': intimate oppression / turns to drowsiness and gives way to sultriness / that my dominant thought undoes / in a sleep not unlike death).[86] The tenth poem, 'Paesaggio' (Landscape) – which Bemporad herself identified as a declaration of poetics – opens a new series where the theme of death interlocks with those of memory and the image of the moon, whilst hinting at the complexity of the process of poetic creation. The image of fresh and living water that quenches thirst stands for the codification of material into poetic form, where thirst metaphorically alludes to the physical necessity of writing. The flow of water and its dynamic vitality symbolise inspiration. However, water acts as a mirror in the second section of the poem and reflects the movements of the joyful women. 'Le donne che lavano le vesti and le ragazze che vanno a stenderle cantando' (The women who wash the clothes and the girls who lay them out singing) represent the transition from childhood to a more adult age which can still offer glee and joy. The journey of water is also a trip through memory. In the last part of the poem, one idea stands out, namely Bemporad's fear that her obsessive desire to make sense of the world through writing ('la smania di / comporre l'ignoto in forma certa': the mania to / arrange the unknown into a definite form)[87] may ruin the innocence of the heart, taking away her childhood. Featuring the themes of memory, nostalgia for childhood and the search for inspiration, the poem is replete with Leopardian echoes. In particular, the very last line bears a striking similarity to the following passage from a letter written by Leopardi to Pietro Giordani (30 April 1817):

> Da che ho cominciato a conoscere un poco il bello, a me quel calore e quel desiderio ardentissimo di tradurre e far mio quello che leggo, non han dato altri che i poeti e quella smania violentissima di comporre, non altri che la natura e le passioni, ma in modo forte ed elevato, facendomi quasi ingigantire l'anima in tutte le sue parti, e dire fra me: questa è poesia, e p[er] esprimere quello che io sento ci voglion versi e non prosa, e darmi a far versi.[88]
>
> Ever since I began to know beauty a little, that heat and that burning desire to translate and to make mine that which I read, has been given to me by none other than the poets and that violent mania to create by none other other than nature and the passions, but in a strong and elevated way, making my soul almost magnify in all its parts and saying to myself: this is poetry, and to express that which I feel, verse not prose is needed and I give myself to making verses.

The intertextuality of this line not only further confirms Leopardi's influence on Bemporad's poetic thought, but reasserts Bemporad's understanding of the importance of inspiration and its interconnectedness with the practice of translation. Leopardi's presence is further explored via the image of the moon which features as the elected confidante of Self and a symbol of Light in the dark nights in the next three poems. A text dedicated to Leopardi ('a Leopardi') occupies the central position of this 'moon' triptych (the other two poems are: 'Malinconica immagine su tutto' – Melancholy image over everything – and 'Nasce la luna come rossa aurora' – The moon is born like rosy dawn) where death features as a vertiginous presence. The poem 'A Leopardi' is an interesting mix of Leopardian and Sophoclean motifs. The image of a solitary girl returning to her house introduces the image of a grave ('io vedo spalancarsi / la sepoltura': I see the tomb open wide) recalls both Electra's desire for death and the concluding lines of Leopardi's *A Silvia*.[89] Five more poems interrogate the theme of death through an excursus on memory in the *Esercizi*. The section ends with the poem entitled 'Epilogo' in which we find two vocatives at the beginning of the poem which may reminiscent of Electra's lament over past events. The pure act of waiting for shadow ('attesa purissima dell'ombra') is a symbolic anticipation of death, expressed by the analogue of eternal Night ('notte eterna'). The thematic word of the entire section ('ombra') is then paired with an adjective ('tragica'). It would be hard not to recognize Sophocles' influence in this passage, the solitude of his heroes always on the edge of ultimate despair and darkness. Death, suffering, misfortune and vain fate fill Bemporad's poetic imagination in this first section of the *Esercizi*. To these themes Bemporad adds the Leopardian themes of lost youth, memory and nostalgia. The ambiguous laughter, another thematic presence of the 'Diari' always featuring in connection with a female figure, alludes to the painful stages of solitude and hostility experienced by Electra throughout the play. Time, another theme dominating Electra's condition, becomes fundamental in Bemporad's poetry. Just as Electra cannot recognize the paedagogus or Orestes because too much time has passed and she has lost the perception of time, so Bemporad's poetic Self appears crystallized in a timeless mask.

The tragic space of Electra's lament, her nightly wakening spent in endless lament, her life as deprivation (and therefore difference) from the very beginning can all be read as metaphors for Bemporad's poetic Self, to the point that the entire section of the 'Diari' could be read as a variation on the Electra theme. If Leopardi's discovery of the Ancients shaped his 'poetica della ricordanza' (poetics of memory),[90] Bemporad's encounter with Greek tragedy prompted the formalization of a poetics of death. Her investigation of the frail fate of the human being results in an endless lament that merges with a desire for death. The dark night of the tragic hero is Bemporad's permanent poetic condition. From this space she explores the themes of abandonment (often shaped in the image of a lost youth) and of desire for emptiness. Her lament moves from poem to poem, finding in them the only solace possible: reunion with her 'forma sorella', of which the reunion between Orestes and Electra is a parallel. This union is celebrated by a later poem entitled 'Forma sorella' (in the section *Esercizi*), which Bemporad herself described as one of the most important of her poetic collection. The negative particle 'Non' as the first word of the poem anticipates the appearance of the Night ('la marea della notte': the tide of the night) and of Sleep ('cadenza di sonno': cadence of sleep) at the end of the composition, thus enclosing the entire text in the semantic field of Death. Water (referenced in the text by the 'ruscello di seta': stream of silk) as the poetic process is where the 'forma sorella' – Bemporad's poetic persona – mirrors herself ('ti specchi': you mirror yourself is also reminiscent of Foscolo's sonnet to Zacinto) and dives in ('immergi'). The 'piede esiguo chiuso' (small foot closed) is the means through which this immersion can take place. It alludes to the metrical and rhythmic aspect, recalled through the classical terminology of the 'piede', of the poetic process. The first poetic unit depicts Bemporad's access to her poetic Self. This passage is mediated through the reflection of the poetic persona in the practice of poetry (symbolized by water) and the active development of the poetic word is made possible by metrics ('il piede esiguo / chiuso in conchiglia d'ostrica vi immergi': the small foot / closed in an oyster shell you plunge there). The second and third units of the composition describe the dialogue between the poetic Self and poetry as a dance. The use of verbs expressing physicality such as 'si distende' (spreads out), 'strofina' (rubs), 'si allunga' (stretches out), 'accarezza' (caresses) create dynamic images. Towards the end of the poem the 'sete d'amore' as 'grande bestia' (great beast) identifies the origin of Bemporad's poetic drive. This 'thirst for love' is always experienced through the Night, as the last line informs us.[91] The reconciliation of the element of desire with that of Night as the fundamental components of this identity echoes Electra's tragic condition and shows, once more, the impact that this figure had on Bemporad's poetic imagination. 'The sadness [...] of life that' the Greeks 'do not attempt to mitigate', to use Woolf's words in her essay 'On Not Knowing Greek',[92] is a cornerstone of Bemporad's poetic quest and the object of her poetic contemplation. Translating Greek tragedy, confronting that sadness, exerted significant influence on Bemporad's articulation of her lexicon. Her interpretative translation of Sophocles' *Electra*, theoretically informed by Leopardi's ideas on the poetic function of translating the Classics and practically performed using the plastic model, was an 'experience' that prompted a 'reflection' on her own poetic voice. By translating Greek tragedy, Bemporad embarked on a process of becoming which led her to find and voice the 'forma sorella' of the *Esercizi*. In this journey Electra provided a model, a paradigm which Bemporad used to reassert the urgency and necessity of poetry.

4

Creative Pedagogy and Poetic Translation

Camillo Sbarbaro's, Pier Paolo Pasolini's and Giovanna Bemporad's Commitment to Education

The relationship of Camillo Sbarbaro and Giovanna Bemporad with Greek literature was chiefly expressed in their poetic translations of Greek tragedy. However, these experiences are part of a wider and much more articulated discourse on the classics. Sbarbaro and Bemporad not only extensively translated works of classical literature, but also taught Greek and Latin in schools and as private tutors. Their teaching experience began in the period in which they translated Greek tragedy. In Sbarbaro's case, there is evidence that he taught Sophocles' *Antigone* at a state school in Genoa in 1927. As far as Bemporad is concerned, the dates of her manuscripts show that she translated Greek tragedy at roughly the time when she taught Greek and Latin in Pier Paolo Pasolini's school in Friuli.

Through the study of Sbarbaro's and Bemporad's experiences as teachers of Greek and Latin, this chapter aims to offer a perspective on their engagement with the classical legacy complementing their translation activity.

Sbarbaro and Bemporad had very different teaching experiences; yet, their relationship with teaching and their pedagogic approach are informed by similar ideas. Their reflections on teaching and on learning per se reveal the most palpable dissimilarity. Sbarbaro devoted significant attention to this aspect. His prose collections and his letters present many passages on the role of education and on his pedagogic methodology, often in connection with his thoughts on translation. Unlike Sbarbaro, Bemporad made no explicit theoretical reference in her creative work to her teaching experience, even though this silence should not be taken as a sign of little importance towards her teaching commitment. If we exclude her remarks in a memorial piece for Pasolini, the sources for her teaching experience are limited to Pasolini's biographers who quote Bemporad among the friends who came to teach in Friuli in 1942. Thanks to Pasolini's biographers, it is possible to form an idea of the kind of educator that Bemporad was and of her teaching approach. The charismatic nature of her teaching and her performative readings of her translations, followed by an oral commentary,[1] anticipate, in a sense, the performativity of her famous public readings of her translation of Homer's *Odyssey*. This way of teaching creates a tight intersectionality between her translation practice and the performative aspect of her lectures.

Sbarbaro, Bemporad and Pasolini aimed at letting the learning experience unfold as a real event in the student's life, through which the individual developed his/her independent thought by gradually discovering his/her real object of interest. With a different degree of theoretical awareness, they were attempting to change the cultural and social canons on which education is founded in the direction of what Andrea Zanzotto defined, using an oxymoronic expression, the *pedagogia apedagogica*.

The use of the Classics in the context of education must be considered in light of the specifics of the historical period in which they lived and operated, bearing in mind that Fascism – which came into power in 1922 – impacted on these poet-translators' lives. It is therefore even superfluous to mention that their faith in the Classics, also as pedagogical tool, had nothing in common with the clumsy attempt of cultural appropriation and instrumentalization of the values of the classical civilization perpetrated by the Fascism.

Sbarbaro, Bemporad and Pasolini, in his Friulian years, aimed at reshaping the role and the function of the educator through an innovative teaching methodology which placed at its centre the translation of the Classics as a moment of genuine dialogical exchange between the student and the teacher. Their interest in Greek poetry, so far explored through the filter of their poetic translations of Greek tragedy, has therefore to be assessed in light of their pedagogical commitment. The Classics are not only a source of personal poetic inspiration, but also a means of reasserting the vital role of poetry in education.

Camillo Sbarbaro: Teacher of His *prediletto* Greek

Camillo Sbarbaro started his teaching activity by invitation from the established philosopher and pedagogist Adelchi Baratono (1875–1947). Baratono had been Sbarbaro's professor of philosophy at the Liceo Classico (from 1905 to 1908) and afterwards became a close family friend. In 1919 Baratono asked the poet to tutor a mature student who needed help with Greek and Latin. The student, Luxardo Lelio di Costante, was a migrant recently returned to Italy from America. Lelio di Costante wanted to graduate in Literature and Philosophy at the University of Genoa, but had no knowledge of Greek and Latin and was therefore in need of private tutoring.[2] This is the beginning of Sbarbaro's career as a teacher. Clelia Sbarbaro, the poet's sister, recalled this episode in her biographical notes, *Camillo Sbarbaro nei ricordi della sorella* (1970):

> Tornò alla vita civile con i nervi a pezzi e per qualche tempo fu sordo e cieco a quanto gli accadeva intorno, cupamente chiuso in sè. [...] Questo stato di cose, che durò alcuni mesi, fu troncato di colpo da una delle sue impensate decisioni: accettò la proposta fattagli dal professor Adelchi Baratono, di portare alla laurea in lettere un non più giovane italo-americano del tutto impreparato in latino e greco.[3]
>
> He returned to civilian life with his nerves in pieces and for some time he was deaf and blind to what was happening around him, gloomily closed within himself. [...] This state of affairs, which lasted some months, was suddenly cut short by one of his unexpected decisions: he accepted the proposal made to him by Professor Adelchi Baratono to tutor a not-so-young Italian-American, completely untrained in Latin or Greek, for their literature degree.

This brief excerpt captures a challenging period of the poet's life. After the poet had returned from war, it appears that he was suffering from depression. He resigned from his job at the Ilva ironworks and began a way of life that will later be labelled a period *maudit*.[4] Clelia Sbarbaro noted that the difficulty involved in this first teaching assignment was the main aspect to convince Sbarbaro to take up the job ('L'impegno non era da poco, ma è probabile che a deciderlo fossero proprio le difficoltà'; The task was weighty, but it is likely that the difficulties were precisely what persuaded him to take it on.). As we will see from other sources, the more problematic the student's situation, the more interested Sbarbaro appeared to be. Moreover, Sbarbaro had to refresh his knowledge of Greek and Latin because he had not been using these languages since high school. Delving into the revision of his knowledge of Greek and Latin added to the complexity and intensity of the commitment.[5] However, Sbarbaro successfully saw it through: the word spread, and Sbarbaro soon became the teacher of 'impossible cases', tutoring only one student at a time.[6] This preference helps us to understand why Sbarbaro did not want to become a schoolteacher, a decision he made after teaching in two schools. The poet spent the academic years 1925–6 and 1926–7 at the Istituto Calsanzio in Cornigliano teaching Greek and Italian. In 1927 he took up a teaching post at the Istituto Arecco in Genoa.[7] Carlo Bo, then a student at the Istituto Arecco, had Sbarbaro as a teacher of Greek, an experience that changed his life, as Bo later recalled in a now famous piece titled 'Com' era Sbarbaro'. Among other things, Bo's remarks on Sbarbaro's teaching methodology are perhaps the most enlightening ones:

> Sbarbaro non era un professore né insegnava come un professore: era piuttosto un innovatore senza dirlo ma sicuro del proprio metodo che era poi quello della partecipazione, della comunicazione fra discente e docente.[8]
> Sbarbaro was not a teacher nor did he teach like a teacher: rather he was an innovator without saying but sure of his own method which involved participation, communication between teacher and student.

This brief fragment taken from the lengthy memorial 'Com' era Sbarbaro' – the most extensive source that we have on Sbarbaro as teacher – underlines the crucial importance that teaching had in Sbarbaro's poetic life. By comparing, later on in the passage, his teaching methodology with his commitment to carry on research on lichens as an independent and world-renowned scholar, Bo sees an illuminating analogy between these 'marginal' activities. By choosing to be a private tutor and an 'amateur botanist', Sbarbaro made it clear that he had no desire to be associated with any official institution or any kind of professionalism. The poet did not miss a single occasion to challenge the traditional idea of the teacher and the role of schools. Instead, he proposed empathy as the foundation of the educational deed. Bo points out that Sbarbaro could not have been labelled a standard teacher: he was, indeed, an innovator. The innovative feature of this method, labelled by Bo as 'metodo della partecipazione', (a method which involves participation) is confidently put into practice by the teacher, almost as if Sbarbaro did not know how to teach otherwise. After this, Bo describes one of Sbarbaro's lessons, thus giving us an insight into the practical reality of the poet's teaching: they translated Sophocles' *Antigone* in class and Sbarbaro read the tragedy by giving an almost interlinear translation. The aim of this kind translation was to avoid any kind of commentary or literary criticism, letting the bare Sophoclean word shine. The effects appeared to be extremely positive, at least in Bo's case: the pupil was fascinated by the poetic word. Sbarbaro's goal was to divest the text from all the secondary apparatuses (commentaries, schools of thoughts, interpretations). Sbarbaro's 'metodo della partecipazione' is discussed by Angelo Barile in 'Testimonianza per Camillo Sbarbaro':

> Fino a questi ultimi anni Sbarbaro si è aiutato a vivere traducendo e dando lezioni di latino e greco (il prediletto suo greco). Non dico del lavoro di traduttore, ma quello delle lezioni non è stato propriamente per lui un lavoro, tanto lo ha sempre fatto di suo genio. Fatica senza fatica. Il suo impegno, il suo scrupolo era solo eguagliato dal piacere che provava e che partecipava vivamente agli allievi.[9]
>
> Up until those final years, Sbarbaro earned a living translating and giving Latin and Greek lessons (Greek being his favourite). I am not talking about his translation work, but his teaching was not really a job for him, he always did it from his own ingeniousness. Effort without effort. His dedication, his meticulousness, was only equalled by the pleasure he felt and warmly shared with his students.

Another reference touching on the joys of teaching deployed according to Sbarbaro's method is found in a passage of his *Fuochi fatui* (1956), where the poet himself stigmatizes the idea of professional teaching:

> Quando m'avvien di dire che a insegnare mi animo e né lo scolaro né io avvertiamo il passare del tempo. Se chi ode è un insegnante, mi oppone un viso opaco o apertamente beffardo: a chi vuol darla a bere?[10]
>
> When I happen to say that teaching enlivens me and that neither the student nor I notice the passage of time, if the person listening is a teacher, they look at me with a blank or openly derisive face: who are you trying to kid?

Sbarbaro draws a subtle, yet very defined, line between teaching and being a professional schoolteacher. For him, *insegnare* (to teach) is one with *animarsi* (to cheer up): teaching lifts up his spirit, time is forgotten. The passage shows us that Sbarbaro fastidiously avoids applying the noun *insegnante* to himself, pointing at the fact that the poet by no means wanted to be included in the category of professional teachers. Drawing again from Bo's testimony, we are told by his pupil that, one day, Sbarbaro suddenly disappeared. Lagorio confirms this piece of information explaining the poet's sudden decision to abandon his school in Genoa. In January 1928 all the professors at the Istituto Arecco were offered *la tessera fascista*.[11] The following day a medical certificate arrived at the school, declaring Sbarbaro was unfit to teach because of heart problems. This is to be understood, according to Lagorio, as the formal reason for the poet's departure. However, beyond Sbarbaro's evident repulsion towards the Fascist regime, the episode of the *tessera fascista* offered the poet the opportunity to distance himself from the role of professional teacher.[12] The poet remained a private tutor of Greek and Latin for the rest of his life. His decision to leave school helps us to appreciate all the more profoundly his pedagogical ideas and how these influenced his poetic life. In a telling passage of *Fuochi fatui* – the poet's only testimony from this time – he presents his colleague Ettore Maestroni at the Istituto Calsanzio:

> Dove sei, che è di te, Ettore Maestroni? A dispetto dell'accrescitivo da cattedra universitario, m'era collega in uno di quegli istituti dove, per motivi di economia, all'insegnante non si chiede la laurea. [...] Amabile uomo; ma, anche per me, avvistarlo per strada era tentare la fuga. Acchiappato t'inchiodava tra le spinte della folla all'orlo d'un marciapiede e, alzata la manina didattica, dava il via al suo dire; inutile protestare urgenze, non avevi scampo. [...] Con questa disposizione a ascoltarsi, in cattedra trionfava.[13]
>
> Where are you, what has become of you, Ettore Maestroni? Notwithstanding the augmentation of university professorship, he was my colleague in one of those institutions where, for economic motives, no degree is required of the teacher. [...] Likeable man; but, even for me, to see him on the street was to attempt to flee. Having seized you, he would trap you between the shoving of the crowd on the edge of the pavement and, raising his little didactic hands, he would give way to his speech; useless to protest urgency, you had no escape. [...] With this disposition to listen to his own voice, he triumphed in his professorship.

The passage, one of the many satirical descriptions in Sbarbaro's *Fuochi fatui*, offers a valuable insight into the poet's ideas about schools and teachers. His colleague Ettore Maestroni argues powerfully for Sbarbaro's strong disagreement with the rhetoric of bombastic teaching. The comically pompous incipit sets the tone for the entire passage, which critiques the uselessness of posturing in pedagogy. The surname is already a caricature, 'Maestroni' meaning 'big teacher'. Sbarbaro underlines such an enhancement in the name ('accrescitivo da cattedra universitaria') – as if university lecturers should have a more pompous name than schoolteachers – in complete contrast with the humble school. The Istituto Calsanzio was one of those schools where, for economic reasons, the teachers were not required to hold a degree in order to teach. Sbarbaro uses this information in two ways. Firstly, it underlines the fact that he does not have a degree and that he is a schoolteacher purely because of occasional and randomly favorable circumstances. Secondly, it helps him to build an ironically bittersweet portrayal of Ettore Maestroni. What Sbarbaro presents in this passage is the caricature of the institutional notion of a teacher. Not only does he dismiss any kind of social prestige attached to the profession, but he also ridicules those teachers who believed in it and allowed it to become an important aspect of their role. Maestroni literally functions as a negative model. However, behind the ironic description of his colleague it is possible to find room for empathy and humanity, which are the reasons why Sbarbaro decided, after all, to include this passage in his collection. Towards the end, we can see how Sbarbaro found in Maestroni's way of teaching the innocent desire to find solace in words, or to say it with Lagorio 'si teneva su con le parole'.[14] Maestroni works as the perfect antinomy of what he, Sbarbaro, believed in, and did, as a teacher, or in other words exemplifies the difference between the teacher who loves to listen to himself rather than listening to the students.

The Tenets of Sbarbaro's Pedagogical Work

Sbarbaro's creative work reflects the deep and wide-ranging discourse on education thus underlining the interplay between poetry and pedagogy. The Ettore Maestroni sketch and the brief passage on the positive effects of teaching are only two of the numerous passages that highlight the poet's views on learning. His major prose collections[15] are home to a variety of references and thoughts, detailing his views on pedagogy and teaching. Among these, a corpus of letters titled *Trama delle lucciole* contains a significant number of references to Sbarbaro's teaching activity, testifying to a longstanding and intense commitment. A letter dated Genoa, 9 September 1937 offers a precious insight into the effects that teaching had on the poet:

> Caro Angelo,
> [...] Io non so se sto bene o male: buono certo, perché ogni giorno mi mette buono la bastonatura di sei ore di lezione ed altrettante di preparazione [...] Ma mi sorride il pensiero che fra dieci giorni o poco più mi porterò a spasso per mano come un bravo ragazzino che se lo ha meritato.[16]

> Dear Angelo,
> [...] I don't know whether I'm well or not: good certainly, because every day the thrashing of six hours of lessons and as many of preparation does me good [...] But I smile to think that in ten days or so I will take myself for a walk like a good little boy who has deserved it.

Alongside an improvement in his morale, in this letter Sbarbaro hints at a contradiction between labour and pleasure ('mi mette buono la bastonatura'). Interestingly, the co-existence of labour and pleasure recalls Bo's reading of Sbarbaro's poetic work and creates a parallel between the experience of being a teacher and that of being a poet.[17] Another letter, dated Genoa, 17 January 1926, sheds light on the ethical implications of the 'contradiction' of teaching:

> Quel calore che è ancora in me lo metto tutto quotidianamente nell'insegnamento; che mi lascia come una spugna strizzata. È la mia ultima nobiltà e la distrazione che mi allevia l'attesa.[18]
>
> Every day I put all of the energy that is still in me into teaching, which leaves me like a wrung sponge. It is my last dignity and the distraction which eases the wait.

The poet admits that he puts all the energy ('calore') left in him into teaching, thus disclosing its enlivening, ennobling ('la mia ultima nobiltà') effect on his existence. Indeed, it is a very ethical experience, a preparation for death ('mi allevia l'attesa'). The fundamental importance of teaching in his everyday life is evident in another letter, dated Genoa, 3 January 1936:

> Caro Angelo,
> [...] Lavoro a rottadicollo (ma non per me); sono 3 giorni, se oggi è il 3, che non esco. Persino l'erbario (alle mie spalle dorme). Il commercio quotidiano coi Grandi è per me piacevolissimo (sono un insegnante nato).[19]

Dear Angelo
[...] I work at breakneck speed (but not for myself); if today is the 3rd, I haven't gone out for three days. Even the herbarium (it sleeps at my back / which lies behind me). Daily commerce with the Greats is so pleasing to me (I'm a born teacher).

The letter showcases an interesting example of intertextuality where we can see Sbarbaro interweaves a nexus between his reality as a teacher and translator of Classics and Niccolò Machiavelli's regenerative dialogue with *antiqui huomini* described in his letter to Francesco Vettori. More generally, Sbarbaro's thoughts on education can be divided into three kinds: his personal memories as a student, the irreverent recollections of his own teachers, and his reflections on the role of school and teaching. These thoughts are interconnected with notations on translation of the classics, making the correlation between translation, pedagogy and poetic voice very close.

Following the chronological order, let us examine the poet's personal memories as a student. At the beginning of *Fuochi fatui*, Sbarbaro's last book, we read:

> L'anno che nel passaggio alla seconda liceo fu consentito di scegliere tra il greco e la matematica, i condiscepoli che optarono per questa lessero sulla loro lavagna: 'A noi le violette di Saffo, a voi un mazzolino di segmenti.'[20]
>
> The year when, in the passage to the second class, it was permitted to choose between Greek and mathematics, the fellow disciples who chose the latter read on their blackboard: 'To us the violets of Sappho, to you a bouquet of segments.'

This memory appears in the opening pages of the book, immediately after the poetics, *Ars iners poetica*. Such vocabulary as 'passaggio' and 'condiscepoli' conveys a ritual dimension. 'A noi le violette di Saffo', a quote from Alcaeus, makes Sappho the symbol of the whole of Greek literature. The solemn atmosphere is mitigated by the ironic phrase 'a voi un mazzolino di segmenti', but the superiority of Greek over mathematics is stressed all the more forcefully by the extension of the botanical metaphor to the mathematical term 'segmenti'. In another passage of *Fuochi fatui*, the poet traces the origin of his passion for literature back to his 'ginnasio' days and informs us that he infected his schoolmates with it:

Ragazzo, raggranellavo i soldi e da Varazze andavo a piedi a Savona per acquistare magari 'La signora Autari'. In ginnasio della mia sete di letture contagiai i compagni; leggevamo quel che capitava, libri innocenti e proibiti alla rinfusa. Allarmato dall'estendersi dell'epidemia, il clero locale intervenne: il parroco bandì dal pulpito la crociata, il curato improvvisatosi braccio secolare entrò nelle case a sequestrar libri. Alla voce del pastore, il paese si sollevò; io fui additato come la pecora nera; le famiglie ci diedero la caccia, ci frugarono addosso, scovarono libri fin sotto i materassi. Aizzati dalla persecuzione, escogitammo per il corpo del reato, i nascondigli più imprevedibili. Il giovedì, giorno di vacanza, io lo passavo in un orto; rimuovendo da una muriccia di fascia certa pietra, ritiravo, invaso da formiche, 'Resurrezione' (che lessi sino in fondo con una costanza di cui sarei oggi incapace). La cosa arrivò al punto che il vescovo se ne interessò; disapprovata dall'alto, la persecuzione ebbe termine e con essa, nei miei compagni, la scarlattina.[21]

As a boy, I would scrape together my money and go on foot from Varazze to Savona to buy maybe *La signora Autari*. In high school, I infected my companions with my thirst for reading; we would read whatever came to us, innocent and forbidden books at random. Alarmed by the spread of the epidemic, the local cleric intervened: the parish priest announced the crusade from the pulpit, the curate, improvised secular arm, entered houses to seize books. At the priest's call, the town rose up; I was held up as a black sheep; our families hunted us down, rummaged through our things, unearthed books even under our mattresses. Incited by the persecution, we devised the most unpredictable hiding places for the evidence. On Thursdays, a holiday, I would go by a vegetable garden; removing certain stones from a dry-stone wall, I would retrieve, covered in ants, *Resurrection* (which I read from cover to cover with a perseverance I would be incapable of today). Things came to a point when the bishop became involved; disapproved of from on high, the persecution ended and with it, in my companions, the fever.

Sbarbaro recalls the supreme pleasure of reading Leo Tolstoy's *Resurrection* during the holidays, alone in the vegetable garden, digging the book out of its hiding place. The pleasure of reading is empowered by prohibition. This episode shows that questioning authority is a fundamental spur to intellectual growth. The same idea can be found in a slightly different context:

Se leggi un autore, per quanto grande, a un giovane, non lodare tutto come fanno impunemente i chiosatori di Dante. Corri piuttosto censurando il rischio di sbagliarti. Solo così egli ti crederà quando esclamerai.[22]

> If you read an author, however great they might be, to a child, do not praise everything like Dante's commentators do. Rather run the risk of being wrong by criticizing. Only then will the child believe what you say.

Sbarbaro here transfigures one of his memories as a student in order to provide an example for a correct and sincere reading of an author. Sbarbaro challenges the poetic authority of Dante as a means to awaken critical thinking in the student. The presence of censorship is here a completely different kind. Used in an antinomic relationship with the action of praising ('lodare'), Sbarbaro proposes to use censorship to show the student that authors, no matter how canonical, need to be addressed with a critical attitude to fully appreciate their value. The example of the Dante scholars also serves as an anti-model for those who aim to kindle passion and trust in their students. From his memories as a student Sbarbaro derives a whole pedagogy. The poet still reasons as a student even while he must act as a teacher. Another memory of his school days is illuminating:

> Ragazzo, finiti gli esami, cacciavo la testa sotto il rubinetto nella insensata speranza di cancellare sin la traccia di ciò che avevo studiato. Ma studiare, specie a quell'età, incide si vede il cervello di solchi come un disco. Non è molti anni, dormivo ancora sotto l'incubo d'un esame da dare e mi capitava di svegliarmi con sulle labbra le parole: 'Tiro da A una retta a ...'. La lavagna era quella, orizzontale, del liceo e il problema che dimostravo, quello della perpendicolare a due sghembe.[23]
>
> As a boy, when exams were finished, I would run my head under the tap in the senseless hope of removing all trace of what I had studied. But studying, especially at that age, carves grooves into the brain like a disc. It is not many years (up until not so long ago), I would still sleep with the nightmare of having an exam to take and I would wake with the words 'Draw a straight line from A ...' on my lips. The school's blackboard showed a horizontal line while my solution to the maths problem showed a perpendicular line to two crooked ones.

Sbarbaro codifies his school experience as shocking, its legacy as a nightmare. Education is symbolically described as a contamination that Sbarbaro desires to wash away thus showing early awareness that the school experience was for him a sort of violence. However, Sbarbaro's views on school are not entirely as catastrophic as it might appear from this fragment. Notwithstanding his unremitting criticism towards the school system, Sbarbaro was able to interact with positive models while a student. The poet's memories of his own teachers offer valuable insight into the poet's pedagogic ideas, showing his models and anti-models. The poet himself provides us with the names of his own teachers. Don Giacomo Gresino, his old professor of Greek, a priest, comes across as a very positive model. He appears in *Cartoline in Franchigia*, a book composed of letters written by Sbarbaro to his childhood friend Angelo Barile:

> Le poesie. A Don Gresino (il salesiano che mi insegnò gli elementi di greco) per la stima che di lui conservo avevo mandato quella 'a mio padre', pubblicata sulla *Riviera Ligure*. Mi scrive: 'Se non ti offendi, ti dico schietto che da te mi aspettavo di molto meglio.' Non per questo mi sto convincendo (e amaramente rallegrandomi) che i miei versi piaceranno a pochissimi.[24]
>
> The poems. To Don Gresino (the Salesian who taught me the rudiments of Greek) for the esteem in which I hold him, I had sent the poem 'to my father' published in *Riviera Ligure*. He writes to me: 'If I may, I say frankly that I expected better of you.' Not for this I am convincing myself (and bitterly cheering myself up) that my verses will please very few.

Sbarbaro seems to trust Don Gresino's judgement. The fragment, composed with an almost illogical syntax, does not create a nexus of causality between Don Gresino's opinions and Sbarbaro's standpoint on the reception of his own poetry. Don Gresino is here pictured more as an occasion to reflect on his own poetry. Respect for the teacher's judgement, here shown by the poet's decision to send him the poem 'A mio padre', is then reinstated in another section of *Fuochi fatui*:

> Vento, sole, appetito e neanche una parola di letteratura: mi sono rinfrescato l'anima. Ma ce l'ho con te e te lo dico subito. Le cosette che scrivo sono, questo è certo, il meglio di me. Ora, come sono difficile a far amicizia, anche più sono geloso di quello che scrivo; perciò appena te le ho lette, dimenticatene ti prego anche il titolo. Se no ... Dal Beigua si vedeva il Monviso e il monte Rosa. Su un muretto ho scritto: *Montagne, amiche mie uniche, io sono / per la vita e la morte tutto vostro*. Buffone, ha commentato Don Gresino. A ragione.[25]
>
> Wind, sun, appetite and not even one word of literature: my soul is refreshed. But I'm angry with you and I'm telling you straight away. The little things I write, and this is certain, are the best of me. Now, like I find it harder to make friends, I am also more jealous of what I write; so as soon as you

have read my writings, please forget them all, even the title. If not ... From Beigua one could see Monviso and Monte Rosa. On a little wall I wrote: *Mountains, my only friends, I am all yours / for life and death*. Fool, commented Don Gresino. He's right.

Both passages show Sbarbaro's affection for his old professor of Greek. Lagorio stressed the importance of this relationship for Sbarbaro's approach to classical literature:

> La brusca rudezza del prete, la sua cultura non manualistica, ma nutrita del contatto continuo coi classici, l'ampiezza degli interessi, lasciarono una traccia profonda in Sbarbaro: ne è la prova più sicura l'aver sottoposto a lui più tardi i suoi versi.[26]
>
> The brusque rudeness of the priest, his knowledge, not textbook but nourished by continual contact with the classics, the breadth of his interests, left a profound trace on Sbarbaro; even more certain proof of it lies in the fact he later presented his verses to him.

The importance of Don Gresino in Sbarbaro's relationship with classical literature is more than a 'traccia profonda'. It is a very precise influence: Don Gresino's continuous contact with the classics and his anti-academic approach modelled Sbarbaro's way of teaching. Sbarbaro's request for Don Gresino's approval for his poetic compositions could also be read in a symbolic way. By asking his old teacher of Greek to read his own poetry, Sbarbaro metaphorically asks the classics for poetic approval thus unveiling the creative spur that he assigned to the knowledge of classics. The interplay between Sbarbaro's poetic universe and his relationship with the classics filtered by education shows in another passage focusing on Don Gresino's personality. A piece entitled 'Visita al collegio', from the book *Scampoli* (1960), offers a detailed description of the priest which can help us to further appreciate Sbarbaro's affection towards his former teacher of Greek:

> Nel parlatorio dove son venuto a cercare dell'antico maestro, riprovo il disagio che già da ragazzo. [...] Ritrovo nel maestro i bruschi modi che amo. Propone con mio sollievo un'arrampicata all'aperto. [...] Qualcosa a questo punto passa nella voce del maestro; l'ha alzata ad affrettare disinvoltura; non vorrei fosse a causa di questo incontro. Per uno simile, un giorno che ci accompagnava in una passeggiata collegiale, la voce, mi sovviene, gli era uscita così diversa da non lasciarmela riconoscere; perchè, già allora, m'era

venuto di pensare che la via scelta dal maestro doveva condurre più presto alla santità che alla pace. [...] Lo guardo. Che vita deserta. Di genitori, non ho udito da lui come ne avesse avuto. Dalla sua terra, più del disamore per il borgo nativo *tutto ciottoli e buine,* lo tiene lontano la paura, come di versiera, della sorella; miscredente e accesa socialista, che non ha voluto rivederlo da quando, ordinandosi, ha disertato secondo lei il suo posto di stenti. I colleghi, coi quali per principio è solidale, uno ad uno li vede quali sono e gli sfuggono sul loro conto parole senza carità. Appena usciti dalla scuola, gli alunni si rifanno della passata soggezione non salutandolo; avvicinati, non nascondono impazienza e distacco. Di tanti che in una vita d'insegnamento gli son passati sotto gli occhi, il mio è l'unico viso che gli ricompaia qualche volta davanti.[27]

In the parlour where I went to seek out my old teacher, I feel again the unease I felt as a boy. I find again the brusque ways that I love. To my relief he proposes a climb outside. [...] At this point something happens in the teacher's voice; it has risen to hurried flippancy: I do not want it to be caused by this meeting. At a similar meeting, one day he accompanied us on a school walk, I remember his voice came out so differently that I could not recognise it; because, even then I had begun to think that the way chosen by the teacher would lead sooner to holiness than peace. [...] I look at him. What a desolate life. Of parents, I have heard nothing from him, as if he never had them. More than lack of love for its *pebbles and buine,* fear keeps him distant from his native town, fear as though of a witch, of his sister; unbelieving and intense socialist who did not want to see him again since in being ordained, in her opinion, he deserted his place of struggle. His colleagues, with whom he is in principle sympathetic, one by one he sees what they are and unkind words about them escape him. As soon as they leave school, the pupils make up for their past respect by not greeting him; close to, they do not hide impatience and indifference. Of the many that have passed under his eyes as a teacher, mine is the only face that sometimes reappears before him.

The passage begins with Sbarbaro recalling his old teacher's beloved manners. The teacher and the former pupil decide to take a walk, metaphorically recalling the teacher's arduous path through life ('un'arrampicata all'aperto') and a welcomed exit from the schoolrooms. Sbarbaro focuses on the teacher's life, showing a deep affection and a sense of profound empathy. Roles are well defined. Don Gresino is always referred to as *maestro*. Sbarbaro calls himself the schoolboy ('ragazzo') or simply one of the many students taught by Don

Gresino. The melancholic, yet affectionate tone of the passage defines Sbarbaro's lovely homage to his old teacher, whose most precious lesson is his relentless yet modest devotion to teaching.

A significant anti-model, on the contrary, query is the professor of Italian literature Pietro Fiammazzo to whom Sbarbaro devotes a long, ironic description in his *Gocce* (1963):

> Lo vedo ancora il *mio* dantista, nell'aula gelida, chiuso nel soprabito dove non una sola asola era sbottonata, ritto in piedi alto com'era presso la cattedra che sfiorava appena del gomito, sogguardandoci distante e sospettoso di dietro le lenti in equilibrio precario e segnando il tempo con la lunga appuntitissima matita brandita in aria scandire appoggiando sulle dieresi: *Quale nei plenilunii sereni Trivia ride tra le ninfe eterne* ..., citazione prediletta che a causa dei nostri cachinni e rumoreggiamenti inconsulti di rado riusciva a condurre a termine e interrompeva allora per esclamare col suo Autore: *O terreni animali, o menti grosse / sciocche*. [...] Il bilancio che a fin d'anno chi ci tenesse poteva fare era quindi lo stesso che onestamente lui faceva ad ogni fine lezione: tutto ciò che della Commedia ritenevamo, per averli le mille volte uditi, erano i due versi menzionati in principio e neanch'essi avremmo saputo reperirli nel testo. Le forti emozioni, si dice, sono mute; e forse il suo amore per Dante era troppo perchè potesse comunicarlo.²⁸

I can still see my *dantista*, in the freezing classroom, wrapped in an overcoat on which not a single buttonhole was undone, standing upright and tall as he was beside the lectern that just brushed his elbow, peering at us, distant and suspicious from behind his precariously balanced glasses and marking the time with a long, sharp pencil brandishing in the air to punctuate and emphasise the diaeresis: *Quale nei plenilunii sereni Trivia ride tra le ninfe eterne* ... (As on calm, moonlit nights / Diana smiles amongst the eternal nymphs ...) favourite quotes which, due to our outbursts of laughter and sudden clamouring, he rarely managed to complete and would then interrupt to exclaim, like his author: *O terreni animali, o menti sciocche* (Oh earthbound animals, oh coarse minds ...). [...] The report that those who cared could make at the end of the year was therefore honestly the same that he made at the end of every lesson: all we could remember of the *Commedia*, having heard them a thousand times, were the two verses mentioned at the beginning and even those, we would not have known where to find them in the text. Strong emotions, it is said, are mute; and perhaps his love for Dante was too great for him to be able to communicate it.

The difference between the model and the anti-model is evident from the style of the fragment itself. For Don Gresino, Sbarbaro employs a pathetic and emotional register, whereas for Fiammazzo he uses an ironic and sarcastic style. Fiammazzo comes across as an unreliable source of information from the way in which he is presented. The 'aula gelida' immediately anticipates the dry and cold nature of his teaching. Fiammazzo's pedantic approach, towards which Sbarbaro is clearly hostile, is epitomized in the way he reads. The teacher is entirely concentrated on the perfect diction and on the pronunciation of dieresis. Philological expertise, knowledge of prosody and a tedious display of variants also demonstrate Fiammazzo's hyper-academic approach.

As is evident from this memory Sbarbaro entirely rejected this approach. The lack of communication with the students, evidenced by the fact that the professor was not even aware of the students' protests, is highlighted throughout the entire passage. Such a critique finds its peak in the final paradox of the teacher who, for loving the subject too much, cannot communicate it.

Besides the satirical description of teachers we have just seen, there are several passages expressing the poet's own radical ideas about school. In *Fuochi fatui*, such passages are grouped together and presented as a negative summary on teaching:

> Al motto che campeggia sulla facciata: Non scholae sed vitae: 'Si scrive così ma si legge: Non discenti sed docenti.'
> Laurea è dispensa da imparare: il pezzo di carta su cui ci si siede per difendere l'alfine acquisito diritto all'ignoranza.
> Ministro della Pubblica Istruzione, mi scalzerei il posto col primo provvedimento: abolirei le scuole. L'istruzione tornerebbe a essere quello che è: il privilegio di chi lo merita. Il quale non avrà bisogno di insegnanti: imparerà da sé – che è il solo modo di imparare.
> Prova a chiedere a chi la parla dalla nascita gli elementi della sua lingua; al corridore, come si va in bicicletta . . . Insegnare si può solo quello che non si sa.[29]

> To the motto that dominates the façade: Non scholae sed vitae: 'It is written thus but read: Not pupils but teachers.'
> A degree is an exemption from learning: the piece of paper on which one rests to defend the acquired right to ignorance.
> Ministry of Public Education, I would get rid of the place as a first measure: I would abolish schools. Education would return to what it is: the privilege

of those who deserve it. This will not need teachers: one will learn independently – which is the only way to learn.
Try asking a speaker from birth the elements of their language, the racer how to ride a bike ... One can only teach what one does not know.

This sequence of thoughts condenses Sbarbaro's critique of the school system. In sum, teaching is self-teaching, or making oneself learn from what one does not know. The poet begins by accusing the school of mystifying its function. He then faults higher education for offering degrees as a means to dismiss intellectual commitment instead of fostering the individual's responsibility in learning. Sbarbaro eventually and climactically postulates a condition, apparently paradoxical and somewhat reminiscent of the Socratic approach, in which teaching is based solely on ignorance. In other words, a teacher can only teach what he does not know. Sbarbaro's ideas are not as naïve as they might seem at first glance. From an eccentric position, but, evidently, from his experience as a teacher of classics, Sbarbaro engages with two major issues in modernity: the role of school and of the transmission of classical literature. His fierce criticism of his hyper-academic teachers may remind us of Michel de Montaigne's stark opposition to pedantry in relation to the transmission of classical civilization.[30] In the famous metaphor of the bees and flowers (which has a very long tradition, going all the way back to Plato), Montaigne pinpointed the vital function of the Ancients:

> Les abeilles pillotent deçà delà les fleurs, mais elles en font après le miel, qui est tout leur: ce n'est pas thym ni marjolaine; ainsi les pièces empruntées d'autrui, il les transformera et confondra, pour en faire un ouvrage tout sien, à savoir son jugement.[31]
>
> The bees plunder flowers here and there but they then make a honey which is all their own: it is not thyme or marjoram. So pieces borrowed from others he will transform and mix to make a work all his own, that is, his judgement.

It is evident how Montaigne considered the classics a vital source of inspiration ('les fleurs') for the Moderns ('les abeilles') who, thanks to the Ancients' mediation, can develop their inherent nature ('un ouvrage tout sien').[32] In opposition to the true *connoisseurs* are the pedantic imitators of the Ancients, parasites who spoil their noble function.[33] The generosity of the Classics and the critique of psittacism, i.e. parrot repetition, resonates in Sbarbaro's thoughts on school. As a teacher of classics, Sbarbaro not only condemned the pedantic attitude, stressing the damage such an approach could bring to the true knowledge of the classics, but also fostered a personalized didactics which could assist the student in the discovery of his/her true object of interest. Sbarbaro conceived the study of the classics as a shared experience in which the student and the teacher are equally participating at the same level. Among the many passages stressing this aspect, the dialogic nature of this experience is particularly evident in one of his *Trucioli dispersi*:

> Conquistai la fiducia della nuova scolara, prevenendola che del greco non so l'alfabeto.[34]
>
> I won the trust of the new pupil by warning her that I do not know the Greek alphabet.

Behind Sbarbaro's provocative statement we should read a twofold agenda. First, it reveals a substantial critique of the canonical method of teaching Greek in schools. By telling the student that he, the tutor of Greek, does not know the Greek alphabet he immediately distances himself from the traditional, Fiammazzo-like way of teaching Greek in school. Indeed, he questions the very principle of educational authority. Secondly, it is evident how Sbarbaro uses a paradox to put forward his own 'metodo della partecipazione'. The poet undermines his own authority by declaring his gaps in knowledge, aiming at putting himself on the same level as the student. Sbarbaro's criticism towards the limitations of classical education in an institutional system bears interesting analogies with Friedrich Nietzsche's polemical attack on the so-called classical education in the homonymous fragment taken from *Daybreak: Thoughts on the Prejudices of Morality*:

> *The so-called classical education.* – [...] the squandering of our own youth when our educators failed to employ those eager, hot and thirsty years to lead us towards *knowledge* of things but used them for a so-called 'classical education'. The squandering of our own youth when we had a meager knowledge of the Greeks and the Romans and their languages drummed into us in a way as clumsy as it was painful and one contrary to the supreme principle of all education, that one should offer food only to him *who hungers for it*! [...] What we felt instead was the breath of a certain disdain for the actual sciences in favour of history, of 'formal education' and of 'the classics'!

And we let ourselves be deceived so easily! Formal education! Could we not have pointed to the finest teachers at our grammar schools, laughed at them and asked: 'are they the products of formal education? And if not, how can they teach it? And the classics! Did we learn anything of that which these same ancients taught their young people? Did we learn to speak or write as they did? Did we practice unceasingly the fencing-art of conversation, dialectics? Did we learn to move as beautifully and proudly as they did, to wrestle, to throw, to box as they did? Did we learn anything of the asceticism practiced by all Greek philosophers? Were we trained in a single one of the antique virtues and in the manner in which the ancients practised it? Was all reflection on morality not utterly lacking in our education – not to speak of the only possible critique of morality, a brave and rigorous attempt to *live* in this or that morality? Was there ever aroused in it any feeling that the ancients regarded more highly than the moderns? Were we ever shown the divisions of the day and of life, and goals beyond life, in the spirit of antiquity? Did we learn even the ancient languages in the way we learn those of living nations – namely, so as to speak them with ease and fluency? Not one real piece of ability, of new capacity, out of years of effort! [...] For the proud conceit of our classics teachers goes far in imagining they are as it were *in possession of the ancients* that they transfer this arrogance to their pupils, together with the suspicion that such possession, while it certainly does not make us happy, is good enough for poor, foolish, honest old book-dragons: 'let these dragons brood over their hoard! For it will be worthy of them!' – it is with this silent thought that our classical education is concluded. – This can no longer be made good – so far as we are concerned! But let us not think only of ourselves.[35]

In this splendid passage, Nietzsche outlines the problematic complexity of classical education, touching on such fundamental themes as the 'hunger for knowledge' and teachers' communication of the Classics. The shortcomings of formal education are primarily connected to the fact that the students do not experience a real desire for knowledge. Nietzsche almost seems to postulate an anthropologically necessary reason for learning. Sbarbaro's *fuoco fatuo* 'L'istruzione tornerebbe a essere quello che è: il privilegio di chi lo merita'[36] (Education would return to what it is: the privilege of those who deserve it). strongly echoes Nietzsche's view on the 'hunger for knowledge' as 'the supreme principle of all education.' Moreover, Nietzsche's critique of 'our classics teachers' helps us to appreciate Sbarbaro's profound resilience towards formal education. Nietzsche laments that teachers of classics developed a despotic possession and failed to communicate and teach the most valuable of all lessons one could learn from the classics, namely *the reflection on morality*. Such deficits lead to a certain kind of deception as well as failure to deliver to the students the complexity entailed in the knowledge held by the Greeks. Sbarbaro's critique of compulsory education and shallow academism were the reasons why Sbarbaro himself quit his own 'formal' education. As a student, he did not pursue higher education. Nonetheless, his passion for the Classics was not thwarted. When he had the opportunity of becoming a private tutor of Classics, he promptly devised a new didactic method. In an autobiographical piece written in the form of an interview, 'Visita al maestro',[37] he constructs his professional trajectory in a most memorable manner:

- Maestro ... – esordisco.
- ... di scuola. E nemmeno: non ho la laurea né diploma.
- [...]
- Sai piuttosto come andò che non proseguii, come si dice, gli studi? – E racconta: – Quando uscii dal liceo, mio padre era vecchio e si viveva in tre sulla pensione di maggiore del Genio. Quel che s'augurava, e al più presto, era di vedermi impiegato; ma s'arrese alle insistenze dei miei insegnanti. Un mattino, Benedetta mi accompagnò alla stazione, mi consegnò trenta lire, un calamaietto tascabile e con questo viatico m'imbarcai per Firenze: si trattava di vincere una borsa di studio a quell'Istituto di Studi superiori. [...]
- Fatto sta che il mattino dopo, invece di avviarmi verso piazza San Marco per sostenere la prima prova, passava una fanfara militare e mi accodai. Scarto, di cui ancora ringrazio il Cielo –.
- Insegna, però ... – osservai.
- Già; e dalla fine della prima guerra. Ritornato dal fronte e liberatomi con un cavillo dall'impiego – altro scarto che benedico – riaffrontati col solo aiuto del vocabolario l'odioso latino e il diletto greco, cimentandomi direttamente coi testi; e in capo a qualche mese di duro lavoro, fui in grado di assitere uno studente universitario nella traduzione di Pindaro ... Sì, perchè – ricòrdatelo, figliola – imparare si può solo da sé. Le scuole ci sono per chi insegna –.[38]
- Teacher ... – I begin.

- ... of school. And not even: I don't have a degree or a diploma.
- [...]
- You know how it was that I did not continue, as they say, my studies? – And he says: When I left high school my father was old and three of us had to live on his engineering corp pension. What he hoped, and as soon as possible, was to see me employed; but he gave in to the insistence of my teachers. One morning, Benedetta took me to the station, gave me 30 lire and a pocket inkwell, and with these supplies I set off for Florence. I was going to win a scholarship to study at the Institute of Advanced Studies. [...].

  The fact was next morning rather than making my way to Piazza San Marco to sit the first test, a military band went past and I got in line. A deviation for which I still thank heaven.
- But you teach ... I observed.
- Right. Since the beginning of the first war. Returning from the front and, on a technicality, freed from employment – another deviation I'm thankful for – with the sole aid of a dictionary, I again confronted hateful Latin and beloved Greek, grappling directly with the texts. And within a few months of hard work, I was able to help a university student translate Pindar. Yes, because – and remember this child – you can only learn on your own. Schools are there for the teachers.

The poet boils down his professional and personal life into two *scarti* originating from the same root, touching again on the fundamental role of necessity as the engine of learning experience, a necessity which – it is worth underlining again – must be awakened within the pupil. The almost invisible assistance of the so-called teacher (Sbarbaro uses the verb 'assistere'), a linguistic instruction solely based on dictionaries – interestingly there is no mention of the use of grammars – and close reading of the texts ('cimentandomi direttamente con i testi') are Sbarbaro's teaching tools. The passage highlights a recurring feature of Sbarbaro's thought, which here finds its application to the educational context. The poets' hostility towards any institutionalized and formalized scenario becomes all the more intense when applied to the learning experience. By revisiting his juvenile memories relating to his own choices to reject formal education, Sbarbaro legitimizes his perceptions as a student towards the institutionalized learning environment whilst linking his life as a student and as teacher.

Ricordo di Giorgio Labò: The Unexpected Gifts of Teaching Latin

The letters and the aphoristic thoughts scattered throughout Sbarbaro's poetic work provide us with a clear picture of the poet's ideas about school and teaching. Yet, Sbarbaro worded his most profound reflections on the relationship between student and teacher in a memorial for one of his former students. The eulogy 'Ricordo di Giorgio Labò' was composed by Sbarbaro in 1946 for the commemorative volume *Un sabotatore: Giorgio Labò*.[39] Unfortunately, Sbarbaro failed to submit his piece on time.[40] He finally published the *Ricordo di Giorgio Labò* only in 1969 (700 copies), twenty-five years after Labò's death.[41] Labò (1919–44), a student in the faculty of architecture, was called to arms during the Second World War. He joined the GAP (Gruppi di Azione Patriottica) as a sapper, but was captured by the German troops on 1 February 1944, tortured and eventually killed after refusing to provide information about his fellow soldiers.[42] Sbarbaro privately tutored Giorgio Labò when he was at the 'ginnasio' and later at the 'Liceo', and his personal relationship with Labò as a student largely informs the 'Ricordo'. The learning aspect is so prominent that the essay could be considered a pedagogical treatise on the teaching of Latin language and literature. The notion of teaching, however, ends up expanding into a metaphor for the nature of interaction with the other subjectivities.

The essay can be divided into four sections. The first section sets the foundation of Sbarbaro's teaching philosophy. A psychological assessment of the pupil's personality informs the second section. Here, we also find the 'golden' rules of Sbarbaro, concerning the study of Latin grammar, syntax and literature. The third section takes a moral turn. Sbarbaro, indeed, realizes that what will stay with the student is not the subject taught but, more probably, some inherent qualities that he conveyed as a teacher and as a human being. At the same time, this section develops the two-way relationship between student and teacher as it demonstrates the nature of the lesson that Sbarbaro learned from his pupil. The fourth and last section fulfils the dramatic duty of bidding the final farewell to the student. Focusing on the poignant beauty of Rapallo's maritime setting, the poet makes the seashore into a symbol of the passage from life to death where voices are muted. Silence remains the only option thus mercilessly iterating the impotence of art and poetry in the face of death.

Quite effectively, Sbarbaro begins the text with the image of a voice emerging from a class of students:

> Se insegnando si avesse presente in chi può cadere, la nostra voce sarebbe meno sicura. Sorpresa che riserva una scolaresca! dal suo anonimo quasi sempre un volto si stacca che avevamo confuso con gli altri; dal brusio di tante, prima o poi una voce si leva che – s'anche parla un linguaggio non nostro – col suo accento di convinzione ci turba e ci costringe in ascolto.[43]
>
> If when teaching one would have present upon whom (our voice) could fall, our voice would be less secure. A surprise that saves a schoolchild. From anonymity a face almost always detaches itself that we have confused with the others; from the buzz of many, sooner or later a voice rises up which – even if it does not speak our language – with its accent of conviction unsettles us and forces us to listen.

The reference to a language that is not 'of our own' highlights the dialogical dimension at the heart of Sbarbaro's teaching approach. The element of difference creates a stimulating disturbance enforcing the act of listening and thus initiating the dialogue with others. Whose voices are most likely to rise? Is there a way to recognize the type of student from the voice? These are Sbarbaro's questions.[44] The surprise, according to Sbarbaro, never comes from the model student, the one who consistently agrees with the teacher on the majority of things:

> Con Giorgio la sorpresa fu doppia: a quella di rivelarsi di punto in bianco qualcuno, egli aggiunse – impartita in silenzio – una lezione di vita. Avviene così che ad un'età in cui per apprendere è tardi ci troviamo costretti a rientrare nei banchi.[45]
>
> With Giorgio the surprise was twofold: to that of revealing himself all of a sudden to be someone, he added a life lesson, given in silence. It thus happens that at a late age for learning, we find ourselves obliged to return to the school desks.

Labò's surprising role even made the teacher swap roles. The latter thus became the student and Labò the teacher, an exchange particularly dear to Sbarbaro, the one on which his 'metodo della partecipazione' is based. Sbarbaro then focuses on Labò's personality:

> Scolaro modello Giorgio non fu. E non tanto perché indocile e caparbio – solo chi è vuoto è anche pronto ad accogliere un contenuto purchessia – ma

perché delle cosiddette materie di studio non ce n'era una, ch'io sappia, dalla quale non aborisse: resistenza a ciò che ci è inflitto che lascia, a quella età, presentire un carattere.[46]

Giorgio was not a model student. And not so much because he was wild or obstinate – only one who is empty is also ready to accommodate whatsoever content – but because of the so-called subjects of study there was not one, that I know of, which he did not detest: resistance to that which is inflicted on us which, at that age, foretells character.

It becomes clear that Sbarbaro is attempting to establish a parallel with his own personality. In the same way that Labò was not a model student so was Sbarbaro not a model teacher, and this similarity is the reason why the student and the teacher got along well from the start:

> Con me Giorgio si trovò subito a suo agio; sentì subito di non aver più a che fare con un insegnante di professione che s'attedia al suono della propria voce. Ad imparare non si annoiò più per la semplice ragione che a insegnarli io mi divertivo.[47]

Giorgio found himself immediately at ease with me: he immediately felt he wasn't dealing with a professional teacher who grew bored of the sound of his own voice. He was no longer bored with learning for the simple reason that I enjoyed teaching him.

As Sbarbaro has also indicated elsewhere, the enjoyment experienced by the tutor is what triggers the student's intellectual involvement. Moreover, Sbarbaro's pride in not being a professional teacher pairs with his satisfaction of being able to help a non-model student. Just as Labò did not find professional teachers stimulating because they did not seem to enjoy teaching, so Sbarbaro did not enjoy teaching a class in which the number of students prevented him from developing a personalized approach. It is evident that pleasure and enjoyment in the learning activity were important for both for the non-model student and non-professional teacher and were possible only in a one-to-one dimension. On these premises, Sbarbaro seeks to establish a 'trust-based relationship' with the student from the very beginning and in order to do this he uses a technique with which we are by now familiar:

> Per cominciare m'accaparrai la sua fiducia sparlandogli della scuola in genere come di un istituto fatto più per il comodo dei maestri che per l'utile degli scolari; e del latino che vi si insegna come di una lingua artificiale,

fissata dal cattivo gusto dei grammatici con una rigidità che, sebbene pigli Cicerone a modello, neppure il modello si salva per essa da mende.[48]

To start with I gained their trust by badmouthing school in general as an institution made for the comfort of teachers rather than the advantage of students: and Latin, which is taught as an artificial language, fixed by the bad taste of grammarians with a rigidity which, even though it takes Cicero as its model, not even the model is saved by it from flaws.

It is important to bear in mind that Sbarbaro did not change ideas nor he did contradict himself on the views shared with Labò at the beginning of their relationship. This way, he won the student's confidence and empathized with him, who so fiercely rejected every single subject, resisting the school system as a whole. Very likely, Sbarbaro projected his own past as student onto Labò's. Once the bond was created, Sbarbaro had to attend to the difficult task of demonstrating that Latin is not the artificial language experienced by Labò with other teachers. But how did Sbarbaro succeed? How was Sbarbaro's Latin different from the Latin taught in schools? And how did Sbarbaro demonstrate that the school serves teachers more than it does serve the student?

The third section of the *Ricordo* is devoted to the demonstration that Latin can be taught as a living language. Sbarbaro explains his teaching method with practical examples:

Venire a sapere che nello stesso latino 'aureo', contrariamente a quanto gli avevano detto, accanto a *potest* s'incontra *potestur*; che persino il soggetto in accusativo che viene riprovato come l'errore per eccellenza può giustificarsi con ottimi testi alla mano; apprendere che, visto senza paraocchi, il latino è una lingua non meno libera e viva d'ogni altra, lo tirò da un incubo.[49]

To learn that in that same 'golden' Latin, contrary to what they had told him, next to *potest* one can find *potestur*; that even the subject in the accusative, which is condemned as an error *par excellence*, can be justified with the best texts to hand; to learn that, seen without blinkers, Latin is a language as free and alive as any other, pulled him from a nightmare.

Sbarbaro shows his student that Latin is no artificial language, as the so-called exceptions demonstrate (*potest/potestur*). By showing the variety in morphology and syntax, he establishes a comparison between Latin and any other living language, where exceptions are not perceived as such. Sbarbaro's emphasis on exceptions parallels his own and Labò's situation, themselves exceptions as a teacher and a student. The effects of concrete examples have on Giorgio are linked to the sensation of coming into bright sunlight after a period spent in the dark:

> Se sai che uscendo trovi il sole, ti rassicuri meglio a restare provvisoriamente nel buio d'una stanza; e saputo che si poteva camminare spedito, a procedere con le pastoie Giorgio prese il gusto che si trova a cimentarsi in una scommessa.[50]
>
> If you know that going out you will find the sun, you reassure yourself better staying for a little in the darkness of a room; and knowing that he could walk quickly, Giorgio developed a taste for proceeding with the shackles similar to that which one finds in taking on a challenge.

The poet prides himself on having been able to communicate to Labò that the hardest part of language learning was propaedeutic to the future beauty of literature. This is an essential step in the awakening of the student's involvement. Once the student's interest is aroused, Sbarbaro's task became easier. The poet resorted to a visual aid to familiarize the student with logical analysis:

> Intanto poiché a precludergli l'accesso al ginnasio superiore era l'analisi logica, pensai di presentargli questo spaventacchio che sta sulla soglia a scoraggiare chi entra, sotto aspetto coloristico: il soggetto era rosso, blu l'oggetto e i vari complementi si spartivano fra loro colori assortiti. La novità della cosa lo incuriosì. Brandendo matite multicolori aggrediva la frase da tradurre e la convertiva in una tavolozza. Avevo svegliato la sua attenzione: il più era fatto. Quello che sinallora era stato un supplizio diventava uno svago.[51]
>
> Meanwhile, since logical analysis was keeping him out of middle school, I thought of presenting this discouraging fright that sits on the doorstep in terms of colour: the subject was red, the object blue and the various complements divided between their assorted colours. The novelty of the thing intrigued him. Brandishing coloured pencils, he attacked the phrases to be translated and converted them into a palette. I had awoken his attention: the greater part was done. That which had up to then been a torture became an amusement.

The colours strategy captures the student's attention and awakens his curiosity. At the same time, the comparison between the sentence and the palette symbolically anticipates Labò's interest in De Chirico's art. With equal pedagogical commitment, Sbarbaro devises a practice in which the teacher induces the student to correct the mistakes he (the teacher) has deliberately made:

> Quando nello svago dava segni di stanchezza, gli sottentravo come discente; ed ero io allora a spropositare a tutto spiano in rosso e in blu e lui a correggermi vittorioso.[52]
>
> When in leisure he showed signs of tiredness, I would take on the position of student; and then it was I who got everything wrong in red and blue like there was no tomorrow and he who corrected me, victoriously.

By making mistakes on purpose, the teacher stimulates the student's attention and boosts his confidence.

What about dictionaries and grammars, the fundamental tool of classical education? Sbarbaro did not make any use of them:

> (Gli avevo annunciato che non si aprirebbe una grammatica e mantenni la promessa: l'essenziale delle forme si imparò a furia di esercizio. Il parco uso che fece sempre del vocabolario lo portò alla peggio a creare qualche innocuo neologismo.)[53]
>
> I had told him that he shouldn't open a grammar book and he kept his promise: he learnt the fundamentals of the conventions by doing lots of exercises. The careful use he always made of the dictionary led him at worst to create some harmless neologisms.

The teacher wanted his student to have a totally anti-academic learning experience. Sbarbaro's motto 'cimentandomi direttamente coi testi'[54] is put into practice also in his tutorials with Labò. Latin syntax is then introduced through a few examples, as is characteristic of Sbarbaro's pedagogy:

> Così quando in quarta si dovette affrontare la sintassi, alla astrattezza – spesso astrusa e sempre ostica – delle regole, sostituii la concretezza degli esempi. Prima che in latino, lo avvezzai a volgere ad alta voce la frase nella forma che assumerebbe nella nuova lingua; a non dire 'piuttosto che servire, preferir morire', ma piuttosto 'piuttosto che servisse', facendogli notare, come in questo caso, la maggiore aderenza dell'espressione (in confronto della nostra). Pochi esempi, che avevo cura fossero sempre gli stessi, smaltivano pagine e pagine di regole. Si trovò così presto ad avere in mente una specie di sintassi figurata; un repertorio di frasi italiane (atteggiate alla latina) da servirgli da falsariga nel tradurre e d'un suono così insolito al nostro orecchio da stamparvisi per sempre.[55]

> So when in the fourth year he had to confront syntax, in place of abstractness – often abstruse and always arduous – I substituted the concreteness of examples. Before doing it in Latin, I got him used to saying the phrase out loud in the form which it would take in the new language; not to say 'rather than to serve, prefer to die', but rather 'rather than serve', making him note, as in this example, the greater cohesion of the expression (in comparison with ours). A few examples, that I took care were always the same, got rid of pages and pages of rules. Quickly he found that he had in mind a sort of illustrated syntax; a repertoire of Italian phrases (composed in a Latin manner) that served him as examples in translation and of a sound so unusual to our ear as to imprint upon it forever.

'Sintassi figurata' is indeed a highly peculiar strategy based on analogy and difference. First, Sbarbaro shows the similarity of Italian syntax to that of Latin. A repertoire of Italian sentences, modelled on a Latin structure, becomes the point of reference for the student when they have to translate from Latin into Italian. Difference is then used as a mnemonic strategy: because the sound of these sentences is so unusual the student is bound to remember them. Sbarbaro also uses one of the examples ('piuttosto che servire, preferir morire') to refer to and anticipate Labò's tragic end: Labò preferred to die instead of betraying his fellow partisans.

As far as the teaching of literature is concerned, Sbarbaro returns to the philosophy of one of his *Trucioli dispersi*:

> In liceo il mio compito fu più lieto. Ormai si trattava di fargli gustare gli Autori e bastava per questo liberarli dall'aura imbecille di intoccabilità della quale testi e scuole li circondano e che allontana chi sarebbe degno di accostarli perché in quella ammirazione ad ogni costo subodora a ragione una truffa.[56]
>
> In high school my task was happier. By then it was about making him savour the Authors and to do this it was enough to free him from the idiotic aura of untouchability with which texts and schools surround them and that alienates anyone who would be worthy of approaching them, because in that admiration at all costs the student rightly smells a fraud.

The poet challenges all a priori admiration for Classical authors. Such 'aura imbecille d'intoccabilità' precludes a sincere appreciation of the author and it is Sbarbaro's first objective to question such an approach. The teacher can speak with an authoritative voice on this matter only if he shows the students that he is capable of criticism:

> Solo trovando liberamente a ridire in Omero come in Dante, correndo cioè – piuttosto di mentire – il rischio di ingannarsi, si acquista credito agli occhi dello scolaro quando gli si addita questa o quella bellezza o quando più eloquentemente gliela sottolinea la voce lisa di commozione di chi per la centesima volta si rilegge con lui quel canto o quel verso.[57]
>
> Only by freely finding something to criticize in Homer as in Dante, that is – to speak plainly – by running the risk of being wrong, does he acquire credit in the eyes of his pupil when he points out to him this or that beauty or when it is more eloquently highlighted for him by the worn voice of emotion of one who rereads that canto or that verse with him for the hundredth time.

This passage concludes the sections of the treatise devoted to Sbarbaro's methods of teaching Latin. Most importantly, this illuminating fragment pinpoints the act of reading and rereading the set texts as one of the cornerstones of Sbarbaro's relationship with his teaching of the Classics.

In the last and fourth section, Sbarbaro demonstrates once more how school is not the ideal place for learning. According to this view, it is entirely vain to think that subjects taught in school will remain in a person's memory. The dialogue-based pedagogy appears all the more necessary. Labò's progress, in the study of both Latin language and literature, coincided with a personal maturity, which became a symbol for the mutual enrichment of the teacher and the student:

> Senonché non è mai quello che ci si propone che si insegna davvero e in modo durevole; sì qualche cosa che esorbita dai programmi e che – come convinzione privata – a farne parte abbiamo il ritegno che s'ha a trasmettere un contagio. Ma le convinzioni vitali traspirano da noi nostro malgrado; e forse a mia insaputa avevo portato Giorgio a vedere nell'arte la sola consistenza, se, allo scadere del mio compito, quando già m'appagavo d'averlo passo passo condotto dalla proclamata ammirazione per il Giusti a quella per il Leopardi, ebbi la gioia di sentirlo impetuosamente interrompermi per partire lancia in resta contro un critico ostile alla pittura di De Chirico e manifestarmi l'urgente bisogno di controbatterlo su un giornale. [...] Ma – ciò che ancora non avevo visto abbastanza – nonché dell'arte, della stessa accettazione della vita era per lui presupposto la libertà e più imperioso d'ogni parola da dire, l'odio per la prepotenza.[58]

However, it is never what one intends that one really teaches in a lasting way; there is something that exceeds the curriculum – like personal convictions – and to avoid letting it in we show the same restraint as when not wanting to transmit an infection. But our fundamental convictions sweat out of us in spite of ourselves; and perhaps unconsciously I had led Giorgio to see in art the only substance, if, at the end of my task, when I had already satisfied myself by having step by step led him from the proclaimed admiration for Giusti to that for Leopardi, I had the joy of hearing him impetuously interrupt me to resolutely burst forth against a hostile criticism of De Chirico's picture and show me the urgent need to counterattack in the paper. [...] But what I had not yet seen enough of, however, was that he presupposed freedom not only of art but of life as well, and, more pressing than every word to be said, that he hated abuse.

The value of teaching goes beyond the subject taught. The poet acknowledges that his legacy as a teacher is more connected with his own ideas than with literature. Although he avoided sharing his views on life with Labò, he did compare his 'convinzione privata' to a contagious disease that he was very careful not to transmit to anyone. He realized that his influence, though, needed no words. Labò's desire to support publicly Giorgio de Chirico's art (which to the poet signifies courage and a striving for freedom) was indeed interpreted by Sbarbaro as a proof of his influence. Labò's struggle for these ideals when he was only a student forebodes, in Sbarbaro's description, his commitment as a partisan during the Second World War:

> Imbattutosi, dopo una prepotenza organizzata a governo che, giovinetto aveva dovuto subire, in un'altra, tetra e gelida come una macchina e straniera per giunta, era prevedibile che Giorgio l'avrebbe affrontata piuttosto che acconciarsivi.[59]
>
> Undefeated, after one government of organized bullies that he had had to endure as a young man, in the face of another, dark and frozen as a machine and foreign to boot, it was predictable that Giorgio would confront it rather than submit to it.

Sbarbaro here alludes to the torture and imprisonment of Giorgio who refused to betray his fellow partisans and was therefore killed. Instead of dwelling on Labò's death, Sbarbaro shifts the focus to the lesson that he was able to draw from his student:

A Giorgio devo d'aver conosciuto da presso un eroe. Egli ha dato per me contenuto a un'abusata figura rettorica, della quale i tempi, che di eroi spesseggiavano, avevano più che mai portato a diffidare. Tra troppi eroi a loro insaputa, Giorgio fu eroe di sua scelta, davanti a se stesso e in silenzio. Ai genitori che di lui vivevano lascia per sopravvivere l'orgoglio di averlo avuto per figlio; a chi gli insegnò, il più alto e severo degli insegnamenti; alla patria umiliata, perché si salvi, l'esempio della sua serietà e del suo silenzio.[60]

To Giorgio, I owe having known a hero up close. He gave substance for me to an abused rhetorical figure, which the times, full of heroes, have more than ever led us to distrust. Amongst too many heroes unknown to themselves, Giorgio was a hero by choice, ahead of himself and in silence. To those parents who outlived him, he left pride to live on in having had him for a son; to his teacher, the greatest and most severe of lessons; to his humiliated country, so it may be saved, the example of his honesty and his silence.

For Sbarbaro, Labò revived the meaning of a rhetorical figure (the hero) that was used up. Interestingly, just as Latin was a dynamic and varied language for Sbarbaro, so does Labò appear to him a hero not in a rhetorical manner, but as a reality. In other words, in the same way that Sbarbaro was able to show Labò that Latin was a free language and very much alive, Labò was able to demonstrate to Sbarbaro that the hero was not just a rhetorical conceit but a reality, equally alive.

In a cyclical structure, the end of the essay on Labò reconnects with the beginning. Labò's voice, when he was a student, rose above the rest and asked to be heard. As the life progressed, that voice held great surprises for his teacher. The roles were soon reversed: Labò taught Sbarbaro a life lesson. Yet, for Sbarbaro, it is again the merciless principle of Necessity to control his destiny. Now in the role of the student, the poet cannot raise his voice and be heard by his teacher, and hero, Labò, and his voice is instead silenced in the face of death.

By tracing the beginning of Sbarbaro's experience as a teacher and mapping its development through his life, it is possible to unravel the poet's pedagogic engagement with the classics. The analysis of all the references to education in his poetic work demonstrates a persistent interest in the classical legacy and its connection to didactics. The most unique aspect of Sbarbaro's discourse rests on the interplay between his ideas on pedagogy and his own poetic discourse. His teaching experience became part of his poetics, thus asserting the creative function the poet assigned to the knowledge of the Classics. His 'metodo della partecipazione' based on a strong dialogical approach and tailored to the individual needs of each student, aimed at fostering a learning experience of mutual enrichment based on the direct knowledge of classical poetry. Conceived in those terms, Sbarbaro's teaching activity proves to be of highly ethical stance. The poet as a teacher revived the study of classical civilization as a means to foster self-awareness and awaken the individual's creative responsiveness.

Giovanna Bemporad Teacher of Greek and Latin in Pier Paolo Pasolini's *scuola irregolare*

Bemporad became involved with education when she taught Greek and Latin in Pier Paolo Pasolini's school in Friuli. The two poets knew each other and collaborated consistently throughout their life, sharing a passion for poetic translation. Bemporad's teaching experience was indeed one of their various collaborations, as she herself recalls in a memorial piece written for Pasolini:

> [Ho] vissuto a Casarsa in quotidiano contatto con Pasolini ed è stato il periodo più intenso della nostra amicizia, dopo il sodalizio bolognese. Mi trovavo là soltanto per insegnare greco e latino nella piccola scuola improvvisata di Pier Paolo, alla fine della guerra perchè i ragazzi del luogo e dei paesi intorno non rischiassero di morire sotto i bombardamenti andando in treno a Udine. Insegnavo greco e latino, o greco e inglese, come sostiene Nico Naldini, perché – a quanto pare – come dice Sbarbaro in una sua nota poesia: '[...] i ricordi son mani che non giungono a incontrarsi.' Comunque sia, ho avuto per scolari, più o meno miei coetanei, Nico Naldini e il fratello di Pier Paolo, Guido, a cui ho dato qualche lezione di letteratura italiana per l'esame di terza Liceo.[61]
>
> I lived in Casarsa in daily contact with Pasolini and it was the most intense period of our friendship after our Bolognese association. I only found myself there to teach Greek and Latin in Pier Paolo's little improvised school at the end of the war so the children of the town and those surrounding it didn't have to risk death in the bombings by taking the train to Udine. I taught Greek and Latin, or Greek and English as Nico Naldini maintains, because – it seems – as Sbarbaro says in his well-known poem: '[...] memories are hands that do not reach each other to meet'. Whichever it is, I

had my more or less contemporaries for students, Nico Naldini and Pier Paolo's brother Guido, to whom I gave some lessons in Italian literature for his third year exam in high school.

By emphasizing that her students were her own age, she constructed herself as an *enfant prodige*, while underlining the unconventional nature of the school itself. The phrase 'piccola scuola improvvisata' creates a powerful contrast with the noble duty that the school was fulfilling. The importance assigned to education emerges all the more if one considers the historical circumstances in which the independent school was established and operated. As Bemporad tells us in this excerpt, her teaching involvement is strongly connected to her friendship with Pasolini. They became friends during the years 1939–40, in Bologna. Bemporad was still in school (although she would not stay there much longer), at the Liceo Galvani, and had already become famous for her poetic translations of Virgil's *Aeneid*. Pasolini, who had just enrolled at the University of Bologna, was then creating a group of literary friends.[62] According to Bemporad, their first encounter happened precisely because Pasolini showed an interest in her poetic translations.[63] The poet needed contributors for his literary magazine *Il Setaccio* and asked Bemporad to help him. As we read in Enzo Siciliano's biography of Pasolini:

> Pier Paolo la cercò: – lei frequentava la scuola a Bologna, al liceo Galvani: – Pier Paolo le offrì la collaborazione al 'Setaccio'. I due divennero amici, e si incontrarono anche spesso nella casa bolognese di lei, – un enorme stanzone, un tavolo vastissimo e carico oltre misura di libri.[64]
>
> Pier Paolo sought her out – she was attending the Liceo Galvani in Bologna, – and invited her to contribute to Il Setaccio. The two became friends, and even met frequently at her home in Bologna – a huge room, with a vast table overflowing with books.[65]

Pasolini had a peculiar faith in the combination of literature and friendship, 'una comunione letteraria' to put it in Siciliano's words.[66] Bemporad agreed to collaborate with his school in the name of a similar faith, almost a religion of poetry. Her first visit to Casarsa, where the school was to be founded, took place in May 1943:

> Alla fine di Maggio Giovanna Bemporad è la prima degli amici bolognesi a venir ospite per qualche giorno a Casarsa. Giovanna, innamorata della luna,

vede le sue luci sfolgorare libere nella vasta campagna, durante le notti dell'oscuramento. Accetta di buon grado le amicizie paesane di Pier Paolo e già pensa a un suo possibile trasferimento a Casarsa dove le minacce della guerra e delle persecuzioni razziali sembrano ancora lontane.[67]

At the end of May, Giovanna Bemporad is the first of the friends from Bologna to be a guest at Casarsa for a few days. Giovanna, in love with the Moon, sees its light shine freely in the vast countryside during the nighttime blackouts. She willingly accepts Pier Paolo's country friends and already contemplates a possible move to Casarsa where the threat of the war and the racial persecutions still seem far off.

This passage is from one of her future pupils, Domenico Naldini, describing Bemporad's stay in Casarsa. Naldini's idyllic description of the Friulian landscape, epitomized in Bemporad's fondness for the moon, is spoiled by the jarring reference to Fascism. Although he hypothesizes that Bemporad's move to Casarsa was due to her Jewish origins, in fact it was not until September 1943 that Pasolini asked her to join him in Friuli:

I bombardamenti creano difficoltà anche ai ragazzi di Casarsa che frequentano le scuole di Pordenone e di Udine; nasce cosí il progetto di una scuoletta privata. A due chilometri da Casarsa, oltre la ferrovia, c'è il paese di San Giovanni di cui Versuta è la più lontana appendice verso il Tagliamento. In una casa abbandonata, di una certa dignità borghese, con due corridoi centrali al piano terra e al primo piano, con le stanze disposte ai lati, Pier Paolo e cinque suoi amici aprono alla fine di settembre una scuola con tutte le regole delle iscrizioni e degli orari. Pier Paolo insegna materie letterarie e storiche, Cesare Bortotto scienze, Riccardo Castellani matematica e Giovanna Bemporad, richiamata subito da Bologna, greco e inglese. La scuola di San Giovanni, come primo esperimento didattico dura molto poco perchè a metà novembre il provveditore agli studi di Udine manda una diffida amministrativa. La scuola viene chiusa e gli insegnanti decidono di continuare le lezioni ciascuno a casa propria.[68]

The bombings also create difficulties for the children from Casarsa who go to school in Pordenone and Udine; so the project of the little private school is born. Two kilometres from Casarsa, beyond the railway, there is the town of San Giovanni of which Versuta is the most distant part towards Tagliamento. In an abandoned house, with a certain middle-class dignity, with two central corridors on the ground and first floors and rooms off to the sides, Pier Paolo and five of his friends open a school at the end of

September with all the regulations for enrollment and timetable. [...] Pier Paolo teaches literature and history, Cesare Bortotto science, Riccardo Castellani mathematics, and Giovanna Bemporad, immediately called from Bologna, Greek and English. The San Giovanni school as a first didactic experiment did not last long because in the middle of November the school inspector from Udine sends an administrative injunction. The school is closed and the teachers decide to continue the lessons each in their own home.

Naldini stresses Pasolini's social agenda behind this didactic project. The private school aimed at complementing the public system which was under the strain of war. Unfortunately, once the government declared the school illegal, the students started withdrawing. Between January and February 1944, Pasolini's experiment was definitively over.[69] As Naldini remarks, friendship ('philia') was the leading criterion of the experiment. Bemporad was one of the 'cinque amici' who made the school possible. More importantly, Bemporad was the first one to be called to teach in Casarsa.[70] The lack of a comprehensive scholarly study on the school of San Giovanni makes Naldini's memories a fundamental source. However, in his reconstruction of the school – he was one of the students attending – Naldini failed to highlight the school's poetic scope, by far the most prominent feature of the didactic experiment. Enzo Siciliano and Andrea Zanzotto underlined the uniqueness and the importance of this feature. Siciliano connected Pasolini's attraction for teaching with a project of linguistic renovation:

> Ho parlato di immaginazione didascalica. In Pasolini era fortissima la tensione idealistica del maestro, – modulo sublimato d'una pulsione omoerotica. Questa tensione nutriva anche un possibile concetto di letteratura: lo nutriva d'un certo qual volontarismo. Il poeta desiderava 'il ritorno a una lingua più vicina al mondo':- tuttavia, il mondo non intendeva scoprirlo individualmente, ma in comunità, coralmente. A questo fine si profilò la scuola. [...] Per pochissimi alunni Pasolini aprì la scuola a Casarsa, in casa. Insegnò ai ragazzi, accanto ai classici italiani, greci e latini, come scrivere poesia friulana: la lirica pura e la *vilota*.[71]
>
> I have mentioned 'didactic imagination'. In Pasolini the idealistic tension of the teacher was very strong – the sublimated form of a homoerotic drive. This tension also nourished a possible conception of literature, willed in a sense by the poet's desire for a 'return to a language closer to the world'. He

did not, however, mean to discover the world individually, but as part of community, as the member of a chorus. The school was formed to that end. [...] Pasolini opened a school for a handful of students in his home in Casarsa. Along with the Italian, Greek, and Latin classics, he taught the children how to write Friulian poetry: the pure lyric and the villotta.[72]

The school's end was to create an environment for Pasolini's new idea of literature. The discovery of this new concept of literature was to be experienced alongside the students, to whom Pasolini and Bemporad taught poetic composition,[73] and with the other teachers involved in his school. Pasolini's *didactic imagination* applied to a collective project having poetry at its core is key to our understanding of Bemporad's teaching commitment. In his essay 'Pedagogia', Andrea Zanzotto further developed the connection between pedagogy and literature postulating that Pasolini's enquiry as a whole revolved around the idea and the function of education.[74] In Zanzotto's view, poetry and pedagogy not only intersect but constitute the basic identity of Pasolini's poetics as a whole. Through the categories of 'poesia didascalia' and 'pedagogia apedagogica' Zanzotto systematized the poetic meaning of Pasolini's didactic experiment:

> Ma prima di tutto esisteva per lui la poesia, o meglio l'arte anche il più possibile polimorfa, didascalia proveniente da tutto, rivolta a tutto, eppure crescente anche da sé e in sé.[75]
>
> But before everything for him was poetry, or better the art that is also the most polymorphous, teachings coming from everything, addressing everything, yet also growing by itself and in itself.

The prioritization of poetry as the highest form of pedagogy suggests a totalizing, self-containing and quasi-pantheistic dimension of literature. To better understand the implications deriving from this standpoint, Zanzotto employed the Freudian infantile polymorphous perversity to define Pasolini's 'poesia-didascalia'. Zanzotto highlighted the fertile anomie ('fertile anomia') entailed in the psychoanalytic category thus helping us to visualize Pasolini's attempt to redefine the concept of education outside normative models:

> Da ciò la sua ricerca, fino all'ossessione, di quello che si vorrebbe chiamare un 'iperspazio' ove costituire un'etica, una pedagogia futuribili e aperte al massimo, apedagogiche.[76]

Hence his search, even obsession, for what one might call a 'hyperspace' in which to establish an ethics, a pedagogy that was feasible and open, if anything, to the unpedagogical.

It is precisely within this non-normative attitude that we need to read Bemporad's presence in Pasolini's school. Indeed, Pasolini wanted Bemporad to be part of this 'iperspazio'. She had what was needed: religious devotion to poetry and an outsider status. Bemporad brought to the school anti-conformism and freedom of expression. As Siciliano wrote, Bemporad arrived in Casarsa with her 'leggenda umana e letteraria' (personal and literary legend). Her past as a student is telling of how she conceived the relationship between institutional learning and her dedication to poetry. In an illuminating autobiographical fragment, Bemporad reflects on her relationship with school:

> Quel distacco [from school] fu una cosa naturale, in un certo senso scritta nel mio destino. Io con la scuola non legavo, così come non legavo con la famiglia, specialmente con mia madre. A dire proprio tutta la verità sono stata una contestatrice avanti lettera. Avevo scelto, per una forma di protesta esistenziale, di andare in giro senza scarpe, di non lavarmi, di non pettinarmi, di usare un linguaggio brutale. Non è vero però che portavo i pantaloni, come vuole una certa leggenda: indossavo una giacchettina nera e un gonnellino nero di quaranta anni prima, che avevo scovato in un ripostiglio. Per le strade, i ragazzi mi ridevano dietro, mi insultavano. Ma io nemmeno me ne accorgevo. Avevo un gran fuoco dentro, mi sentivo una vestale della poesia.[77]

> That detachment [from school] was natural, in a certain sense written in my fate. I did not connect with school, like I did not connect with family, especially my mother. To say the whole truth, I was an objector ahead of my time. I had chosen, through a form of existential protest, to walk around without shoes, to not wash, to not comb my hair, to use rough language. It's not true though that I wore trousers as a certain legend says: I wore a black jacket and a little black skirt from forty years before that I had found in a broom cupboard. On the street, children would laugh at me, insult me. But I didn't even notice. I had a great fire inside, I felt myself to be a Vestal of poetry.

Bemporad's totalizing devotion to literature was not compatible with institutional learning. It is interesting to see how Bemporad connects her decision to quit school to a far more structured project in which even her personal appearance also plays a role. The protest against a 'normal way' of existing within a bourgeois society informs her decision to reject social conventions, such as personal hygiene and physical appearance.[78] The combination of 'gran fuoco della poesia' (indeed, the very self-identification with an ancient virgin priestess) and the 'protesta esistenziale', coupled with her uncompromising adhesion to poetry, perfectly fits in the 'iperspazio apedagogico' of Pasolini's school. Students indeed were fascinated by her mysterious appearance and manners. Siciliano offers a sample of her hypnotizing readings in Casarsa:

> Nella piccola aula casalinga di Casarsa, Giovanna Bemporad trascinava gli uditori leggendo i *Sepolcri* foscoliani. Anche Guido Pasolini era fra loro e a occhi sgranati seguiva la lettura e il commento, per intero dominato dall'idea 'bella' del morire per la patria.[79]

> In the little classroom in the Pasolini house in Casarsa, Giovanna Bemporad's listeners were carried away by her reading of Foscolo's *Sepolcri*. Guido Pasolini was there too, and wide-eyed he followed the reading and discussion, wholly enthralled by the 'beautiful' idea of dying for the fatherland.[80]

This excerpt provides a clear example of Bemporad's approach to teaching. The word 'trascinava' conveys the performative core of her method, based on her recitals of the texts. The theatrical delivery was also in line with Pasolini's teaching agenda. In a passage from the *Diario di un insegnante* Pasolini underlined the importance of a dramatic approach to teaching.[81] Elio Pagliarani has already pointed out the peculiarity of Bemporad's reading. The two met in Viserba in 1938 when they were both teenagers:

> Ebbi la ventura di incontrare nella prima adolescenza una Pizia adolescente, autentica sacerdotessa di Apollo (si misurava già con Omero) musicale fin negli ingorghi più intrigati delle viscere, come chiariva subito la sua voce; [...] Giovanna Bemporad mi declamava 'Felicità raggiunta fra i capanni/ o 'Sbarbaro, estroso fanciullo' I più facili epigrammi / le notti estive a spiaggia in mezzo ai corpi degli amanti ...' E certo mi declamava soprattutto 'Il canto di un pastore errante', e ancora mi declamava 'Il canto di un pastore errante' quella volta che fummo colpiti dalla Military Police con abbaglianti e canilupo alle tre e mezza di notte sulla spiaggia del Lido di Venezia l'estate del '46 [...] Nel '44 o '45 Giovanna ebbe occasione di declamare nel Veneto

il *Faust* nell'originale tedesco davanti a un plotone d'esecuzione tedesco: anche quelli riconobbero la Pizia...[82]

I had the fortune to meet a teenage Pythia in my early adolescence, an authentic high priestess of Apollo (she was already contending with Homer), musical all the way into the most knotted blockages of her viscera, as her voice immediately showed; [...] Giovanna Bemporad recited to me 'Happiness met amongst the huts / o 'Sbarbaro, brilliant boy' The easiest epigrams / summer nights on the beach amidst the bodies of lovers...' And especially she recited 'The Song of the Wandering Shepherd' that time we were arrested by the Military Police with search lights and police dogs at half past three in the morning on the Venice Lido beach in the summer of '46 [...]. In '44 or '45 in Veneto, Giovanna had the occasion to recite *Faust* in the original German before a German firing squad; they too recognized the Pythia.

While remembering Bemporad's readings of Leopardi, Montale and Goethe, Pagliarani made Bemporad a symbol of Ancient Greece, the interpreter of the Pythian oracle herself. Her literary precocity is stressed in the adjective *adolescente*. While Bemporad referred to herself as a 'Vestale della poesia', hinting at the religious dimension of her devotion to poetry, here Pagliarani suggests a comparison with the prophetic and maniac obsession experienced by the oral poets described in Plato's *Phaedrus*.[83] The reference to the poetic frenzy underlines the oral dimension of Bemporad's relationship with poetry and simultaneously implies that the poetic word held a daimonic function for her. Pagliariani's remarks on the inherent musicality and on the clarity of her voice should be read in connection with the fact that Bemporad changed her voice when reading, as if seized by supernatural forces.[84]

In the school, her lessons knew no time limit. The *comunione letteraria* involved students and teachers alike:

Facevano scuola di mattina. Il pomeriggio passeggiavano per i campi: un gran parlare di poesia e libri, ma ancora di più, come fra giovani di buone letture, della vita e della morte. La morte era una presenza ossessiva, obbligata, manieristica, nell'immaginario di Giovanna. [...] A cena, in casa – Giovanna mangiava con i Pasolini, e dormiva presso alcuni loro parenti, – era una gara a scrivere *vilote*. Pier Paolo ne dettava una via l'altra. Insegnavano ai loro studenti quelle canzoni. Altro divertimento: amavano entrambi il Foscolo: delle *Grazie* versificavano le parti incompiute. E fra i due era un punto d'onore scrivere il perfetto endecasillabo: più legata al formalismo neoclassico Giovanna, più libero nell'invenzione Pier Paolo. Si dicevano l'un l'altro che sarebbero stati i poeti della loro generazione. [...] Una delle *vilote* scritte da lui diceva: *Zovinuta blancia e rosa / Con chel stras di vestidin / La to musa dolorosa / A someja al me destin*. Giovanna Bemporad aveva dettato la musica per altre due quartine, dedicate ai cinquecento anni della parrocchia di Casarsa. [...] Musica profana, sempre della Bemporad, per quest'altra quartina: [...].[85]

They taught in the morning. Afternoons they walked in the fields. They talked a lot about poetry and books, but even more, as between well-read young people, about life and death. Death was an obsessive, necessary, and artificial presence in Giovanna's imagination. [...] At home in the evening (Giovanna ate with the Pasolinis and slept at the house of some of their relatives), they held a contest in writing villotas. Pier Paolo composed them one after another. They taught their students these songs. Another diversion: they both loved Foscolo, and versified the unfinished parts of the *Grazie*. And between the two it was a point of honour to write the perfect hendecasyllable. Giovanna was more bound by neoclassical formalism, Pier Paolo freer in invention. They told themselves that they would be the poets of their generation. [...] One of his villotas ran *Zovinuta blancia e rosa / Con chel stras di vestidin / La to musa dolorosa / A someja al me destin*. Giovanna Bemporad had composed the music for two other quatrains celebrating the five hundred years of the Casarsa parish church. [...] Secular music, also by Bemporad, for this other quatrain [...].[86]

Afternoon and evening walks with the students enhanced the collective dimension of the *cenacolo letterario* of which the school was part. In particular, the endless discussions on poetry *en plein air* symbolically recall the dialogical dimension of learning in Socrates' Greece. Through the exercise of composing *vilote* (a traditional polyphonic song with a variety of metrics, dating back to the fifteenth century), the teachers encouraged the students' creativity whilst fostering an appreciation for the cultural local heritage. The passage reveals the interplay between the didactic activity and Bemporad's and Pasolini's poetic inventiveness. In this kind of environment, it is evident how Bemporad's teaching aimed at freeing the Classics, and their legacy, from the penalizing constraints of the traditional learning experience as it happened in regular schools. Bemporad staged a play of sorts where she herself performed as a modern rhapsode, allowing the student audience to experience every text as an ancient text. Thanks to her amazing mnemonic powers, Bemporad could perform long extracts and capture the students' attention for a prolonged time, as in ancient ritual performance. Her mnemotechnic skills were indeed an essential part of her way of working. Bemporad herself confessed that while translating and composing poetry she constantly read aloud the passages translated in order to hear the sounds of her verses and in order to possess the oral dimension of the poetry. The role of educator/perfomer assumed by Bemporad in Casarsa would continue after the school. Bemporad devoted her entire life to poetic translation and performative readings of the Classics both as a means of self-education and as a means to enact the communal experience of poetry. Although Bemporad's experience as a teacher was brief and was unique in her life, her time as a teacher of Latin and Greek in Casarsa is crucial in her trajectory as a verbal artist and a most active defender of the classics within the modern tradition.

Conclusion

Mapping the response of the cultural and literary agents involved in the twentieth-century Italian reception of Greek tragedy has enabled us to pinpoint the originality and peculiarity of Sbarbaro and Bemporad's approaches to the translation of Greek tragedy, which have been examined in this book from different angles. The Italian context revealed its dynamic and multifarious nature, presenting itself as an open issue gravitating around an institution (INDA) which has now been active for more than a century and which is increasingly receiving scholarly attention.

The comparative study of Sbarbaro and Bemporad's translations of Greek tragedy, which were completed in the 1940s and are therefore an active part of the environment, demonstrated the key role played by the classical legacy in their literary life. Diverging from the majority of twentieth-century Italian translators who mostly translated for performance purposes, their work on Greek tragedy is disengaged from any theatrical commitment as well as from ideological filters or conceptual categories. Instead of using the tragic paradigm as a means of inspiration for their own dramatic art or for fostering classicizing aesthetics and poetics, the poetic versions of Sophocles' plays by Sbarbaro and Bemporad focused on the purely linguistic characteristics of the original. Choosing poetic translation as the key activity to shape their dialogue with Greek tragedians and grounding their interpretation on the internal theatricality of the tragic word, Sbarbaro and Bemporad enhanced the intrinsically dialogical nature of both the tragic genre and translation. There is an element of reciprocity at the heart of these poet-translators' relationship with Greek tragedy. On the one hand, their work on Sophocles disclosed new aspects within the tragic text they translated. On the other, they were enriched, and somewhat transformed, by this translation experience with regards to their own poetic discourse: tropes, themes and poetic identities appeared more clearly defined as a result of their dialogue with Greek tragedy. The discovery of this increased transparency to themselves, triggered by this translation experience, informs another practice that intersects with that of translation: their teaching activity. Sbarbaro and Bemporad's teaching commitment is a further similarity bridging the journey of these two poet-translators, analysed together in this book with the aim of bringing to the fore the (shared) originality of their approach to the tragic paradigm.

Assuming that translation of Greek tragedies functions as a case study of their wider translation activities, I identified a common denominator among their works as translators of Greek tragedy, poets and teachers of Classics. Sbarbaro and Bemporad's experiences as teachers of Latin and Greek drew extensively on their activities as translators, as well as on their poetic agendas, thus charging the triad of Classics, poetry and translation with pedagogical commitment. Besides exploring shared traits, I also demonstrated that Sbarbaro and Bemporad each had very original translation methodologies and pedagogical ideas on the Classics, and I analysed each author as an individual case.

I have conducted my study by taking into account examples of two Greek tragedies: Sophocles' *Antigone* in Sbarbaro's translation and Sophocles' *Electra* in Bemporad's translation. The tragedies have been the object of close reading. This analysis prompted a discussion of Sbarbaro and Bemporad's engagement with Greek tragedy from two perspectives. The first addresses the poets' translation methodologies, which within the field of translation studies can be located within the set of approaches focusing on the reflective nature of translation practice and on its plasticity as a privileged means for advancing a more dynamic exchange between the concepts of authorship and translatorship. Sbarbaro fostered a *poetica dell'aderenza* for his translation of Sophocles' *Antigone*, an approach which was put into practice through a staunchly literal translation. Adherence to the verbal fabric of the Greek somewhat contrasted with the openness of the rhythmic prose which he chose for his translation of the *Antigone*, giving birth to a most original oxymoron. Sbarbaro's desire to adhere to the original stemmed from his reverence towards the Greek tragedians, as I demonstrated through an analysis of some relevant letters. At the heart of his 'bare' approach was the belief that Sophoclean poetry had a core which would reveal itself only by a word-for-word translation. In so doing, Sbarbaro charged Sophoclean poetry with a somewhat biblical aura, that of sacred revelation, recalling Benjamin's take on interlinear translation expounded in his seminal essay on the task of the translator.

Bemporad instead professed that she believed in the 'tradizione filologico-umanistica', according to which a perfect solution ('una resa felice') had to be found out of a set of variants.[1] My study of her translation of Sophocles' *Electra* has shown this quest for a 'resa felice', which she only later theorized in her essay on Homer's *Odyssey* (1989). In her translation of Sophocles, Bemporad chose the closed measure of the hendecasyllable, the same metre she used for her own poetry and for the majority of her poetic translations. My study of Bemporad's 'tragic' hendecasyllables revealed, especially in the lyrical sections, a tendency towards the expansion of rhythmical units beyond their syllabic constraints. In this way, Bemporad overcame the verse constraints by exploiting the hendecasyllable's rhythmical potential. In this practice, I identified Bemporad's desire to reproduce Electra's endless lament, the main theme of the play itself. Both Sbarbaro and Bemporad's translation methodologies are inspired and ruled by an element of constraint. Within the space of a given structure, they both devised strategies to overcome its limits and use it as a creative resource and a means of exploring new meanings, making translation into an inventive and poetically inspiring activity.

The second perspective unravels the process by which Sbarbaro and Bemporad's translation experience interweaves with their lyrical production and, ultimately, reflects on their poetics and shaping of poetic personae. I have shown how, to describe his task as a translator, Sbarbaro developed a metaphor which he then extended to his poetic activity as a whole: the metaphor of the translator 'che cammina sulla corda' (who walks on the rope). This image chiefly expresses a sense of adherence to the text and the limited freedom of expression that he felt he had when translating Greek tragedy. The necessity of 'walking on a rope' then acquired a symbolic meaning and stimulated a wider reflection on the aim of his poetry and on his poetic awareness. In my discussion I argued that this image triggered another powerful metaphor, that of 'scrittura sotto dettatura', which opens Sbarbaro's declaration of poetics in *Fuochi fatui*, a miscellany of metapoetic meditation and remarks on the activity of translation. The poet who writes 'sotto dettatura' (under dictation) expresses that very same constraint experienced by the translator who 'cammina sulla corda', establishing a parallel between Sbarbaro as a translator of Greek tragedy and Sbarbaro as a poet, thus connecting the author's two literary periods. Moreover, in *Fuochi fatui*, the poet declares that he has understood the meaning of his poetic quest and asserts his desire to reconnect with his beginnings, namely with his first collection of poems, *Pianissimo*. In light of this, the echoes of *Pianissimo* present in his translation of *Antigone* create a strong connection between Sbarbaro's poetic themes and those of Greek tragedy.

My analysis revealed how Bemporad's translation of Sophocles was a key moment in the development of her poetic persona. Her interest in Electra's character appears from the start from her decision to translate only *The Libation Bearers* (which focuses on Electra) out of the trilogy of Aeschylus' *Oresteia* and, subsequently, Hofmannsthal's *Elektra*, which largely drew from Sophocles' interpretation of Electra. In Sophocles' play, the character of Electra is to be read together with her other constitutive half, her brother Orestes, with whom she constantly longs to reunite. The only solace she can find are her laments and the hymns to death that she sings. This figure of a character who lives a half-life is, I have argued, what intrigued Bemporad. In my analysis of the 'Diari' – a section of Bemporad's *Esercizi* – I have shown how, similarly to Electra, Bemporad's poetic persona is constantly longing to reunite with her other constitutive half, her 'forma sorella', that is poetry. My comparative analysis of Bemporad's translation of Electra and of her *Esercizi* has demonstrated how the endless lament and the constant desire for death experienced by the poetic self, especially in the 'Diari', are profoundly indebted to Electra's condition. The tragic heroine, her endless quest for the other half, her nightly terrors consoled only by her hymns to death are all to be read as a set of metaphors for Bemporad's endless longing to be reunited with poetry. Moreover, a number of symbols and personifications of Death in the 'Diari', such as Shadow ('Ombra'), Darkness ('Tenebra') and Night ('Notte'), shape Bemporad's poetics of death after the model of Electra. Adopting the Leopardian model of translation of the Classics as poetic apprenticeship, Bemporad not only finalized her poetic themes and shaped her poetic persona but made her translation of Sophocles a milestone of her literary trajectory.

As mentioned before, Sbarbaro and Bemporad's appropriation of the Classics as sources of poetry and inspiration was deeply connected with their experiences and commitments as teachers. Sbarbaro's lifelong teaching activity must be placed under the sign of radical freedom: the poet categorically refused to be part of any schooling institution. Such a decision was informed by a precise belief: Sbarbaro strongly opposed the scholastic system, as he believed that it was an obstacle to a real learning experience. However, Sbarbaro's radical view on learning was not an a priori rejection of the system as a whole but was informed by his own schooling experience. By choosing to be a private tutor, Sbarbaro had the opportunity to develop his own pedagogy in opposition to the institutional one. His 'metodo della partecipazione' and his strong dialogical approach, tailored to the needs of the individual students (Sbarbaro only taught one-to-one), aimed at fostering a learning experience of mutual enrichment based on direct knowledge of classical poetry. Conceived in those terms, Sbarbaro's teaching activity was of a highly ethical stance. The poet as a teacher revived the study of classical civilization as a means to promote self-awareness and awaken the individual's creative responsiveness. Sbarbaro's peculiar way of finding, step by step, the most adequate pedagogy for every student somewhat recalls the poetic and translation process of finding, word by word, the right solution for every composition. The parallel between poetry and teaching produced actual intersection. Significantly, Sbarbaro included his reflections on teaching in his poetic collections, which stresses all the more clearly the creative function he assigned to the knowledge of and to the teaching of Classics.

While Sbarbaro taught almost his entire life, Bemporad was a teacher of Latin and Greek for only a few months. The uniqueness of her experience as a teacher is mostly due to the context in which she taught. Bemporad was a teacher at Pier Paolo Pasolini's private school. Differently from Sbarbaro's one-to-one lessons, Bemporad had an entire class to teach and lived together with teachers and students in a sort of commune where the learning experience was constantly revived in a number of ways (metrical competitions, walks, theatrical projects and poetic compositions). A key element in Bemporad's methodology as a teacher was the use of dramatic art and translation. In line with Pasolini's theoretical writing on the importance of the theatre and translation in pedagogy, Bemporad was a performer-teacher. Her lessons focused on dramatic readings of her own translations. As a teacher of Classics, Bemporad put great emphasis on the oral transmission of literature (a model of delivery she used until the end of her life). In her lessons/performances, she acted out long extracts of her translations of the Classics by heart. Teaching Classics in Pasolini's school was, above all, a transformative poetic experience for Bemporad: the transmission of classical poetry allowed her to change into a modern rhapsode. Ultimately, my analysis of Sbarbaro and Bemporad's pedagogical commitment has revealed that their teaching aimed to free the Classics from that aura of conformism associated with the traditional method of teaching Greek and Latin in schools. Moreover, both poets placed the translation from classical languages as the centre of their teaching activity and pedagogical reflections. In different ways and with different agendas, both poets developed a teaching approach in which translation held a creative role and was employed as a means of exalting the poetic function of the Classics.

This study of Sbarbaro and Bemporad's poetic translations of Greek tragedy enriches the ever-growing field of study interrogating the dialogue of twentieth-century Italian poetry with the classical legacy. From a stylistic point of view, the analysis of their engagement with Greek tragedians revealed how both poets investigated the lyrical possibilities of the tragic genre by means of translation. At the same time, their rhythmical translations of Sophocles helped their lyrical voices and provided models for their poetic personae. Revealing their proximity to the sensibility of the movement expounded in *La Voce* and to the experience of Hermeticism, Sbarbaro and Bemporad's exploration of lyrical possibility via the translation of Greek tragedy reasserts the centrality of the comparative approach with respect to literature and its genres.

The comparative analysis of these two authors – addressed in their work as poets, translators and teachers – offered in this book sheds light on novel achievements within the twentieth-century Italian reception of Greek tragedy, and within the landscape of scholarship on Sbarbaro and Bemporad. Furthermore, tracing Sbarbaro and Bemporad's relationship with the Classics from a comparative perspective hopefully complements the approach of addressing this topic by taking isolated cases of single authors. This work aims at encouraging further studies on the intersections between Sbarbaro's literary periods, unearthing the osmotic links between his poetic discourse and his translation practice whilst calling for a less compartmentalized outlook on his work as a poet-translator as a whole. These findings could open up new perspectives addressing all his translations from the Classics and the interplay with his poetic universe. It is my hope that this book will provide a solid basis for advancing the interest in Bemporad's literary production, spurring us to broaden our understanding of her work on the Classics well beyond her published translations of Homer and to take full stock of Bemporad's contribution to the history of twentieth-century Italian translations of Greek tragedy, which still remain entirely unpublished in her vast archive.

Notes

Introduction

1 The debate on the role, the function and the values of Modern and Classical literatures intersects with the so-called *Querelle des Anciens et des Moderns*, which manifested itself in the seventeenth century, recalling and encompassing ideas that already been posited well before by Petrarch's protohumanism as Fumaroli highlights in his seminal essay 'Les abeilles et les araignées' in Anne-Marie Lecoq, *La Querelle des Anciens et des Modernes: XVII–XVIII siècles* (Paris: Gallimard, 2001), 7–218.

2 On this see Marcello Ravesi, 'La polemica classico-romantica in Italia' in Sergio Luzzatto and Gabriele Pedullà (eds), *Atlante della letteratura italiana* (Turin: Einaudi, 2012), 14–25; Fabio Camilletti, *Classicism and Romanticism in Italian Literature: Leopardi's Discourse on Romantic Poetry* (London: Routledge, 2016).

3 On this see Paolo Zoboli, *La rinascita della tragedia: Le versioni della tragedia greca da D'Annunzio a Pasolini* (Lecce: Pensa Multimedia Editore, 2004). While it is true that performance informed and shaped the language of translation of Greek drama of some classical scholars, it was by no means a widespread conviction amongst the community of classical scholars that it should do so. On this point see Sara Troiani, *Dal testo alla scena e ritorno: Ettore Romagnoli e il teatro greco*, Collana Labirinti, Università degli Studi di Trento (Dipartimento di Lettere e Filosofia: Trento, 2022), 25–36.

4 On INDA's beginnings and its ties with D'Annunzio see Giovanna Di Martino, 'L'*Agamennone* di Eschilo: Italianità e Sicilianità alla vigilia della grande guerra', *FuturoClassico*, 5 (2019): 174–208.

5 The community of Italian classicists was quite divided on the issue of performance translation. For a good survey of this aspect see Troiani, *La polemica antifilologica tra 'ellenismo artistico' e italianità della cultura*, 25–36.

6 The bibliography on this aspect is vast. Recent scholarship in classical reception has come to appreciate the modernist nature of Fascism's appropriation of the classics, particularly in the theatrical realm. Recently on this aspect: G. Di Martino, E. Ioannidou and S. Troiani, 'Performing Ancient Greece in Fascist Italy:

Modernism and the Classical', *Classical Receptions Journal, Special Issue: A Hellenic Modernism: Greek Theatre and Italian Fascism*, 16, no. 1 (2024); Patricia Gaborik, *Mussolini's Theatre: Fascist Experiments in Art and Politics* (Cambridge: Cambridge University Press, 2021); Emilio Gentile, 'The Theatre of Politics in Fascist Italy' in G. Berghaus (ed.), *Fascism and Theatre: Comparative Studies on Aesthetics and Politics of Performance in Europe 1925-1945* (Oxford: Berghahn Books, 1996), 72–93; R. Griffin, 'Fascism's Modernist Revolution: A New Paradigm for the Study of Right Wing Dictatorships', *Fascism*, 5, no. 2 (2016): 105–29.

7 Anna Benucci Serva (ed.), *Cara Giovanna: Lettere di Camillo Sbarbaro a Giovanna Bemporad (1952–1964)* (Milan: Edizioni Archivio del '900, 2004).

8 Montale, 'Camillo Sbarbaro', *L'Azione*, Genova, 16 November 1920; then in Camillo Sbarbaro, *Il Nostro e nuove gocce* (Milan: Scheiwiller, 1964).

9 On this see Laura Vallortigara, '"Nel furore che mi teneva sveglia": La traduzione dell'*Eneide* di Giovanna Bemporad' in Eleonara Cavallini (ed.), *Scrittori che traducono scrittori: traduzioni 'd'autore' da classici latini e greci nella letteratura italiana del Novecento* (Alessandria: Edizioni dell'Orso, 2017), 107–22.

10 On the pair experience–reflection see Antoine Berman, *L'épreuve de l'étranger* (Paris: Gallimard, 1984); Antoin Berman, *La traduction et la lettre ou l'auberge du lointain* (Paris: Éditions du Seuil, 1999).

11 Oreste Macrí, 'La traduzione poetica negli anni trenta (e seguenti)' in F. Buffoni (ed.), *La traduzione del testo poetico* (Milan: Marcos y Marcos, 2004), 243–56.

12 Antonio Prete, 'Le pagine di Leopardi sul tradurre', *Testo a Fronte*, III (1991): 131–4.

13 On this see George Steiner, *Antigones: The Antigone Myth in Western Literature Art and Thought* (Oxford: Oxford University Press, 1984).

14 Peter Szondi, *An Essay on the Tragic*, trans. Paul Fleming (Stanford: Stanford University Press, 2002), 1.

1 Poetic Translations in Context: The Reception of Greek Tragedy in the Italian *Novecento*

1 Paolo Zoboli, *La rinascita della tragedia: Le versioni della tragedia greca da D'Annunzio a Pasolini* (Lecce: Pensa Multimedia Editore, 2004). For the purposes of my research, the value of Zoboli's study rests on his analysis of the historical context and of the most prominent contemporary figures dealing with the classical reception. He considered such important classical scholars such as Ettore Romagnoli and Manara Valgimigli and devoted significant attention to Benedetto

Croce's and Giovanni Gentile's debate on poetic translation. *La Rinascita della tragedia* is therefore a fundamental study if one is to appreciate the breadth and the diversity of the reception of Greek tragedy in the Italian *Novecento*.

2. Among the variety of twentieth-century poets who translated Greek tragedy, I selected Pasolini, Quasimodo and Sanguineti as case studies of poet-translators of entire tragedies, omitting from this study the authors who instead produced partial translations of Greek tragedies. On the blooming of encounters, especially from the 1970s, between Italian poets and the Classics see Federico Condello and Andrea Rodighiero (eds), '*Un compito infinito*': *Testi classici e traduzioni d'autore nel* Novecento *italiano* (Bologna: Bononia Univeristy Press, 2015); Eleonora Cavallini (ed.), *Scrittori che traducono scrittori: traduzioni 'd'autore' da classici latini e greci nella letteraratura italiana del Novecento* (Alessandria: Edizioni dell'Orso, 2017). On the specific case of Giovanni Giudici, translator of Aeschylus, see Caterina Paoli, '"Da quale parte il primo fuoco accenda": *L'Orestea* di Eschilo nella traduzione di Giovanni Giudici', *Istmi: Tracce di vita letteraria*, 35 (2015): 463–94.

3. Gabriele D'Annunzio, 'La rinascenza della tragedia', *La Tribuna*, 2 August 1897, now in Gabriele D'Annunzio, *Scritti giornalistici*, vol. 2, ed. Annamaria Andreoli and Giorgio Zanetti (Milan: Mondadori, 2003), 262 (262–5). On D'Annunzio's theatre see Valentina Valentini, *La tragedia moderna e mediterranea: Sul teatro di Gabriele D'Annunzio* (Milano: Franco Angeli, 1992), especially the chapter 'Il teatro moderno di Gabriele D'Annunzio', 11–58.

4. Valentini, 'Popolo e coro' in *La tragedia moderna e mediterranea*, p. 45, highlighted how D'Annunzio used the term 'popolo' alluding to the anthropological dimension according to which the primitive coincides with the childhood of mankind.

5. Valentini, *La tragedia moderna e mediterranea*, 31 and then Zoboli, *La rinascita della tragedia*, 23, highlighted that D'Annunzio here refers to Friederich Nietzsche's polemic with Richard Wagner, expressed in *The Case of Wagner* now in Friederich Nietzsche trans. Walter Kaufman, *The Birth of Tragedy and The Case of Wagner* (New York: Vintage, 1976), 159. On the influence exerted by Wagner on D'Annunzio's work see Vincenzo Borghetti and Riccardo Pecci, *Il bacio della sfinge: D'Annunzio, Pizzetti e Fedra* (Turin: E.D.T. Istituto Nazionale Tostiano, 1998). More generally, on the influence of Wagner's art on Italian literature see Adriana Guarnieri Corazzol, *Musica e letteratura in Italia tra Ottocento e Novecento* (Milan: Sansoni, 2000), 131–66 (163). D'Annunzio discussed Wagner's work in three articles: 'Nella vita e nell'arte: Il caso Wagner I, II, III', *La Tribuna*, 23 July 1893, 3 August 1893, 9 August 1893, now in D'Annunzio, *Scritti giornalistici*, 2, 233–61.

6. Zoboli, *La rinascita della tragedia*, 23.

7 D'Annunzio, *La rinascenza della tragedia*, 265.
8 Ibid.
9 Gabriele D'Annunzio, 'Discorso agli Ateniesi' in *Il Marzocco*, 28 May 1989, now in Gabriele D'Annunzio, *Scritti giornalistici*, 2, 460–3.
10 In Gabriele D'Annunzio, *Lettere ai Treves*, ed. Gianni Oliva, collaborazione di Katia Berardi e Barbara di Serio (Milan: Garzanti, 1999), 167–8. Valentini, *La tragedia moderna e mediterranea*, 109–10, and Zoboli, *La rinascita*, 9, first drew attention to the importance of this letter.
11 Valentini, *La tragedia moderna e mediterranea*, 25.
12 D'Annunzio's theatrical commitment prompted a conspicuous number of reviews and articles. On this see Anna Baldazzi, *Bibliografia della critica dannunziana nei periodici italiani dal 1880 al 1938* (Rome: Cooperativa scrittori, 1977), especially 89–98, covering the years 1898–1900.
13 On the influence exerted by Greek tragedy on D'Annunzio's theatre see Valentini, 'Travestire il moderno d'antico: Conti, la Grecia e i simbolisti' in *La tragedia moderna e mediterranea*, 31–4. In the same volume, there is a rich bibliography on D'Annunzio's theatre, 335–46.
14 On the theatre of Albano see Valentini, *La tragedia moderna e mediterranea*, 13–14.
15 On Ettore Romanogli see Patricia Salomoni (ed.), *Ritmo, Parole, Musica: Ettore Romagnoli traduttore dei poeti*, Atti del seminario di studi (Rovereto: Edizioni Scripta, 2021); Marina Valensise, *Orestea: Atto Secondo* (Milan: Electa, 2021); Sara Troiani, *Dal testo alla scena e ritorno: Ettore Romagnoli e il teatro greco*, Collana Labirinti, Università degli Studi di Trento (Dipartimento di Lettere e Filosofia: Trento, 2022). Recently a conference entitled 'Ettore Romagnoli e la rinascita del teatro greco nei primi decenni del Novecento' was organized in 2021 in Rovereto by L'Accademia Roveretana degli Agiati di Scienza, Lettere ed Arti (proceedings in progress).
16 Ettore Romagnoli, 'La musica greca', *La nuova antologia*, s. IV, CXVI [CC], 1905, 800: 650–72 now in *Musica e poesia nell'antica Grecia* (Bari: Laterza, 1911), 41.
17 Friederich Nietzsche, *The Birth of Tragedy out of the Spirit of Music* in *The Birth of Tragedy and Other Writings*, ed. Raymond Geuss and Ronald Speirs, trans. Ronald Speirs (Cambridge: Cambridge University Press, 1999), 13–116.
18 Zoboli, *La Rinascita della tragedia*, 126.
19 On the history of INDA and its relationship with classical reception, see E. Ioannidou, G. Di Martino and S. Troiani (eds), '(Re)Living Greece and Rome: Performances of Classical Antiquity under Fascism', *Fascism: Journal of Comparative Fascist Studies*, 12, no. 2 (2023).
20 Ettore Romagnoli, *Nel Regno d'Orfeo: Studi sulla lirica e la musica greca* (Bologna: Zanichelli, 1921), 11. The concept of '*moderno ellenismo*' had been the object of a

Prolusione at the University of Catania in 1906, entitled *Il moderno concetto dell'Ellenismo*.

21 For a concise overview of the various types of classicisms see classica Luigi Enrico Rossi, 'Umanesimo e filologia (A proposito della Storia della filologia classia di Rudolf Pfeiffer)', *Rivista di Filologia e di Istruzione Classica*, 104 (1976): 98–117. On this aspect see also Luciano Canfora, *Ideologie del classicismo* (Turin: Einaudi, 1980).

22 In terms of quantity, his work equals that of Felice Bellotti who, in the nineteenth century, translated the entire corpus of Greek poetry.

23 Ettore Romagnoli, 'La diffusione della cultura classica' in *Vigilie Italiche* (Milan: Istituto Editoriale Italiano, 1919), 89.

24 On the evolution of Greek rhythm see Ettore Romagnoli, *Nel Regno d'Orfeo: Studi sulla lirica e la musica greca* (Bologna: Zanichelli, 1921), 167–71.

25 Ettore Romagnoli, *Musica e poesia nell'antica Grecia* (Bari: Laterza, 1911), 317.

26 George Steiner, *After Babel* (London: Oxford University Press, 1975), 244.

27 Benedetto Croce, *Estetica come scienza dell'espressione e linguistica generale: Teoria e storia*, ed. G. Galasso (Milan: Adelphi, 1990), 87.

28 Croce, *La Poesia* (Bari: Laterza, 1935), 103.

29 Domenico Jervolino, 'Croce, Gentile e Gramsci sulla traduzione' in Giuseppe Cacciator, Girolamo Cotroneo and Renata Viti Cavaliere (eds), *Croce filosofo: Atti del convegno internazionale di studi in occasione del 50 anniversario della morte* (Soveria Mannelli: Rubbettino, 2003), 2 vols, II, 436 (431–41).

30 Steiner, *After Babel*, 251.

31 I quote from Jervolino, 'Croce, Gentile e Gramsci sulla traduzione', 436.

32 Giovanni Gentile, 'Il diritto e il torto delle traduzioni' in *Frammenti di estetica e letteratura* (Lanciano: Carabba, 1920), 369–75.

33 Jervolino, 'Croce, Gentile e Gramsci sulla traduzione', 437: 'Come si vede, in entrambi i filosofi la soluzione all'aporia del tradurre ripropone l'ispirazione di fondo del sistema filosofico: da una parte la filosofia dei distinti, dall'altra l'unità dell'atto spirituale. Questo conferma la rilevanza teoretica della questione, apparentemente marginale, della traduzione.'

34 On this topic, apart from Zoboli, 'La speculazione filosofica: Croce e Gentile' in *La rinascita della tragedia*, 73–9, see also Simone Giusti, 'Tradurre per comprendere: Gobetti tra Croce e Gentile' in Simone Giusti, *La congiura stabilita: Dialoghi e comparazioni tra Ottocento e Novecento* (Milan: Francoangeli, 2005), 39–53.

35 Antoine Berman, 'L'emprise philologique' in *La traduction et la lettre ou l'auberge du lointain* (Paris: Éditions de Seuil, 1999), 118.

36 Ibid., 119.

37 Gennaro Perrotta, 'Intelligenza di Giorgio Pasquali', *Primato*, IV, I, 1 Gennaio 1934, 5–6.

38 Giorgio Pasquali, 'Traduzioni, classici e antichi' in *Filologia e Storia* (Florence: Le Monnier, 1998), 35.
39 Giorgio Pasquali, 'Arti e studi in Italia nell'ultimo venticinquennio: Gli studi di greco', *Leonardo*, I, no. 12 (1925): 261–5, now in *Scritti filologici, II, Letteratura latina Cultura Contemporanea Recensioni*, ed. F. Bornmann, G. Pascucci, S. Timpanaro, introduction by A. La Penna (Firenze: Olschki, 1986), 736–51. Pasquali's polemics on the role of translation is informed by his belief that translation cannot be considered a satisfactory form of exegesis. On Pasquali's translations see A. Ronconi, 'Il filologo' in L. Caretti (ed.), *Per Giorgio Pasquali: Studi e testimonianze* (Pisa: Nistri-Lischi, 1972), 116–17. On the position of the rest of the classical philologists see Fausto Giordano's introduction to the volume Giorgio Pasquali, *Filologia e Storia* (Florence: Le Monnier, 1998), III–XXI. In his introduction, Giordano quotes, together with Romagnoli and Fraccaroli, the other classical philologists who believed in the importance of the '*traduzioni estetizzanti*' such as Domenico Comparetti, Girolamo Vitelli, Ermenegildo Pistelli and Nicola Festa (the founders of the 'Società Italiana per la diffusione degli studi classici' and of the journal *Atene e Roma*).
40 Pasquali here quotes Giuseppe Fraccaroli and Ettore Romagnoli as the two emblematic cases, probably the most famous ones, of classical scholars who devoted particular attention to the practice of translation from the Classics.
41 In addition to this, Pasquali saw a substantial difference between a 'classical text' and an 'ancient text'. According to Pasquali, only classical texts deserve to be translated and therefore made accessible to everyone, whereas the ancient texts must remain object of the specialists' attention. These positions are discussed in the chapters 'Traduzioni, classici e antichi' (31–8), 'Classici e antichi, traduzioni e commenti' (39–43) and 'Classici, antichi e studio storico' (44–9) in *Filologia e storia*. Giordano discussed the importance of such a difference in shaping a view of the Greek and Latin cultures not as a normative model to be imitated (*umanesimo*), but as a stratified civilization in need of a set of specific skills and learned approaches. Giordano agrees with Sebastiano Timpanaro, who in his review of the second edition of *Filologia e Storia* credited Pasquali with the merit of having discarded the *umanesimo* root – present in Wilamowitz's conception of classical philology – from his own philological approach; see Sebastiano Timpanaro, 'Recensione a Giorgio Pasquali, *Filologia e storia*, nuova edizione con una premessa di Alessandro Ronconi, Firenze, Le Monnier, 1964, x–96', *Critica Storica* IV (1965): 565–6.
42 On Pasquali's pedagogic interest see Giorgio Pasquali, *Università e scuola* (Florence: Sansoni, 1950).
43 Manara Valgimigli, 'Del tradurre poesia antica' in *Del tradurre e altri scritti* (Milan-Naples: Ricciardi, 1957), 20.

44 Manara Valgimigli, *Eschilo: Le Coefore* (Bari: Laterza, 1948), 7–8.
45 On this Jean-Pierre Vernant and Pierre Vidal-Naquet, *Oedipus in Vicenza and in Paris: Two Turning Points in the History of Oedipus* in *Myth and Tragedy in Ancient Greece*, trans. Janet Lloyd (New York: Zone Books, 1990), 361 (361–80).
46 Manara Valgimigli, *La Orestea: Agamennone, Coefore, Eumenidi. Eschilo* (Florence: Sansoni, 1948).
47 I quote from Marcello Gigante, *Gennaro Perrotta e Benedetto Croce* in *Giornate di studio su Gennaro Perrotta*, ed. Bruno Gentili; Agostino Masaracchia (Pisa-Rome: Istituti Editoriali e Poligrafici Internazionali, 1996), 146 (129–52).
48 Aurelio Privitera, 'La storia della letteratura greca di Gennaro Perrotta' in *Giornate di studio su Gennaro Perrotta*, 21–39.
49 Masaracchia, 'Gli scritti sulla tragedia greca' in *Giornate di studio su Gennaro Perrotta*, 76–7.
50 Giuliana Cardinali, 'Ricordo di Gennaro Perrotta' in *Giornate di studio su Gennaro Perrotta*, 118.
51 Masaracchia, 'Gli scritti sulla tragedia greca', 89: 'Uno degli aspetti più nuovi e moderni dell'opera di Perrotta è la sua opera di traduttore (Perrotta's translation practice is one of the most innovative and modern aspects of his work.'
52 Zoboli, 'La riflessione dei traduttori (1900–1920)' and 'La riflessione dei traduttori (1921–1960)' in *La rinascita della tragedia*, 80–4 and 120–4, highlight the lack of a theoretical debate on translation also among the translators themselves, who mostly appeared to be concerned with the formal issue of choosing between verse and prose.
53 On the history of classical scholarship in eighteenth-century Germany and on the creation of the paradigm known as *Altertumswissenschaft* see Katherine Harloe, *Winckelmann and the Invention of Antiquity: History and Aesthetics in the Age of Altertumswissenschaft* (Oxford: Oxford University Press, 2013), especially part 2 *On the Contours of Das Altertum and the Possibility of its Recovery: Heyne versus Wolf*, Chapter 6 ('Heyne, Winckelmann, and Altertumwissenschaft'), 162–91.
54 Sotera Fornaro, 'Christian Gottlob Heyne dans l'historie des études classiques', *Revue germanique internationale*, 14 (2011): 15–26.
55 On the figure of C. G. Heyne see Ulrich Schindel, 'C.G. Heyne' in Ward W. Briggs and William M. Calder III (eds), *Classical Scholarship: A Biographical Encyclopedia* (New York: Garland Publishing, 1990), 176–82.
56 Sotera Fornaro, p. 5, compares Heyne's questions to those posed by Levi Strauss: 'Heyne se demande [...] pour parler comme Lévy-Strauss, pourquoi il existe des differences entre les cultures malgré l'uniformité de l'esprit humain.'
57 From M. Cowan, *An Anthology of the Writings of Wilhelm von Humboldt: Humanist without Portfolio* (Detroit: Wayne State University Press, 1963), 79.

58 On Humboldt's reforms see 'Humboldt Education Reforms' in Martin Bernal, *Black Athena: The Afroasiatic Roots of Classical Civilisation*, vol. I (London: Free Association Books, 1987), 285–8.
59 F. Boiardi, 'La riforma della scuola di Gabrio Casati' in *Il parlamento italiano* (Milan: Nuova CEI Informatica, 1988), 317–18.
60 Humboldt's Hellenocentrism exerted a significant influence on classical scholarship. Werner Jaeger's monumental *Paideia* is, perhaps, the most famous example of the Hellenocentric principle and of its pedagogical application. On the influence exerted by Jaeger's thought see W. M. Calder III, *Werner Jaeger and Richard Harder: an Erklärung*, QS, 9 (1983), 19 ff.; W. M. Calder III, 'Werner Jager' in *Classical Scholarship: A Biographical Encyclopedia* (New York, 1990), 219 ff.; W. M. Calder III (ed.), *Werner Jager Reconsidered*, Illinois Classical Studies, Supplement 3 (Atlanta: Scholars Press, 1992); C. Franco, *Werner Jager in Italia: il contributo di Piero Treves*, QS, 3 (1997), 51 ff.; Canfora, *Ideologie del classicismo*, 218 ff.; Jas Elsner, 'Paideia: Ancient Concept and Modern Reception', *International Journal of Classical Tradition*, 20 (2013): 136–52.
61 I here refer to the anthropological notion of conglomerate introduced by E. R. Dodds in 'Plato, the Irrational Soul, and the Inherited Conglomerate' in *The Greeks and the Irrational* (Los Angeles: University of California Press, 1951), 207–35.
62 Lucio Bertelli, 'J.E. Harrison e "Ritualisti di Cambridge": la riscoperta del "primitivo"' in *Ítaca: Quaderns Catalans de Cultura Clàssica*, 21 (2005): 118.
63 Robert Ackerman, *J.G. Frazer: His Life and Work* (Cambridge: Cambridge University Press, 1903), 26.
64 On this see Ackerman, *The Myth and Ritual School: J. G. Frazer and the Cambridge Ritualists* (New York and London: Routledge, 2002). See also *The Cambridge Ritualists Reconsidered: Proceedings of the First Oldfather Conference, Held on the Campus of the Univeristy of Illinois at Urbana-Champaign April 27-30 1989*, ed. William M. Calder III in *Illinois Classical Studies*, Supplement 2 (Atlanta: Scholars Press, 1991).
65 On Jane Harrison see Lucio Bertelli, 'J.E. Harrison e "Ritualisti di Cambridge": la riscoperta del "primitivo"', 111–38. See also Renate Schleisier and Jane Ellen Harrison in Ward W. Briggs and William M. Calder III (eds), *Classical Scholarship: A Biographical Encyclopedia* (New York: Garland Publishing, 1990), 127–41; Mary Beard, *The Invention of Jane Harrison* (Cambridge, MA: Harvard University Press, 2002).
66 On Gilbert Murray see Robert Fowler, 'Gilbert Murray' in Briggs and Calder III (eds), *Classical Scholarship*, 321–34.
67 On F. M. Cornford see Douglas Kellog Wood and F. M. Cornford in Briggs and Calder III (eds), *Classical Scholarship*, 23–36.

68 Bertelli, 'J.E. Harrison e "Ritualisti di Cambridge": la riscoperta del "primitivo"', 120–1.
69 Jean-Pierre Vernant and Pierre Vidal-Naquet, *Myth and Tragedy in Ancient Greece*, trans. Janet Lloyd (New York: Zone Books, 1990).
70 Vernant and Vidal-Naquet, 'Tensions and Ambiguities in Greek Tragedy' in *Myth and Tragedy in Ancient Greece*, 29–48 and 21–2.
71 On Giorgio Pasquali's relationship with the world of German philology see C. J. Classen, *Giorgio Pasquali, un italiano come mediatore della scienza tedesca*, 'QS', 13, 1987 (p. 6). The dependence of Pasquali's philology on Wilamowitz is discussed by B. Bravo, 'Giorgio Pasquali e l'eredità del XIX secolo' in M. Bollack and H. Wismann (eds), *Philologie und Hermeneutik im 19. Jahrhundert*, II (Göttingen: 1983), 333–58. See also Giorgio Pasquali, *Storia dello spirito tedesco nelle memorie di un contemporaneo* (Milan: Adelphi, 2013).
72 On the relationship between the philological approach and the literary criticism inspired by Aestheticism in the Italian *Novecento* see G. Vitelli, *Filologia classica... e romantica*, ed. T. Lodi (Florence: 1962), 133–43.
73 Romagnoli's aesthetic theories are discussed in his *Minerva e lo scimmione* (Bologna: Zanichelli, 1917) and in *Lo scimmione in Italia* (Bologna: Zanichelli, 1919).
74 On this topic see J. Taminiaux, *Le théâtre des philosophes: La tragédie, l'être, l'action* (Grenoble: Jérôme Million, 1995); D. Schmidt, *On Germans and Other Greeks: Tragedy and Ethical Life* (Bloomington, IN: Indiana University Press, 2001); Peter Szondi, *An Essay on the Tragic*, trans. Paul Fleming (Stanford, CA: Stanford University Press, 2002); M. Thibodeau, *Hegel et la tragédie grecque* (Rennes: Rennes University Press, 2011); Joshua Billings, *Genealogy of the Tragic: Greek Tragedy and German Philosophy* (Princeton, NJ: Princeton University Press, 2014).
75 A concise overview of the vast debate on the concept of tragic is offered by Carlo Gentili and Gianluca Garelli, *Il tragico* (Bologna: Il Mulino, 2010).
76 Szondi, *An Essay on the Tragic*, 1.
77 Szondi, *An Essay on the Tragic*.
78 According to Szondi the philosophy of the tragic begins with Friedrich Wilhelm Joseph Schelling.
79 The bibliography on this topic is vast. Recently, Cristina Savettieri devoted critical attention to this matter, also discussing the Italian situation, in her article 'Tragedia, tragico e romanzo nel modernismo', *Allegoria*, XXIII (2011): 45–63. The article offers a useful discussion of the status quo of criticism on the tragic and the tragedy.
80 Giorgio Bárberi Squarotti, *Le sorti del 'tragico': Il Novecento italiano: romanzo e teatro* (Ravenna: Longo Editore, 1978). In his analysis, Squarotti aligns with George Steiner's argument in his *The Death of Tragedy* (London: Faber & Faber, 1995).

81 For a concise overview of the overlap between the reception of the tragic and the reception of Greek tragedy see Andrea Rodighiero, *La tragedia greca* (Bologna: Il Mulino, 2013), 7–10.
82 Aspects of this debate are outlined in the introduction to the re-edition of Remigio Sabbadini's *Il metodo degli umanisti*, ed. Concetta Bianca (Rome: Edizioni di Storia e Letteratura, 2018).
83 Oreste Macrí, 'La traduzione poetica negli anni trenta (e seguenti)' in F. Buffoni (ed.), *La traduzione del testo poetico* (Milan: Marcos y Marcos, 2004), 243–56.
84 On this see Emilio Mattioli, 'Storia della traduzione e poetiche del tradurre (dall'umanesimo al romanticismo)' in Rosita Copioli (ed.), *Tradurre poesia* (Brescia: Paideia, 1983).
85 Yopie Prins, *Ladies' Greek: Victorian Translations of Tragedy* (Princeton, NJ: Princeton University Press, 2017), 38.
86 On alternative forms of theatricality and performativity see Olga Taxidou, *Greek Tragedy and Modernist Performance: Hellenism and Theatricality* (Edinburgh: Edinburgh University Press, 2023).
87 Bonnefoy started to translate in the 1950 but published his reflections on this experience only in 2015.
88 Yves Bonnefoy, 'Jouer Hamlet dans le noir' in *L'hésitation d'Hamlet et la décision de Shakespeare* (Paris: Seuil, 2015), 145.
89 Ibid., 139.
90 Ibid., 121.
91 Ibid., 142.
92 Giovanna Bemporad's translation of Sophocles' *Electra*, ms.
93 Sophocles, *The Electra of Sophocles*, ed. with introduction and notes by Sir Richard Jebb (Cambridge: Cambridge University Press, 1894).
94 Camillo Sbarbaro, *Sofocle: Antigone* (Milan: Bompiani, 1943), 15.
95 Sophocles, *The Antigone of Sophocles*, ed. with introduction and notes by Sir Richard Jebb (Cambridge: Cambridge University Press, 1891).
96 To name a few, Gennaro Perrotta with *Prometheus Bound* (1954) and Leone Traverso with *Hippolytus* (1956). It was only after the 1960s that poets began to collaborate with INDA and produce poetic translations for the stage.
97 Zoboli, *Rinascita della tragedia*, 131.
98 On Pasolini's rewriting of the Oedipus myth see Giacomo Trevisan, 'Edipo all'alba "Io griderò chiara e intatta la mia vergogna"': Studio su "Edipo all'alba" di Pier Paolo Pasolini' in *Studi Pasoliniani*, 2 (Pisa–Roma, 2008), 37–55.
99 The fragments are now in Massimo Fusillo, *La Grecia secondo Pasolini: Mito e cinema* (Florence: La Nuova Italia, 1996), 243–6.

100 I discuss Pasolini's school and Bemporad's experience as a teacher in Chapter 4 of this book.
101 Pier Paolo Pasolini, 'Dal diario di un insegnante' in *Pier Paolo Pasolini, Romanzi e Racconti*, 2 vols, I, ed. Walter Siti and Silvia De Laude (Milan: Mondadori, 1998), 1136.
102 Ibid.
103 Now in Pier Paolo Pasolini, *Teatro*, ed. Walter Siti and Silvia De Laude (Milan: Mondadori, 2001), 1013–124.
104 Pier Paolo Pasolini, 'Lettera del traduttore' now in Pier Paolo Pasolini, *Teatro*, 1007.
105 On Pasolini's translation of Aeschylus see Luigi Enrico Rossi, 'L'approccio non classicistico di Pasolini alla tragedia attica' in Tullio De Mauro and Francesco Ferri (eds), *Lezioni su Pasolini* (Ripatransone: Edizioni Sestante, 1997), 123–31.
106 Pasolini, 'Lettera del traduttore', 1008.
107 On the category of transhistoricity see Vernant and Vidal-Naquet, 'The Tragic Subject' in *Myth and Tragedy in Ancient Greece*, 237–48.
108 Stefano Casi, *I teatri di Pasolini* (Milan: Ubulibri, 2015), 93: 'Dopo la traduzione per Gassman, il teatro è diventato per Pasolini una precisa realtà e non più solo metafora di grandezza o proiezione della tragedia personale, e le tracce rimaste nei suoi scritti marcano questo cambiamento.'
109 Between 1965 and 1966 Pasolini wrote six tragedies: *Orgia, Affabulazione, Pilade, Bestia da stile, Porcile, Calderón*. Among those, Casi focuses on the connections of these tragedies with Pasolini's translation of Greek tragedy: 'due opere, concepite in stretta connessione con la tragedia classica: *Pilade*, ideale continuzione dell'*Orestiade*, e *Affabulazione*, che reinterpreta le sofoclee *Trachinie* ed *Edipo re*. Intanto si perdono per strada altre ipotesi come quella di un "poema drammatico" dal titolo *Malcom X* e della tragedia *Teorema*, che dopo la scrittura dei primi monologhi muta percorso trasformandosi in ipotesi di sceneggiatura, così come la rilettura di *Edipo re* di Sofocle lo convince a progettare un film si questa storia' (p. 142). In addition to this, Pasolini wrote *Manifesto per un nuovo teatro*. On the 'cultural ritual' that the *Manifesto* was supposed to create, see David War's introduction to his English translation of the *Manifesto* in *Pier Paolo Pasolini: Contemporary perspectives*, ed. Patrick Rumble and Bart Testa (Toronto: University of Toronto Press, 1994), 152–4. The interest in Greek mythology and Greek tragedy has been traced as one of the '*costanti tematiche*' in Pasolini. On this see Massimo Fusillo, *La Grecia secondo Pasolini*, 6.
110 On the impact that Pasolini's translation had see Federico Condello, 'Su Pasolini traduttore classico: Sparsi rilievi tra fatti e leggende', *Semicerchio*, XVLII, no. 2 (2012): 8–17.

111 Quasimodo translated the following tragedies: Sophocles' *Oedipus Rex* (Milan: Bompiani, 1946); Sophocles' *Electra* (Milan: Mondadori, 1954); Aeschylus' *Libation Bearers* (Milan: Bompiani, 1949); Euripides' *Hecuba* (Urbino: Argalìa, 1962); Euripides' *Herakles* (Urbino: Argalìa, 1966). Some tragedies are now colllected in in *Tragici greci tradotti da Salvatore Quasimodo: Le coefore di Eschilo, Elettra di Sofocle, Edipo re di Sofocle* (Milan: Mondadori, 1963). On Salvatore Quasimodo's translations of Greek tragedy see Danilo Ruocco, *Salvatore Quasimodo e il teatro* in *Quasimodo*, ed. Alessandro Quasimodo (Milano: Mazzotta, 1999), 169–81. A list of all the tragedies translated by Quasimodo is included in *Quasimodo*, ed. Alessandro Quasimodo, 195–8.

112 Quasimodo's reviews are now collected in Alessandro Quasimodo (ed.), *Salvatore Quasimodo: Il poeta a teatro* (Milan: Spirali Edizioni, 1984).

113 Ruocco, *Salvatore Quasimodo e il teatro*, 172.

114 Ibid., 171.

115 Ibid.

116 Sanguineti's translations of Greek tragedy are now published in Edoardo Sanguineti, *Teatro antico: Traduzioni e ricordi*, ed. F. Condello and C. Longhi (Milan: BUR, 2006). On Sanguineti's translations see Paola Bisulca, 'Il traduttore-attore: Edoardo Sanguineti dietro la maschera degli antichi', Istituto Nazionale del Dramma Antico, http://www.indafondazione.org/it/il-traduttore-attore-edoardo-sanguineti-dietro-la-maschera-degli-antichi/.

117 On Sanguineti's *storicismo assoluto* and the consequence such a position had on his translation activity see Bisulca, *Il traduttore-attore: Edoardo Sanguineti dietro la maschera degli antichi*.

118 Ibid.

119 Vernant and Vidal-Naquet, 'The God of Tragic Fiction', 181–8.

120 Edoardo Sanguineti, 'Introduzione' in Sanguineti, *Teatro antico: Traduzioni e ricordi*, ed. F. Condello and C. Longhi (Milan: BUR, 2006), 19–20. On the risks caused by an alienating approach produced by the use of calque and interlinear translation see the seminal essay of Walter Benjamin, 'The Task of the Translator' in *Illuminations*, ed. and with an introduction by Hannah Arendt (London: Pimlico, 1999).

2 *Parole precise e ispirate*: Camillo Sbarbaro and the Regenerative Function of Translating Greek Tragedy

1 Eugenio Montale, 'Ricordo di Sbarbaro' in *Sulla poesia*, ed. G. Zampa (Milan: Mondadori, 1976), 335, highlights Sbarbaro's exceptional command of Greek language: 'Sbarbaro, uomo coltissimo, traduttore formidabile, eccellente grecista,

sebbene non avesse perseguito gli studi oltre il liceo, credeva fermamente che la vita fosse più importante della letteratura.'

2 The genesis and the composition of the book is tortuous. Paolo Zoboli in the section 'Il terzo libro di Sbarbaro' in Paolo Zoboli, *Linea ligure: Sbarbaro, Montale, Caproni* (Novara: Interlinea, 2006), 251–84, traces the history of the book and of its three editions (1956, 1958, 1962). It is worthwhile noting that the majority of the metapoetic meditations intertwined with the theme of translation are from the section dated 1940–5, the period in which Sbarbaro translated Greek tragedy.

3 Gina Lagorio, *Sbarbaro: Un modo spoglio di esistere* (Milan: Garzanti, 1981) devoted insightful paragraphs to these translations within the wider discourse on Sbarbaro's experience of the Second World War: 'fu così che si poté leggere Sofocle, e fece uno stranissimo effetto, come di ritrovata sorgente o addirittura di riscoperta, in un linguaggio del tutto inusitato. [...] In questo senso, l'accostarsi di Sbarbaro ai tragici greci, segnò nell'incontro dei moderni con gli antichi, la stessa svolta che fu di Quasimodo per i lirici' (250–1).

4 In chronological order: Lorenzo Polato, *Sbarbaro* (Florence: La nuova Italia, 1969, 1974), 124–9; Giorgio Bàrberi Squarotti, *Camillo Sbarbaro* (Milan: Mursia, 1971), 244–9; Vanni Scheiwiller (ed.), *Camillo Sbarbaro. Poesia e prosa* (Milan: Mondadori, 1979), XXXVI–XLVII; Gina Lagorio, *Sbarbaro: Un modo spoglio di esistere*, 359–78.

5 Gina Lagorio, 'Il Ciclope', *Atene e Roma*, n.s. V (1960): 3, 181–4, now in Gina Lagorio, *Sbarbaro controcorrente* (Parma: Guanda, 1973), 255–6.

6 Anna Maria Mesturini, 'Sbarbaro e il Ciclope di Euripide', *Resine* [IV] (1975): 47–54.

7 Anna Maria Mesturini, 'Antigone secondo Sbarbaro', *Resine* [V] (1976): 3–26.

8 Paolo Zoboli, *Sbarbaro e i tragici greci*, established the reference editions used by Sbarbaro for the tragedies translated. For Aeschylus: *Eschyle, tome I: Les Suppliantes – Les Perses – Les septe contre Thèbes – Prométhée enchainé*, ed. and trans. P. Mazon (Paris: Les Belles Lettres, 1931); *Eschilo, Il Prometeo legato*, con commento di E. Rapisarda (Turin: Società Editrice Internazionale, 1936), Scrittori Greci commentati per le scuole, 77. For Sophocles: *Sophocles, tome I, Ajax – Antigone – Oedipe roi – Électre*, ed. and trans. P. Masqueray (Paris: Les Belles Lettres, 1929) and *Sofocle, Antigone*, con note di Placido Cesareo (Torino: Chiantore, 1926 reprint). For Alcestis: *Euripide, tome I: Le Cyclope – Alceste – Medée – Les Héraclides*, ed. and trans. L. Méridier (Paris: Les Belles Lettres, 1926); *Euripide, Alcesti*, commentata da A. Taccone (Turin: Società Editrice Internazionale, 1930), Scrittori greci commentati per le scuole, 53. I will follow Mazon's, Masqueray's and Méridier's critical editions when referring to the Greek text.

9 Zoboli, *Sbarbaro e i tragici*, 101.
10 Sbarbaro openly expresses this idea about the translation of the *Ciclope* in two letters written to Gina Lagorio between March and April 1960, now in Gina Lagorio, *Sbarbaro controcorrente*, 346–7.
11 All references are from *Camillo Sbarbaro: L'opera in versi e in prosa*, ed. Gina Lagorio and Vanni Scheiwiller (Milan: Garzanti, 1985), 421. From now *OVP*.
12 For instance, Lorenzo Polato, *Sbarbaro* (Florence: La Nuova Italia, 1974), 107–10.
13 See Vanni Scheiwiller's preface to the final edition of Sbarbaro's *opera omnia*, now reprinted in *OVP*, 10.
14 Giuseppe De Robertis, 'Fuochi fatui', *Gazzetta di Parma*, 27 September 1956, now in *Altro Novecento* (Florence: Le Monnier, 1962), 203–4.
15 On the moral dimension of Sbarbaro's poetry: R. Luperini, *Il novecento: apparati ideologici, ceto intellettuale, sistemi formali nella letteratura contemporanea* (Turin: Loescher, 1981), 223–32, describes Sbarbaro's poetry as guided by a 'moralità del conoscere' which coincides with 'autocoscienza'. S. Ramat, *Storia della poesia del Novecento italiano* (Milan: Mursia, 1976), 73–87, described Sbarbaro's poetic experience as an expression of applied ethics, which shares very little with common morality but strives to elaborate his own moral philosophy. See also Carlo Bo, 'Com'era Sbarbaro' in *Atti del convegno nazionale di studi si Camillo Sbarbaro: Spotorno 6–7 Ottobre 1973*, ed. A. Guerrini (Genoa: Resine, Quaderni Liguri di cultura, 1974), 7–20.
16 Polato, *Sbarbaro*, 109.
17 In chronological order: *Resine* (poetry, 1911), *Pianissimo* (poetry, 1914, 1954), *Trucioli 1914–1918* (prose, 1920), *Liquidazione* (prose, 1928), *Trucioli 1914–1940* (prose, 1948), *Rimanenze* (poetry, 1955, 1956), *Fuochi fatui* (prose, 1956, 1958, 1962), *Primizie* (poetry, 1958), *Scampoli* (prose, 1960), *Poesie* (poetry, 1961: contains a new redaction of *Pianissimo, Primizie* and *Rimanenze*), *Gocce* (prose, 1963), *Il Nostro' e nuove gocce* (prose, 1964), *Contagocce* (prose, 1965), *Cartoline in franchigia* (prose, 1966), *Bolle di sapone* (prose, 1966), *Vedute di Genova* (prose, 1921), *Quisquilie* (prose). On this aspect see Alfredo Gargiulo, 'Camillo Sbarbaro' in *Letteratura italiana del Novecento* (Florence: LeMonnier, 1943), 171–6, and Stefano Pavarini, *Sbarbaro prosatore: Percorsi ermeneutici dal frammento alla prosa d'arte* (Bologna: Il Mulino, 1997).
18 Sergio Solmi, *I 'Trucioli' di Sbarbaro* in *Scrittori negli anni* (Milan: Il Saggiatore, 1963), 232–7.
19 Silvio Ramat, '"Pianissimo" di Camillo Sbarbaro' in *La poesia italiana 1903–1943: Quarantuno titoli esemplari* (Venice: Marsilio, 1997), 124–35.
20 The presence of verses dispersed throughout the translation of *Antigone* has been noted by Mesturini, *Antigone secondo Sbarbaro*, and then confirmed by Zoboli,

Sbarbaro e i tragici, who extended the analysis to the translations of *Prometeo Incatenato* and *Alcesti*. Unless otherwise stated all quotations from *Pianissimo* are from the first edition (1914), now in *OVP*. However the second edition of *Pianissimo* (1960), also now in *OVP*, has also been taken into account when there is the need to appreciate a variant dependent on metaphors inspired by the translations of Greek tragedy.

21 On the historical importance of Sbarbaro's prosaic poetry see G. Contini, *Letteratura dell'italia unita: 1861–1968* (Florence: Sansoni, 1968), 726–7.

22 Pier Vincenzo Mengaldo, *Camillo Sbarbaro* in *Poeti italiani del Novecento* (Milan: Mondadori, 1978), 318, associates the used of the *endecasillabo libero* with Sbarbaro's quest for moralism: 'Il tormento moralistico si esprime in *Pianissimo* [...] senza alcuna violenza linguistica esibita, semmai con una sorta di violenza silenziosa e soffocata che si affida all'articolazione nudamente prosastica e anti-melodica del verso, principalmente dedotto, come notava già Cecchi, dai più spogli endecasillabi leopardiani.'

23 As Zoboli, *Sbarbaro e i tragici*, showed at pp. 97–8.

24 Giuseppe Savoca, *Concordanze delle poesie di Camillo Sbarbaro: concordanza, liste di frequenza, indici* (Florence: Olschki, 1989) has been a crucial research tool.

25 Carla Angeleri and Giampiero Costa (eds), *Bibliografia degli scritti di Camillo Sbarbaro* (Milan: All'insegna del pesce d'oro, 1986), 127–61.

26 The translation was published in 1943 as Gina Lagorio, *Sbarbaro: Un modo spoglio di esistere*, 250–1, points out. I give here the full quotation of the edition as recorded by Camillo Sbarbaro's bibliography in Carla Angeleri; Giampiero Costa, *Bibliografia*, 127: *Antigone* (Milan: Bompiani, 1943); 2nd edition: *Antigone* (Milan: Bompiani, 1945).

27 Angeleri and Costa, *Bibliografia*, 127.

28 Ibid., 137.

29 Ibid., 140.

30 For an exhaustive study of these translations see Filippomaria Pontani, '"Gracili avena": le versioni ultime, Pitagora e Pascoli' in *La dorata parmelia: Licheni, poesia e cultura in Camillo Sbarbaro (1888–1967)*, ed. G. Magurno (Roma: Carocci, 2011), 181–205. Gina Lagorio, *Sbarbaro controcorrente*, also places Sbarbaro's translation of Pascoli's Latin works when describing the years 1957–8, p. 297. The translation was published posthumously in 1984: 'Pascoli tradotto da Sbarbaro', ed. Vanni Scheiwiller in *Edizione non venale per gli Amici del Credito Italiani, con due scritti di Eugenio Montale, Manara Valgimigli e tre acqueforti a colori di Enrico Della Torre* (Milan: Scheiwiller, 1984). Vanni Scheiwiller in 'Nota dell'editore': 'Per gli estimatori della poesia di Camillo Sbarbaro le due traduzioni, da lui fatte per la R.A.I., e mai pubblicate, sono un non piccolo avvenimento letterario. Tra le carte

affidatemi per lascito testamentario dal poeta ligure [...]. I due inediti di Sbarbaro sono, più che illustri, accompagnati da un artista finissimo e amico dei poeti come Enrico Della Torre', 97–8.

31 *Caro Bompiani: Lettere con l'editore*, ed. G. D'Ina and G. Zaccaria (Milan: Bompiani, 2007), letter no. 102, p. 89.

32 The scholars who treated the chronology of the translations are: Gina Lagorio, 'Il Ciclope', *Atene e Roma*, 111 (1960); Bàrberi Squarotti, *Camillo Sbarbaro*, 239; Mesturini, *Antigone secondo Sbarbaro*, 3–26; Mesturini, 'Sbarbaro e il Ciclope di Euripide' in *Resine*, 13–14; Gina Lagorio, *Sbarbaro: Un modo spoglio di esistere*, 247–62; Giampiero Costa, 'Camillo Sbarbaro e Vanni Scheiwiller: lettere all'editore' in *Camillo Sbarbaro: Atti della giornata di studio 11 Aprile 2003* (Genova: Edizioni San Marco dei Giustiniani, 2003), 114; Paolo Zoboli, *Sbarbaro e i tragici*, 101.

33 Only two specimens of this corpus of letters exchanged between the poet, the publishing house and his editor in chief at that time, Elio Vittorini, were published in *Caro Bompiani: Lettere con l'editore*, ed. G. D'Ina and G. Zaccaria (Milan: Bompiani, 2007).

34 Zoboli, *Sbarbaro e i tragici*, 51–2.

35 Ibid., 55–6 quotes the letter written by Sbarbaro to Bompiani and dated 'Spotorno, 26 Ottobre 1943'.

36 The letter, dated Spotorno 3 May 1944, is transcribed by Zoboli, *Sbarbaro e i tragici*, 56.

37 Camillo Sbarbaro, *Lettere a Lucia: 1931–1967*, ed. Davide Ferreri (Genova: Fondazione Giorgio e Lilli Devoto – San Marco dei Giustiniani, 2007), 75.

38 Camillo Sbarbaro, *Lettere a Lucia: 1931–1967*, 76.

39 Zoboli, *Sbarbaro e i tragici*, 101.

40 Camillo Sbarbaro, *Lettere a Lucia: 1931–1967*, 77.

41 Ibid., 89.

42 Camillo Sbarbaro, *Lettere a Enrico Falqui: 1928–1967*, ed. Mirco Bevilacqua, Diego Divano and Daniela Carrea (Genova: Fondazione Giorgio e Lilli Devoto – San Marco dei Giustiniani, 2012), 53.

43 Camillo Sbarbaro, *Lettere a Enrico Falqui*, 56.

44 *OVP*, 469. Interestingly enough *diletto* is used as an adjective referred to Greek language in *Scampoli*: 'riaffrontai col solo aiuto del vocabolario l'odioso latino e il diletto greco' in Camillo Sbarbaro, *Scampoli* (Florence: Vallecchi, 1960), n. 32, 86.

45 Joris-Karl Huysmans, *Controcorrente: Traduzione dal francese di Camillo Sbarbaro* (Milan: Rusconi, 1972).

46 The first edition of the translation was published in 1944. Angeleri and Costa, *Bibliografia*, 130, inform us that Sbarbaro wrote the preface to this translation twenty years later.

47 Joris-Karl Huysmans, *Controcorrente*, 341.
48 Another important exchange of letters between Sbarbaro and Einaudi, completely unpublished, corroborates the idea that Sbarbaro's predilection for the Moderns, expressed in the letter to Falqui, is at least ambiguous and it offers a valuable comparison for the translations of the Ancients. From the correspondence emerge several disagreements, or even silences about the works to be translated. The letters, typescripts and manuscripts, are kept in the folder containing letters referring to the period between 25 November 1941 and 12 December 1956, and are kept in Archivio Einaudi.
49 Polato, *Sbarbaro*, 108.
50 Camillo Sbarbaro, *Lettere a Enrico Falqui 1931–1967*, 121.
51 Paolo Zoboli, 'Il motivo di un libro (sulle dediche di Sbarbaro)', in G. Devoto and P. Zoboli (eds), *Camillo Sbarbaro: Atti della giornata di studio. 11 Aprile 2004* (Genova: San Marco dei Giustiniani, 2003), 68–9.
52 Pontani, 'Gracili avena', 203.
53 All references from *Antigone* are from the first edition: Sofocle, *Antigone*, ed. Camillo Sbarbaro (Milan: Bompiani, 1943), 49.
54 Davide Puccini, *Lettura di Sbarbaro* (Florence: Nuovedizioni Vallecchi, 1974), 137–53; Zoboli, *La linea ligure*, 265–84.
55 *OVP*, 421–2.
56 Ibid.
57 *OVP*, 427.
58 *OVP*, 479.
59 Selected parts of these letters, mostly unpublished, are quoted by Zoboli, *Sbarbaro e i tragici*, 101.
60 This is the history of the *Ciclope* editions in brief. The first edition is in prose: Euripide, *Il Ciclope: Dramma satiresco*. Nella versione di Camillo Sbarbaro. Introduzione di G. Galloni, disegni di S. Cerchi (Genoa: Editrice Ligure Arte e Lettere, 1945). After this we have another first edition of the *Ciclope* together with the *Alcesti*: Euripide, *Alcesti. Il Ciclope. Traduzione dal greco di Camillo Sbarbaro* for *Pegaso teatrale. Teatro antico e moderno* (Milan: Bompiani, 1952). The second edition in verse: Euripide, *Il Ciclope. Dramma satiresco di Euripide* (Milan: All'insegna del pesce d'oro, 1960). There is then a third edition: Euripide, *Il Ciclope. Traduzione di Camillo Sbarbaro* (Turin: Einaudi, 1965).
61 Zoboli, *Sbarbaro e i tragici*, 101.
62 Anna Benucci Serva, *Cara Giovanna: Lettere di Camillo Sbarbaro a Giovanna Bemporad (1952–1964)* (Milan: Edizioni Archivio del '900, 2004), 69–70.
63 Carlo Bo, 'Com'era Sbarbaro', 10–11. See also C. Bo, 'Il debito con Sbarbaro' in *Otto studi*, preface by S. Pautasso (Genoa: San Marco dei Giustiniani, 2000), 105–17.

64 George Steiner, *The Death of Tragedy* (London: Faber & Faber, 1961), 6–10.
65 Walter Benjamin, 'The Task of the Translator' in *Illuminations*, ed. and with an introduction by Hannah Arendt (London: Pimlico, 1999), 82.
66 An example of this way of proceeding can be seen in Sbarbaro's translation of the l.590 'κυλίνδει βυσσόθεν / κελαινὰν θίνα' with *nera rena* where the alliteration between κυλίνδει and κελαινὰν is rendered by Sbarbaro with 'nera rena'. Another similar intervention is made by Sbarbaro in the first stasimon at l. 339 where the alliteration of the letter 'α' in the line 'ἄφθιτον, ἀκαμάταν, ἀποτρύεται' is translated with 'immortale, instancabile, affatica'.
67 Antoine Berman, 'Hölderlin: le national et l'étranger' in *L'épreuve de l'étranger* (Paris: Gallimard, 1984), 250–78.
68 Sbarbaro, *Antigone*, 16.
69 Benjamin, 'The Task of the Translator', 82.
70 The other passage is from the translation of Aeschylus' *Prometeo incatenato* and merged as a quote in Sbarbaro's *Trucioli dispersi*, ed. Giampiero Costa and Vanni Scheiwiller (Milan: Libri Scheiwiller, 1986). It is the line 252: 'ΠΡ. τυφλὰς ἐν αὐτοῖς ἐλπίδας κατῴκισα (l. 252P) / Pr. Misi ad abitare in essi le cieche speranze.' Sbarbaro quoted the line on blind hope in one of his *Trucioli dispersi* (Milan: Scheiwiller, 1986), n. [146], 95: '"Misi ad abitare in essi le cieche speranze" si gloria in Eschilo il benefattore degli uomini; ed è in Pindaro la definizione: "Speranze, sogni che si han da desti." Ma l'averne fatto tutta la vita l'esperienza non toglie che l'ultima speranza è anche la più ambiziosa.' As Zoboli demonstrated, p. 98, footnote 274, the line is not part of an original ode but it was attributed to Pindar by Stobeus, and Sbarbaro followed that interpretation.
71 *OVP*, 548.
72 Camillo Sbarbaro, *Antigone*, 75–6.
73 Sophocles, *The Antigone of Sophocles*.
74 Giorgio Barberi Squarotti, *Camillo Sbarbaro*, 52.
75 All references are from Camillo Sbarbaro, *Alcesti: Il Ciclope di Euripide* (Milan: Bompiani, 1952), 69.
76 *Euripides*, trans. David Kovacs (Cambridge, MA: Harvard University Press, 1994).
77 Camillo Sbarbaro, *Alcesti*, 46.
78 *Euripides*, trans. Kovacs.
79 Squarotti, *Camillo Sbarbaro*, 47–60.
80 *OVP*, 25–6.
81 Camillo Sbarbaro, *Antigone*, 78.
82 Sophocles, *The Antigone of Sophocles*.
83 *OVP*, 28.
84 Camillo Sbarbaro, *Antigone*, 15.

85 Sophocles, *The Antigone of Sophocles*.
86 George Steiner, *Antigones: The Antigone Myth in Western Literature Art and Thought* (Oxford: Oxford University Press, 1984), 16–17.
87 *OVP*, 30.
88 *OVP*, 49.
89 *OVP*, 43–4.
90 Sbarbaro, *Antigone*, 81–2.
91 Sophocles, *The Antigone of Sophocles*.
92 For a thorough description of the hymn of the parodos see Mark Griffith, *Sophocles: Antigone* (Cambridge: Cambridge University Press, 1999), 139–43.
93 Camillo Sbarbaro, *Antigone*, 23–4.
94 Sophocles, *The Antigone of Sophocles*.
95 Camillo Sbarbaro, *Antigone*, 30–1.
96 Sophocles, *Antigone of Sophocles*.
97 Griffith, *Sophocles: Antigone*, 165.
98 Sbarbaro, *Antigone*, 32.
99 *OVP*, p. 34.
100 *Alcesti. Il Ciclope di Euripide. Traduzione dal greco di Camillo Sbarbaro*, 5–8.
101 Eugenio Montale, *Sulla poesia*, 337.
102 The title *Fuochi fatui* is the one that the poet had thought of for his very first collection of poems, *Resine*, as the poets says in Camillo Sbarbaro, *Il mio 'primo vagito'*, ed. Giovanni Farris (Savona: Sabatelli, 1982), 5–7.
103 *OVP*, 422.
104 Just to give a couple of examples of compounds and etymological calques created by Sbarbaro to reproduce the original Greek see the parodos of *Antigone* at l. 106 where the adjective 'λεύκασπιν' is rendered with 'biancoscudato'; in *Prometeo incatenato* at l. 88 the adjective 'ταχύπτεροι' is translated as 'aliveloci'.
105 George Steiner, *After Babel: Aspects of Language and Translation* (Oxford: Oxford University Press, 1975), 236–7.
106 Mengaldo, *Camillo Sbarbaro*: '*Pianissimo* rimane certo il documento fondamentale della poesia di Sbarbaro e uno dei capitali del primo Novecento', p. 321.

3 Giovanna Bemporad's Early Translations of Greek Tragedy

1 Let us begin with the number of authors and works translated by Bemporad. In chronological order, these are Virgil's *Aeneid*, Homer's *Odyssey*, Johann Wolfgang

Goethe's *Trilogia della passione*, Novalis' *Inni alla notte* and *Canti spirituali*, Hugo Von Hofmannsthal's *Elektra* and the *Cantico dei cantici*. In addition to this, we should include the translations in her collection of poems *Esercizi*: poems from the *Atharvaveda*, Sappho's fragments (2, 4, 94 and 96), Baudelaire, Verlaine, Rimbaud, Mallarme, Valéry, Hölderlin, George and Rilke. To this list, we should add the significant number of unpublished translations that I was able to discover during my archival research. Bemporad translated the works of G. G. Byron, J. Milton, R. Frost, J. Keats, D. Thomas, P. B. Shelley, W. Shakespeare, P. Eluard, C. De Pizan, H. Von Kleist, G. Trakl, M. Lermontov, A. Machado, Horace, Theocritus, Aeschylus, Euripides and Sophocles.

2 From an interview typescript draft, densely annotated in the author's handwriting, and kept in a miscellaneous folder without a title. This document, together with Giovanna Bemporad's personal library and archive, has been recently acquired by the Centro Apice of the University of Milan.

3 The importance of Bemporad's translation of the *Odyssey*, especially considering the time she devoted to this work, is worth considering. However, due to constraints of space, I cannot treat this aspect in the present chapter. On her translation of the *Odyssey*, in chronological order, see: Fritz Bornmann, 'La traduzione dell'Odissea di Vanna Bemporad', *L'Approdo letterario*, XVII, 53 (1971); Enrico Falqui, 'L'Odissea dal video al testo e la galleria dei traduttori di Omero', *Il Dramma*, 11-12 (November-December, 1970); Pier Paolo Pasolini, 'Odissea', *Nuovi Argomenti*, n.s. 22 (1971); Maurizio Perugi, 'Odissea', *Paragone*, XXII, 254 (1971); Giovan Battista Pighi, 'L'Odissea della Bemporad', *Il Popolo*, 31 January (1971); Emanuele Trevi, 'Giovanna Bemporad: L'Odissea di Omero', *Nuovi Argomenti*, III serie, 46, April–June (1993); Andrea Rodighiero, 'L'Odissea di Giovanna Bemporad' in F. Condello and A. Rodighiero (eds), *'Un compito infinito': Testi classici e traduzioni d'autore nel Novecento italiano* (Bologna: Bononia University Press, 2015), 22–44.

4 In chronological order, the editions of the *Aeneid*, the *Odyssey* and the *Esercizi* are: *Gli eroi: antologia dell'epica per la scuola media*, ed. Lorenzo Braccesi (Bologna: Edizioni scolastiche Patron, 1965); Virgilio, *Dall'Eneide*, Giovanna Bemporad, introduzione di Luca Canali (Milan: Rusconi, 1983); Virgilio, *Dall'Eneide*, Giovanna Bemporad, introduzione di Luca Canali (Roma: Forcom, 2000); Homer, *Odyssey*, trans. Giovanna Bemporad (Turin: ERI, 1968); Homer, *Odyssey*, trans. Giovanna Bemporad (Turin: ERI, 1970); Homer, *Odissea: Canti e frammenti*, trans. Giovanna Bemporad (Florence: Le lettere, 1992). *Esercizi: Poesie e traduzioni* (Venice: Urbani e Pettanello, 1948); *Poesie e traduzioni* (Fermo: Tipografia La Rapida, 1963); *Esercizi: Poesie e traduzioni* (Milan: Garzanti, 1980); *Esercizi vecchi e nuovi*, ed. Andrea Cirolla (Milan: Edizioni Archivio Dedalus, 2010); *Esercizi vecchi*

e nuovi, ed. Valentina Russi (Bologna: Luca Sossella editore, 2011). Unless otherwise stated, all references to the *Esercizi* are from the Garzanti edition, which faithfully reproduces the 1948 edition.

5 In chronological order they are Euripides' *Medea* (10–15 July 1940), *Iphigenia at Aulis* (27 July–3 August 1940), *Hippolytus* (3–8 August 1940), *Heracleidae* (23–6 August 1940), *Bacchae* (12–17 September 1940; here we know the approximate time when the translation was completed: 'notte'), Aeschylus' *Persians* (8 October 1940: the manuscripts are incomplete and we only know when the translation was started); Sophocles' *Electra* (10–20 October 1940) and Aeschylus' *The Libation Bearers* (here too the manuscript is incomplete: we are told that the translation was started on the 21 October 1940).

6 Guido Avezzù described it as a 'trilogia trasversale': 'Eschilo, Sofocle ed Euripide nelle rispettive *Elettra*, a distanza di anni l'uno dall'altro, enfatizzando questa o quella componente della storia, sviluppando questo o quel personaggio, proponendo all'azione esiti qualitativamente diversi, offrono una visione prismatica dell'episodio centrale. A noi, che non possiamo leggere che una parte minima della produzione drammatica antica, questa "trilogia trasversale", priva di paralleli, offre una possibilità unica [...] di esplorare le potenzialità drammaturgiche e i diversi trattamenti di un singolo episodio della narrazione mitica.' *Sofocle, Euripide, Hofmannsthal, Yourcenar. Elettra. Variazioni sul mito* (Venice: Marsilio, 2002), 7–8.

7 Hugo Von Hofmannsthal, *Elettra*, trans. Giovanna Bemporad (Milan: Garzanti, 1981).

8 Paola Magi and Vincenzo Pezzella (eds), *Carlo Izzo: Lettere a Giovanna Bemporad 1940–1943* (Milan: Archivio Dedalus Edizioni, 2013), 21.

9 Giacomo Leopardi to Pietro Giordani in a letter written on the 21 March 1817: 'Ella dice da Maestro che il tradurre è utilissimo nella età mia, cosa certa e che la pratica a me rende manifestissima. Perché quando ho letto qualche classico, la mia mente tumultua e si confonde. Allora prendo a tradurre il meglio, e quelle bellezze per necessità esaminate e rimenate a una a una, piglian posto nella mia mente, e l'arrichiscono e mi lasciano in pace', now in Franco Brioschi and Patrizia Landi (eds), *Giacomo Leopardi: Epistolario*, 2 vols, (Turin: Bollati Boringhieri), I, 71.

10 Giuseppe Ungaretti, 'Difesa dell'endecasillabo' in M. Diacono and L. Rebay (eds), *Vita di un uomo: Saggi e interventi*, (Milan: Mondadori, 1974), 154–69. Bemporad had a long friendship with Giuseppe Ungaretti, who was one of the witnesses at her wedding in 1957. In the video interview with Bemporad edited by Vincenzo Pezzella, *Giovanna Bemporad: A una forma sorella. Intervista video-ritratto* (Milan: Archivo Dedalus Edizioni, 2011), 35, she said 'Ungaretti, e ti ho anche detto che aveva una grande ammirazione per la mia poesia, mi metteva fra i grandi che lui

amava, con mio gran stupore, e poi mi telefonava quasi ogni sera, facevamo, prima che morisse, grandi conversazioni culturali, sulla cultura del Metaponto, perchè lui era lucano, e quindi era molto legato alla cultura della Magna Grecia, un grande personaggio, veramente un grande personaggio e ha lasciato anche degli scritti molto belli.'

11 In his introduction to Bemporad's poetic translation of the *Odyssey* (1970), Umberto Albini was the first to mention Pascoli's influence on Bemporad's work ('Qua e là affiora anche Pascoli, Garcìa Lorca'). Maurizio Perugi, in his review of the *Odissea* in *Paragone*, XXII, 254 (1971): 129–35, further developed Albini's critical input. Perugi argued that Pascoli's influence on Bemporad's *Odyssey* is manifold. First, Perugi pinpointed Bemporad's references to *Traduzioni e riduzioni*. Second, Perugi claimed that Bemporad used Pascoli's *Poemi Conviviali* as a stylistic collection from which she derived stylistic solutions ('Il discorso critico sulla B. acquista un'efficacia euristica ben maggiore appuntandosi sui Poemi Conviviali, considerati in primo luogo nella loro urgenza di copioso serbatoio stilematico'). Third, Perugi summarized Pascoli's impact on Bemporad's modes of constructing the verse. Specifically, the solutions stressed by Perugi are as follows: the prolongation of rhythm beyond the end of the metrical unit ('la tecnica del verso conclusivo, dove il periodo metrico si ferma e si prolunga in una serie plurima di echi timbrici'); the stress on the penultimate syllable through the use of word proparossitone in hiatus ('Ha imparato a sensibilizzare la penultima sede mediante latinismi proparossitoni, con le ultime due vocali in iato'); and last the triggers on vowels in hiatus ('ha imparato a sollecitare le aperture vocaliche in iato, preferibilmente giocando sul timbro cuspidale'). However, once these debts had been identified, Perugi claimed Bemporad's substantial *anti-pascolismo* in her translation of the *Odyssey*. According to Perugi, Bemporad attempted to dismantle the pascolian hendecasyllable from within ('erosione interna che deflagra l'ombrosa sensibilità dell'endecasillabo pascoliano') so as to create a prosaic version of the hendecasyllable ('prosa endecasillabica') by using a number of solutions such as the refusal to use assonances and rhymes. Valentina Russi, touching on Perugi's claim of Pascoli's influence on Bemporad's work, traced the prosodical solutions highlighted by Perugi (namely the stress on the penultimate syllable through the use of words 'proparossitone' in hiatus) in the *Esercizi* as well, especially in the poem *Epilogo*, thus insisting on the continuity between Bemporad's poetic translations and her original poetry. Furthermore, Russi traced the echo of Pascoli's legacy in Bemporad's enactment of the poetic experience as the repetition of an emotional/psychic condition. As further evidence of Pascoli's traces in Bemporad's poetic imagination, Russi quoted the presence of the *assiuolo* and the *viola* in the poem *Madrigale*, and that of the *asfodeli* in *Euridice* as

elements of funereal symbology. 'Esercizi di assoluto: La poesia di Giovanna Bempoard', *Esperienze letterarie*, 3, XXXVI (2011): 70–81.

12 A similar attention to this prosodic experiment is then to be found in her translation of the *Odyssey*. Perugi traces this approach to Pascoli in his introduction to the *Odyssey*. On Bemporad's use of the hendecasyllable in her translation of the *Odyssey* see Rodighiero, *L'Odissea di Giovanna Bemporad*.

13 Paola Magi and Vincenzo, Pezzella (eds), *Carlo Izzo: Lettere a Giovanna Bemporad 1940–1943* (Milan: Archivio Dedalus Edizioni, 2013). A letter dated Venice, 11 April 1941, informs us that Viserba is the place where the two friends met for the first time, p. 71: 'Ricordati che da quando ti conobbi a Viserba ad oggi io sono rimasto sempre allo stesso punto: amico ammirato e senza albagie.' Unfortunately, the book features only Carlo Izzo's letters to Bemporad. It is unknown if Bemporad ever retrieved the letters she wrote to Izzo from his family or not. The editors, in the prefatory note, do not seem to question the status of these documents. In the prefatory note the editors Magi and Pezzella tell us that Bemporad submitted the original letters from Carlo Izzo (already numbered and organized in chronological order). The editors take the fact that we have only Izzo's letters as a given condition. Bemporad herself in the video protrait edited by Pezzella, *A una forma sorella*, p. 17, mentions these letters: 'Però sarebbero da pubblicare [i.e. le lettere], e io qualche volta ne ho parlato con un figlio di Izzo, e proprio perchè gli avevo dato probabimente, o mi doveva restituire le lettere di Izzo, allora gli ho dato un appuntamento addirittura una sera con la moglie, e dato che anche lui amava l'Opera, all'Opera, quello è stato il nostro unico incontro. E, naturalmente, ne abbiamo parlato di questa eventuale pubblicazione, lui pensava che sarebbe stato giusto, perchè di suo padre, in fondo non esiste, tranne questa antologia, non esiste granchè ...' Maria Pia De Angelis and Guido Fink, *'Ecco un libro da scrivere': Lettere di Carlo Izzo a Giovanna Bemporad* in Magi; Pezzella, 8–11, acknowledge the fact that Bemporad's are missing: 'Se le lettere di lei, che non possediamo, rivelano a quanto pare una sorta di "automatismo epistolare" e una certa tendenza all'autodenigrazione (frutto forse di orgoglio, insieme a una comprensibile paura).'

14 Magi and Pezzella, *Carlo Izzo*, 18.

15 The 'errore metrico' to which Izzo refers probably concerns the word 'Acatae'. Bemporad's translation is in hendecasyllables, but in order to respect the metrical framework either 'Acatae' has to belong to the following verse or 'salutano' must be considered hypermetric.

16 Magi and Pezzella, *Carlo Izzo*, 21. Prosodical comments are found in a letter dated 8 October 1941, when Izzo comments on Bemporad's original poetry: 'e il bruco uccidi/ e il fiore che di te respira cali/ insaziata nel mare (perchè la dieresi? O non

vuoi fare un settenario?)' (p. 90). Another time, in a letter dated 5 November 1941, Izzo discusses Bemporad's translation of Byron's *Childe Harold*: 'Ho fatto una sola correzione: "potenza" invece di "violenza" per via della dieresi: meglio starci attenti: anche Praz ci tiene, e Dazzi, come sai, e Traverso, come strasai. Quando si può è certo meglio evitare: ho guardato qualche trattato teorico: soprattutto quando una "u" è seguita da una consonante accentata (p. es. Persüaso) la regola è rigidissima. Quanto al primo settenario sdrucciolo nel martelliano ti dirò che non solo è ammesso ma anzi è preferito, in quanto il martelliano non sarebbe che un tetrametro giambico catalettico' (p. 105).

17 Ungaretti, *Difesa dell'endecasillabo*, 154: 'E l'ha nel sangue [i.e. l'endecasillabo] ogni vero poeta italiano. È l'ordine poetico naturale delle parole italiane.'
18 Izzo is probably referring to Giosuè Carducci's *Odi barbare* (1877). With his *metrica barbara* (an expression created by Carducci himself) Carducci aimed at reproducing the quantitative aspect of Latin in Italian poetry. On Carducci's *metrica barbara* see: Luigi Conte Falcone, *Metrica classica e metrica barbara: L'esametro latino e il verso sillabico italiano. Due saggi critici* (Vienna: 1855); Massimiliano Mancini, *Saggi sulla poesia barbara e altri studi di metrica italiana* (Rome: Manziana Vecchiarelli, 2000); Carlo Caruso, 'Metri barbari e verso libero' in Carlo Caruso and Juan Rigoli, *Poétiques barbares: Poetiche barbare* (Ravenna: Longo, 1998), 209–30.
19 Magi; Pezzella, 26.
20 Ibid., 37.
21 R. C. Jebb, P. E. Easterling and R. Blondell, *Sophocles: Plays. Antigone* (London: Bristol Classical Press, 2004).
22 Magi and Pezzella, *Carlo Izzo*, 80. The translation of *Antigone* is mentioned again in another letter dated Venice, 24 October 1941, where Izzo encourages Bemporad to send her translation to Manlio Torquato Dazzi: 'Certo che dovrai mandare a Dazzi il Macbeth e l'Antigone: Dazzi è sinceerissimamente ammirato di te' (p. 97); and again at p. 104: 'Dazzi mi ha scritto: che aspetta da te il Macbeth [*sic*] e l'Antigone [*sic*] come d'accordo.'
23 Magi and Pezzella, *Carlo Izzo*, 62.
24 Magi and Pezzella, *Carlo Izzo*, 66.
25 Magi and Pezzella, *Carlo Izzo*, 121–2.
26 Pietro Bembo describes the 'verso rotto' as: 'Oltra che ritrovamento provenzale è stato lo usare i versi rotti; la quale usanza, perciò che molto varia in quelli poeti fu, che alcuna volta di tre sillabe li fecero, alcuna volta di quattro e ora di cinque e d'otto e molto spesso di nove, oltra quelle di sette e d'undici, avvenne che i più antichi Toscani più maniere di versi rotti usarono ne' loro poemi ancora essi, che loro più vicini erano e più nuovi nella imitazione, e meno i meno antichi; i quali

da questa usanza si discostarono, secondo che eglino si vennero da loro lontanando, in tanto che il Petrarca verso rotto niuno altro che di sette sillabe non fece.' Dionisotti in the footnote at the passage explains: 'Il Bembo chiama *versi rotti* qui e nel II libro i versi di misura inferiore all'endecasillabo (decasillabo provenzale). Naturalmente l'uso di tali versi non può dirsi *ritrovamento provenzale*, ma il Bembo ha ragione notando il favore che tali versi ebbero nella poesia provenzale e in quella provenzaleggiante italiana.' 'Prose della volgar lingua' in Carlo Dionisotti (ed.), *Pietro Bembo, Prose e rime* (Turin: Unione Tipografica-Editrice, 1966), I, 9, 93.

27 Magi and Pezzella, *Carlo Izzo*, 120. On this see Avanzolini Maurizio, 'L'eterno nemico. Dalla censura libraria all'applicazione delle leggi razziali: il Ventennio fascista nella Biblioteca dell'Archiginnasio', *'L'Archiginnasio', Bollettino della Biblioteca Comunale di Bologna*, CXIV (2019): 487–618.

28 Virgil's *Georgics* are mentioned at p. 21, and *Bucolics* are mentioned at p. 136; G. G. Byron's *Childe Harold's Pigrimage* at pp. 83, 86, 87, 91, 94, 137, 153, 155; W. Shakespeare's *Macbeth* at pp. 17, 37, 74, 76, 97, 104; J. W. Goethe's *Faust*, at pp. 150, 151. A translation of Plato is referenced in a letter dated 31 October 1941, p. 103: 'Anche Platone ora? Ma prenditi tempo.'

29 Virgil's *Georgics* are mentioned at p. 21 and the *Bucolics* at p. 136. On the translation of the *Bucolics* see C. Paoli, 'Translating Virgil at Age Sixteen: Giovanna Bemporad's Bucolics' in *Women and Translation in the Italian Tradition*, ed. Helena Sanson (Paris: Classiques Garnier, 2022), 291–314; C. Paoli, *Virgilio*, Bucoliche. *Traduzione di Giovanna Bemporad* (Urbino: QuattroVenti, 2023). Other translations are mentioned throughout the correspondence: G. G. Byron's *Childe Harold's Pilgrimage* at pp. 83, 86, 87, 91, 94, 137, 153 and 155; W. Shakespeare's *Macbeth* at pp. 17, 37, 74, 76, 97, 104; J. W. Goethe's *Faust* at pp. 150–1; Plato at p. 103.

30 Franco D'Intino, *Giacomo Leopardi: Poeti greci e latini* (Rome: Salerno Editrice, 1999), VII–LXIII. On the importance of these translations in Leopardi's creative process, see also F. De Sanctis, *Leopardi*, ed. Carlo Muscetta and Antonia Perna (Turin: Einaudi, 1983), 18. S. Timpanaro, *La filologia di Giacomo Leopardi* (Roma-Bari: Laterza, 1977), 171–99; F. Figurelli, *La formazione del Leopardi sino al 1819: Lezioni dell'anno accademico 1970-71* (Naples: De Simone, 1971), 37.

31 D'Intino, XII.

32 D'Intino, XXIII: 'Ma giacchè non è possibile, traducendo, riprodurre *fedelmente*, è meglio allora inventare Anacreonte, ricreando a partire da sè, da quello strato profondo e *naturale* che accomuna, al di qua del linguaggio, il poeta antico a quello moderno.'

33 In a letter dated 18 January 1941, Izzo encourages Bemporad to translate in order to foster her poetic voice, p. 33: 'So che tu sei più che una promessa. Ma, non

conoscendo i tuoi versi originali, voglio prima vedere se sono all'altezza delle traduzioni. Ove non lo siano: traduci e aspetta che il tuo mondo fantastico sia all'altezza delle tue possibilità espressive.'

34 From a manuscript sheet contained in a miscellaneous folder labelled in the author's handwriting as 'Miei scritti sulla questione del tradurre' now held at Centro Apice.

35 Bemporad discusses the importance of having 'un temperamento poetico personale' to produce a good translation in her essay 'La traduzione dell'Odissea' in Buffoni, *La traduzione del testo poetico*, 240–1. Similarly, Bemporad discusses her ideas on translation in the essay 'Come tradurre Omero', *Resine: Quaderni Liguri di Cultura*' (Genova: Marco Sabatelli Editore, 2005), 13–16.

36 The idea is also reinstated in a manuscript sheet contained in a miscellaneous folder labelled in the author's handwriting as *Miei scritti sulla questione del tradurre* now held at the Centro Apice.

37 Yves Bonnefoy, 'Le paradoxe du traducteur' in *L'autre langue à portée de voix* (Paris: Éditions du Seuil, 2013), 81.

38 Yves Bonnefoy, 'Signification et poésie' in *L'autre langue à portée de voix*, 97.

39 We can infer from the manuscript that it took Bemporad ten days to complete the translation. The manuscript of 66 sheets (consisting of 17 folios of four sheets, with text on recto and verso) shows the starting date on the top left margin of the recto side of the first sheet, '10 Ottobre 1940', and the end date, '20 Ottobre 1940', on the verso side of the first sheet of the last folio. It is hard to say with certainty where Bemporad was when she translated Sophocles' *Electra*, but we may put forward a plausible hypothesis. Of all the translations composing the 'tragic group', just two manuscripts give the place together with the date: Euripides' *Heracleidae* (26 August 1940) and *Bacchae* (17 September 1940). The place is Viserba, a small town on the Adriatic coast. Thanks to an interview conducted (and edited) by Vincenzo Pezzella in 2011, we know that every summer Bemporad used to spend three months with her family in Viserba. Given that this group of translations on the whole belongs to the period from 10 July to 21 October (the start date of *The Libation Bearers* which is the last text of the group), we can cautiously assume that Bemporad translated these texts in the summer months spent in Viserba. The second possible location is Bologna where she returned immediately after the end of the summer holidays that year. The *Elettra* manuscript is autographed, as are the other manuscripts composing this group of translations. Bemporad's signature appears in full three times in this document. The first time it features above the title ('SOFOCLE-ELETTRA', in capital letters). The second time it appears on the top right margin beneath the sub-title 'traduzione di Bemporad Giovanna'. The third and last time it is at the very end of the manuscript, just beneath the end date and the line 'FINE-ELETTRA'. This last signature is at the foot of the text as a

concluding element of Bemporad's personal note on the tragedy: 'Finito con furia distruggitrice d'ogni ostacolo. Senza fermarmi mai. Né mai mi fermerò! Finché avrò vita. È questa una tragedia divina. Bemporad Giovanna.' *Elettra*'s concluding note is the longest of all the comments that accompany her translations. At the end of her *Medea* Bemporad complains that her pleasure was short-lived: 'Peccato sia finito così presto. Ma troverò da continuare. Divino poeta!' *Iphigenia at Aulis* has no other comment than the following statement of its end: 'Fine della tragedia: Ifigenia in Aulide.' By contrast, the comment at the end of Bemporad's *Hippolytus* stresses the translator's joy: 'Continuerò. È gioia grande.' *Heracleidae* further restates Bemporad's desire to keep translating: 'Continuerò ancora.' *Bacchae* gives us an insight into Bemporad's sentimental state: 'Continuare a tradurre. È l'ultimo conforto che mi resta. Sono molto triste.' Aeschylus' *The Libation Bearers* and *Persians* are incomplete and therefore do not feature any concluding notes.

40 The editions of Sophocles' *Electra* available in 1940 were, in chronological order: C. G. Erfurdt and J. G. Hermann (Leipzig, 1825, with commentary), L. Campbell (Oxford, 1881 with commentary), R. C. Jebb (Cambridge, 1894, with commentary) and A. C. Pearson (Oxford, 1924, edition only).

41 U. Agatodemone, *Sofocle: L'Elettra* (Naples: L. Chiurazzi, 1909); L. A. Michelangeli, *Sofocle: L'Elettra* (Bologna: Zanichelli, 1917); G. La Magna, *Sofocle: Elettra* (Ragusa: Stab. tib. popolare, 1923); Ettore Romagnoli, *Sofocle: Le tragedie*, 3 voll., III (Bologna: Zanichelli, 1926); H. Montesi and N. Festa, *Sofocle: Elettra* (Rome: Ausonia, 1927); E. Bignone, *Le tragedie di Sofocle*, 3 voll., 3 (Florence: Sansoni, 1937–8); E. Turolla, *Sofocle: Elettra* (Milan: Signorelli, 1937).

42 Enrico Turolla, *Elettra. Sofocle. Traduzione con note critiche e sceniche* (Milan: Carlo Signorelli, 1937). Turolla also wrote an essay on Sophocles: E. Turolla, *Saggio sulla poesia di Sofocle* (Bari: Laterza, 1934). Turolla, at the foot of the introduction to his translation, wrote: 'Il testo originale donde è fatta la versione, è quello sostanzialmente del Pearson (Oxford 1923)' (p. 8).

43 The comparison shows Bemporad's lexical borrowings ('madre sciagurata', 'gemito', 'spargi', 'empiamente', 'mano malvagia') while highlighting that Bemporad's oscillation between less archaic choices (like 'morire' instead of the more dramatic 'perire') and more archaic choices ('figliuola') follows metrical reasons; in this case the need to have a trisyllabic word (*fi-gliuo-la*) instead of a disyllabic one (*fi-glia*). Word order is another criterion. Turolla's 'Colui che, da anni lunghi, per inganni, dell'ingannatrice tua madre' is changed by Bemporad who creates three hendecasyllables thoroughly interlaced.

44 E. Bignone and G. La Magna are the two translators who offer translations in verses of Sophocles' *Electra*.

45 For this bibliographic research the catalogue (*regesto*) of translations of Greek tragedy published in 1900–60 produced by P. Zoboli in appendix to his *Rinascita della tragedia*, 179–202, has been an invaluable tool.
46 Salvatore Quasimodo, *Sofocle: Elettra* (Milan: Mondadori, 1954).
47 Giovanna Bemporad, 'La traduzione dell'Odissea' in Franco Buffoni, *La traduzione del testo poetico* (Milan: Marcos y Marcos, 1989), 240–1.
48 On the difference between metre and verse see Nicola Gardini, 'Il metro e il verso' in *Com' è fatta una poesia* (Milan: Sironi, 2007), 103–21.
49 From an interview, typewritten and corrected by the author's handwriting kept in a miscellaneous folder, probably prepared for a possible publication. The title of the interview is 'L'esercizio della scrittura come ascesi spirituale'. The quotation here is Bemporad's answer to the question: 'Quando e perché hai affrontato la prima traduzione?' The material is now held at Centro Apice.
50 For an analysis of Electra's lyric metres see J. H. Kells (ed.), *Sophocles: Electra* (Cambridge: Cambridge University Press 1973), 232–8.
51 On the *colon* as a metrical unit of variable length, see Bruno Gentili and Liana Lomiento, *Metrica e ritmica: Storia delle forme poetiche della Grecia antica* (Milan: Mondadori Università, 2003), 7–8. Bemporad's awareness of rhythmic units when translating from Greek poetry also emerges from the video interview *A una forma sorella*, in which she discusses her translation of the *Odyssey*: 'E stavo anche su una frase d'Omero per dieci ore, capisci? Finché mi veniva la soluzione perfetta, di ogni frase d'Omero, ogni frase, perché, se anche il primo verso veniva, lo travasavo quasi senza difficoltà dal greco all'italiano, al mio endecasillabo, poi gli altri non venivano, non ci stavano dentro. E allora dovevo cambiare completamente l'inizio perché la frase doveva poi venire tutta completa, fino in fondo, fino al punto. Ogni frase cioè non un verso, ma tutta la frase. Questa è stata la grande fatica' (p. 40).
52 Sophocles, *The Electra of Sophocles*, ed. with introduction and notes by Sir Richard Jebb (Cambridge: Cambridge University Press, 1894).
53 The adjective referred to ἀήρ (ether) is ἰσόμοιρ' which literally means 'sharing equally' (LSJ: earth's equal partner air).
54 Studies in *Electra*'s afterlife have shown how this tragedy ultimately raises utterly 'tragic' issues such as strength, misfortune, love, the relationship between freedom and necessity. See Domenico Cianciani and M. Antonietta Vito (eds), *Marguerite Yourcenar-Simon Weil. Elettre: Letture di un mito greco* (Milan: Edizioni Medusa, 2004), 8; Guido Avezzù, *Sofocle, Euripide, Hofmannsthal, Yourcenar, Elettra. Variazioni sul mito* (Milan: Marsilio, 2002), 7–20.
55 In this passage we find lexical choices reminiscent of Leopardi: 'πολλὰς μὲν θρήνων ᾠδάς' (l. 88) is translated with 'infiniti canti lamentosi'. 'Infinito' is used

again for 'πολύς' (l. 89 'πολλὰς δ' ἀντήρεις ᾖσθου') as well as 'canto' in connection with the 'θρῆνος', even when not coupled with 'ᾠδή' (l. 94).

56 George Méautis, *Sophocle: Essai sur le héros tragique* (Paris: Edition Albin Michel, 1957), 234 and 244.
57 Remo Pagnanelli, 'Giovanna Bemporad: poesia e traduzione', *Otto-Novecento*, XII (1988): 214.
58 Ibid., 213: 'L'epigrafe di *Esercizi (a una forma sorella)* rende bene lo sforzo per ri-trovare la parte mancante di sè, la fede nella poesia come modalità della reunione prenatale; il sintagma va letto in una duplice direzione, fecondamente ambivalente: la "forma sorella" è *in primis* la parola, poi, per chi fa poesia, la traduzione e viceversa, in seguito anche la consolatrice Natura. A mio giudizio, è ineliminabile la simmetria psichica con la desinenza "femminile" del vocabolo.'
59 Another phenomenon to observe is Bemporad's use of less archaic language combined with *amplificatio*. Turolla's sentence 'di prole orbato' becomes longer in Bemporad's 'privato dei suoi figli'. The Latin-modelled sentence (verb at the end) 'farò l'eco del mio gemito qui fuori a tutti risuonare' is rendered by Bemporad with a more standard language structure: 'e sino a quando io la vedrò / questa mia luce come un usignolo /privato dei suoi figli echeggerà/ il mio lungo lamento!' Compared to Turolla's translation, Bemporad opts for an agile and less archaic syntax. The comparison between the two translations shows a very different use of punctuation. Turolla's prose uses it in a way that creates several paratactic periods, also in the lyrical sections.
60 Méautis, *Sophocle*, 232: 'Car voilà la vrai nature d'Électre, elle est un cri. Et Sophocle – par ce procédé si frequent chez lui de la repetition – a accentué cette notion. Dans les trois centes vers qui vont du v. 77 au v. 377 on ne voit pas revenir moins de vingt fois des mots qui se rapportent aux plaints, aux gémissements, aux lamentations, aux cris d'Électre.' On this aspect, see Anne Carson, 'Screaming in Translation' in *Sophocles: Electra*, trans. Anne Carson (Oxford: Oxford University Press, 2001), 41–8.
61 Sophocles, *The Electra of Sophocles*.
62 Other passages where Bemporad employs this mechanism are to be found at ll. 258 ff. In this case, Bemporad makes explicit what was left unspecified in the Greek: 'οὐ δρῴη τάδ' ἄν' becomes 'e non piangere'. At ll. 515 ff. Bemporad adds a few words to finish the section with an hendecasyllable: 'ἔλειπεν ἐκ τοῦδ' οἴκου / πολύπονος αἰκία' becomes 'l'affanno e il disonore abbandonò / la desolata casa e il nostro lare.'
63 Sophocles, *The Electra of Sophocles*.
64 Bemporad, *Esercizi*, 15.
65 Bemporad, *Intarsio* in *Esercizi*, 30.

66 Pagnanelli, 'Giovanna Bemporad', 214.
67 Russi, *Esercizi di assoluto*, p. 72: 'In un incontro del 2009 alla Casa Internazionale delle Donne di Roma, Bemporad ha affermato che il nucleo originario delle sue poesie (la sezione "Diari", nella quale l'opposizione giovinezza/vecchiaia è più accentuata) risale a quando aveva quindici anni.'
68 A total number of fifty poems subdivided into seven subsections titled 'Preludio', 'Diari', 'Aforismi', 'Disegni', 'Esercizi', 'Dediche', 'Altri esercizi', hosting, in order of appearance, translations from Atharvaveda, Homer, Sappho, Virgil, Baudelaire, Valéry, Verlaine, Rimbaud, Mallarmé, Hölderlin, George and Rilke.
69 Caroline Malabou, *Plasticity at the Dusk of Writing: Dialectic, Destruction, Deconstruction*, trans. Carolyn Shread (New York: Columbia University Press, 2009).
70 Cf. Emek Ergun, Denise Kripper, Siobhan Meï, Sandra Joy Russell, Sarah Rutkowski, Carolyne Shread and Ida Hove Solberg, 'Women (Re)Writing Authority: A Roundtable Discussion on Feminist Translation' in Louise Von Flotow and Hala Kamal (eds), *The Routledge Handbook of Translation, Feminism and Gender* (London: Routledge, 2020), 7.
71 Russi, *Esercizi di assoluto*, 70.
72 Andrea Zanzotto, 'Dalla trascrizione della trasmissione radiofonica "Giovanna Bemporad e Alda Merini. Conversazione con Andrea Zanzotto" Radio Lugana, 1980', now in Giovanna Bemporad, *Esercizi vecchi e nuovi* (Milan: Archivio Dedalus, 2010), 205–6.
73 Simone Weil, for example, translated and interpreted Sophocles' *Electra* as a means to defy social injustice and, subsequently, as a symbolic figure of the reunion between God and the human being. On this see Cianciani and Vito, *Elettre: Letture di un mito greco*, 81–114.
74 Pier Paolo Pasolini, 'Poesia della Bemporad in Bemporad' in *Saggi sulla letteratura e sull' arte*, 2 vols, I, ed. Walter Siti and Silvia De Laude (Milano: Mondadori, 1999), 294–7.
75 Pagnanelli, *Giovanna Bemporad*, 212: 'Da questa mancanza perenne scaturisce la perennità della differenza'.
76 Ibid., 213–18.
77 These repetitive situations have been again described by Pagnanelli as 'variazioni innestate su connotazioni ritualistiche e ripetitive che aprono al delirio abbandonico, estasi mortuaria e all'incantamento liberatorio' (p. 213).
78 Bemporad herself commented on the nature and content of these poems in the video-interview *A una forma sorella*, p. 43: 'Di color grigio nero, poi, invece, vengono quelle poesie, più o meno derivate dalle traduzioni che io facevo dei poeti simbolisti e sono, in genere, poesie d'amore, dove ho fatto entrare i colori della natura e del mondo circostante, mentre nelle prime (i *Diari*), non faccio altro che

parlare della morte.' Andrea Cirolla, in the preface to *A una forma sorella*, p. 10, also stresses the presence of death in the 'Diari': 'L'idea della morte copre tutto il "libero magistero" casarsese, e sarà del resto il Leitmotiv anche dei "Diari" che proprio in quei mesi la Bemporad andava componendo, e che finiranno stampati a Venezia negli *Esercizi* del 1948, prima tappa di un lungo percorso umano ed editoriale'.

79 Bemporad connects the mask with funereal symbolism in the *Video-ritratto*, p. 26: 'Comunque, tornando all'immagine evocata in questa poesia: "e non scolpita immortalmente vegli/ la mia maschera chiusa in un cristallo" mi è stata suggerita mentre uscivo dalla casa di questo amico, una sera, ho visto sul plinto una riproduzione, un ritratto in cera probabilmente, di un suo antenato. [...] Sono rimasta stupita... per cui, poi, quando ho scritto questa poesia mi è tornata in mente quell'immagine, come qualcosa di funereo, che respingevo, "e non sul plinto immortalmente vegli / la mia maschera chiusa in un cristallo", perchè era chiusa nel vetro, mi ha fatto impressione, come un'immagine funebre e però immortale, cioè funebre per sempre, come se la mia testa fosse destinata a essere scolpita in cera e messa su un plinto per sempre. Mi ha fatto impressione, come una cosa negativa e l'ho messo nella poesia'.

80 Bemporad, 'Mia compagna implacabile la morte' in *Esercizi*, 19.
81 Bemporad, 'Variazione su tasto obbligato' in *Esercizi*, 20.
82 Bemporad, 'Già comincia a segnare luci e ombre' in *Esercizi*, 21.
83 Bemporad, 'Non soccorre all'eclissi vespertina' in *Esercizi*, 22.
84 Bemporad, 'Dolore, che mi seguiti immortale' in *Esercizi*, 23.
85 Bemporad, 'Non farmi così sola come il vento' in *Esercizi*, 24.
86 Bemporad, 'Vorrei gettare ciecamente al nulla' in *Esercizi*, 25.
87 Bemporad, 'Paesaggio' in *Esercizi*, 26.
88 Giacomo Leopardi, *Epistolario 1817*, 94.
89 Several scholars noted the Leopardian echoes in Bemporad's original poetry. Carlo Izzo was the first to trace this influence. In a letter dated 8 October 1941, p. 89, Izzo comments on Bemporad's *liriche*: 'La prima: "Te che nel grembo". Principio troppo foscoliano. Ucciderei i primi tre versi. "Verno" mi pare un' "anticaglia". Più sotto sostituirei "luce" a "lume". La fine è ottima. "Luna, ultima dea." L'intonazione leopardiana è innegabile.' In another letter dated 5 November 1941, p. 106: 'Liriche. Speranza: molto leopardiana: "tali a noi rivela" "pallidi fiori ed erbe". Non è questione di atteggiamento spirituale, ma di musica.' Pier Paolo Pasolini, 'Poesia della Bemporad' in *Saggi sulla letteratura e sull'arte* (Milan: Mondadori, 1999), 295, mentioned Leopardi's influence as far as the hendecasyllable was concerned: 'Il *pastiche* che nasce da un contatto di una poesia folkloristica, e appartenente a un folclore di molti secoli fa e di un ambiente totalmente diverso dal nostro, con un

endecasillabo Petrarca-Tasso-Leopardi (e Monti) riesce quanto mai succoso e suggestivo, con certi suoi toni magico-esoterici, che danno una vocale larghezza all'invocazione ingenua.' Giacinto Spagnoletti, 'Dal risvolto di copertina di Esercizi 1980', now in Giovanna Bemporad, *Esercizi vecchi e nuovi* (Milan: Archivio Dedalus, 2010), 203: 'dalla lirica degli *Esercizi* e che ritroviamo, proprio al colmo della stagione ermetica, quasi dimentica di prendere le distanze, impavida nel ricercare il cuore della nostra creazione poetica (Leopardi innanzitutto), ferma al crocicchio donde partono le grandi arterie del Simbolismo europeo'. Emanuele Trevi, 'Giovanna Bemporad: l'*Odissea* di Omero', *Nuovi Argomenti*, 46 (1993), now in Giovanna Bemporad, *Esercizi vecchi e nuovi*, 220: 'Quello che si legge nella filigrana degli *Esercizi* è un leopardismo integrale, si direbbe "di natura", per opporlo a quel prolisso leopardismo ideologico, di fattura eminentemente cardarelliana, che per molto tempo è stato davvero la malattia infantile del Novecento poetico italiano. Nella Bemporad il ricorso a Leopardi si dà con l'urgenza di un gesto vitale ma certo non premeditato, come il respiro nel sonno. Anche dove questo gesto possa assumere l'aspetto di un vero e proprio mosaico di citazioni, peraltro apertamente confessato con la dedica *a Leopardi* [...] Perché, insomma, Leopardi è qui davvero un maestro di sensibilità più che un serbatoio retorico, e i *Canti* possono venire utilizzati come la chiave d'accesso a quel mondo intimo e segreto che non conosciamo meglio degli altri solo perché ne siamo i depositari.'
90 D'Intino, XLIV.
91 This is the 'vuoto d'amore' mentioned by Pasolini in his review of the *Esercizi*, 294.
92 Virginia Woolf, 'On Not Knowing Greek' in *The Common Reader* (London: Hogarth Press, 1925), 38. On Virginia Woolf and Greek Tragedy see Nancy Worman, *Virginia Woolf's Greek Tragedy* (London: Bloomsbury, 2019).

4 Creative Pedagogy and Poetic Translation: Camillo Sbarbaro's, Pier Paolo Pasolini's and Giovanna Bemporad's Commitment to Education

1 Enzo Siciliano, *Vita di Pasolini* (Milan: Rizzoli, 1979), 84 offers a concrete example of Bemporad's perfomative readings/lessons at Pier Paolo Pasolini's independent school.
2 Paolo Zoboli, *Sbarbaro e i tragici greci* (Milan: Vita e pensiero, 2005), 29–30 traced the student's name in the records of the University of Genoa: 'Nell'annuario della Regia Università di Genova, Luxardo Lelio di Costante da Buenos Ayres' risulta, al n. 18 del 4 anno, tra gli *Studenti iscritti nell'Anno Scolastico 1921-1922* per la Facoltà di Lettere e Filosofia.'

3 Clelia Sbarbaro, 'Camillo Sbarbaro nei ricordi della sorella', *Paragone*, XXI, 248 (1970): 130–6 (132). On this and on the poet's commitment on teaching Latin and Greek as a turning point in Sbarbaro's life see Gina Lagorio, 'L'insegnamento' in *Sbarbaro: Un modo spoglio di esistere* (Milan: Garzanti, 1981), 160.
4 Zoboli, *Sbarbaro e i tragici greci*, 28.
5 According to Lagorio, Sbarbaro's revision of Greek and Latin should be read ('e cominciò la sua opera di recupero delle lingue classiche') as an act of will-power, which played against the sense of annihilation caused by his depression. Sbarbaro's resolute study of Greek and Latin became symbolic of his determination to bring back his desire for life, counterbalancing his death wish. Lagorio, *Sbarbaro: Un modo spoglio di esistere*, 163.
6 Ibid.: 'Rientrato a Genova, Sbarbaro continua il lavoro cominciato e che sarà più suo, il modo di guadagnare che gli piacerà meno e che eserciterà più a lungo, fino alla vecchiaia: a Luxardo, l'italo-americano che conseguì onorevolmente la sua laurea con il prof. Cerrato, si affiancano altri scolari, mandati da Adelchi Baratono, o figli di amici, e altri che vennero dietro il racconto entusiasta dei primi. Sbarbaro dà lezioni di latino e di greco; a un solo scolaro per volta.'
7 Zoboli, *Sbarbaro e i tragici greci*, 32–3.
8 Carlo Bo, 'Com'era Sbarbaro' in *Atti del convegno nazionale di studi su Camillo Sbarbaro (Spotorno 6–7 Ottobre 1973)*, ed. A. Guerrini (Genoa-Spotorno, Resine-Centro Studi Camillo Sbarbaro, 1974), 10–11.
9 Angelo Barile, 'Testimonianza per Camillo Sbarbaro', *Il Letimbro*, 34 (1978): 3.
10 Sbarbaro, *OVP*, 475.
11 Lagorio, *Sbarbaro*, 163.
12 Ibid., 164.
13 Sbarbaro, *OVP*, 488–9.
14 Lagorio, *Sbarbaro*, 158–9.
15 *Trucioli (1914–1918)* (1920, 1948, 1963), *Fuochi fatui* (1956, 1958, 1962), *Scampoli* (1960), *Cartoline in franchigia* (1966), *La trama delle lucciole: lettere a Angelo Barile (1919–1937)* (1979) and *'Trucioli' dispersi* (1986).
16 Sbarbaro, *La trama delle lucciole*, letter no. 59, pp. 108–9.
17 Bo, 'Com'era Sbarbaro', 10–11 connected Sbarbaro's decision to become a teacher to the primary contradiction at the heart of his poetry.
18 Sbarbaro, *La trama delle lucciole*, letter no. 9, p. 33.
19 Ibid., letter no. 46, pp. 87–8.
20 Sbarbaro, *OVP*, 423.
21 Sbarbaro, *OVP*, 438–9.
22 Sbarbaro, *OVP*, 475.
23 Sbarbaro, *OVP*, 441–2.

24 Sbarbaro, *OVP*, 555–6.
25 Sbarbaro, *OVP*, 549.
26 Lagorio, *Sbarbaro*, 58–9.
27 Sbarbaro, *OVP*, 327–31.
28 Now in Sbarbaro, *Trucioli dispersi*, no. 201, 105–7.
29 Sbarbaro, *OVP*, 455–6.
30 In his seminal essay 'Les abeilles et les araignées', Marc Fumaroli assigned a specific importance to Montaigne's thought in the *querelle* between the Ancients and the Moderns. Cf. Marc Fumaroli, 'Les abeilles et les araignées' in Anne-Marie Lecoq (ed.), *La Querelle des Anciens et des Modernes: XVII–XVIII siècles* (Paris: Gallimard, 2001), 7–218 (10).
31 In ibid., 11.
32 Ibid., 11–12.
33 Ibid., 12.
34 Sbarbaro, *Trucioli dispersi*, no. 88, p. 60.
35 Friederich Nietzsche, *Daybreak: Thoughts on the Prejudices of Morality*, trans. R. J. Hollingdale, ed. Maudemarie Clark and Brian Letter (Cambridge: Cambridge University Press, 1997), thought no. 195, 115–16.
36 Sbarbaro, *OVP*, 456.
37 Zoboli, 'Sbarbaro e i tragici greci', 24, pinpointed the history of this interview. The piece firstly appeared with the title 'Intervista al poeta Camillo Sbarbaro' in *Primizie* (1958), edited by Cinzia Fiore. Sbarbaro subsequently edited the interview and decided to include it in *Scampoli* (1960). Eventually, Sbarbaro excluded the passage from the *ne varietur* edition *OVP*.
38 Now in Sbarbaro, *Trucioli dispersi*, no. 129, 88.
39 The volume hosts contributions by Lionello Venturi, Mario Labò (the father), Giulo Carlo Argan, Franco Calamandrei, Alberto Lattuada and Antonello Trombadori.
40 The book has been recently republished: *Un sabotatore: Giorgio Labò*, ed. Francesca Romana Stabile (Rome: Gangemi Editore, 2014).
41 Camillo Sbarbaro, *Ricordo di Giorgio Labò* (Milan: All'insegna del pesce d'oro, 1969). The piece, with a different title *Addio a Giorgio*, also features in *Camillo Sbarbaro: 'Trucioli dispersi'*, ed. G. Costa and V. Scheiwiller (Milan: Libri Scheiwiller, 1986), 121–7.
42 A brief biographical note ('Notizia') is offered in Sbarbaro's *Ricordo di Giorgio Labò*, 7.
43 Ibid., 9.
44 Ibid., 9.
45 Ibid., 9.
46 Ibid., 9–10.

47 Ibid., 10.
48 Ibid., 10.
49 Ibid., 10-11.
50 Ibid., 11.
51 Ibid.
52 Ibid.
53 Ibid.
54 Sbarbaro, *Trucioli dispersi*, no. 129, 88.
55 Sbarbaro, *Ricordo di Giorgio Labò*, 12.
56 Ibid., 12.
57 Ibid., 12-13.
58 Ibid., 3-14.
59 Ibid., 14.
60 Ibid., 15.
61 Giovanna Bemporad, 'Pasolini, amico e antagonista' in D. Ferrari and G. Scalia (eds), *Pasolini e Bologna* (Bologna: Edizioni Pendrangon, 1998), 101.
62 Enzo Siciliano, *Vita di Pasolini* (Milan: Rizzoli, 1979), 54 described the group as follows: 'Concluso il liceo, la cerchia di amicizi diventa più squisitamente letteraria. Compaiono Francesco Leonetti, Roberto Roversi, Fabio Mauri (più giovane d'anni, ma già dotato d'un intuito penetrante), sua sorella Silvana, Luciano Serra, Fabio Luca Cavazza, Mario Ricci, Sergio Telmon, Achille Ardigò, Giovanna Bemporad.' Nico Naldini, *Pasolini, una vita* (Turin: Einaudi, 1989), 40 also included Bemporad among the group of friends that met in 1942: 'Continua a frequentare Guf e Gil dove incontra altri amici, giovanissimi letterati, filosofi, pittori in erba: Fabio Mauri, Fabio Luca Cavazza, Achille Ardigò, Luigi Vecchi, Mario Ricci e la ragazza prodigio Giovanna Bemporad, che a quattordici anni ha già pubblicato la traduzione di alcuni canti dell'*Odissea*.' Stefano Casi, *I teatri di Pasolini* (Milan: Ubulibri, 2005), 27, also pinpointed Pasolini's interest in the cultural ferment of Bologna: 'La stagione 1939/1940, che corrisponde al suo ingresso all'università e all'inizio della sua sistematica attenzione alla realtà culturale che lo circonda ...'
63 On Bemporad's and Pasolini's first meeting we have a number of sources. Bemporad herself, in the aforementioned article 'Pasolini, amico e antagonista', 111 referred to this meeting as follows: 'Ed è appunto nella mia casa di Bologna, nel grande salotto – studio della casa dei miei genitori (lo ricordo ancora con commozione) che è avvenuto il mio primo incontro con Pier Paolo. (Aveva sentito parlare di me e veniva a chiedermi di partecipare con poesie e traduzioni al primo numero della rivista universitaria da lui diretta, "Il Setaccio". Siciliano, *Vita di Pasolini*, 61: 'Arte letteratura, musica, poesia, teatro, cinema, anche politica: tali gli argomenti messi a "setaccio". [...] "Il setaccio" pubblica traduzioni da Saffo, Goethe, Hölderlin

(traduttrice Giovanna Bemporad, che, per ragioni razziali, si firmava Giovanna Bembo), da Machado (grande passione pasoliniana), da Baudelaire.' Naldini, p. 47 also quotes Bemporad as one of the journal collaborators: 'Il direttore del "Setaccio" è Giovanni Falzone, celebratore in versi dell'"Era Fascista". Consulente il pittore Italo Cinti; [...] Collaboratori: Giovanna Bemporad (che nasconde il nome ebraico con lo pseudonimo Giovanna Bembo), Carlo Alberto Manzoni [...].'

64 Siciliano, *Vita di Pasolini*, 63. On Bemporad's eccentric personality see also Naldini, *Pasolini, una vita*, 47 who reports Fabio Mauri's words: 'Insieme, una sera febbrile, andammo a conoscere (fastidiosamente consci della comune precocità) la nostra Georges Sand: Giovanna Bemporad. Giovanna vestiva da uomo. Con i calzoni da avanguardista tirati alle ginocchia sotto un impermeabile privo di ogni colore ... Ci leggeva la *sua Odissea* ...'

65 Enzo Siciliano, *Pasolini: A Biography*, trans. John Shepley (London: Bloomsbury, 1987), 58.

66 Siciliano, *Vita di Pasolini*, 54.

67 Naldini, *Pasolini, una vita*, 54.

68 Naldini, *Pasolini, una vita*, 62. On this see also Barth David Schwart, *Pasolini Requiem* (New York: Pantheon Books, 1992), 239.

69 Siciliano, *Vita di Pasolini*, 84: 'I ragazzi versavano alla scuola una piccola tassa: utile a pagare l'affitto del locale dove avvenivano le lezioni. Sopravvennero complicazioni burocratiche. Il provveditorato agli studi di Udine, sulla base di notizie raccolte, diffidò Pasolini dal proseguire nella sua attività. Tra il gennaio e il febbraio 1944, i ragazzi disertarono: la Bemporad appunto partì.'

70 Naldini, *Pasolini, una vita*, 54.

71 Siciliano, *Vita di Pasolini*, 79–80.

72 Ibid., 75.

73 Ibid., 82–3.

74 Andrea Zanzotto, 'Pedagogia' in *Aure e disincanti* (Milan: Mondadori, 1994), 141–52. Jennifer Stone, 'Pasolini, Zanzotto, and the Question of Pedagogy' in Patrick Rumble and Bart Testa (eds), *Pier Paolo Pasolini: Contemporary Perspectives* (Toronto: University of Toronto Press, 1994), 40–53 discussed the intersection between Pasolini's pedagogy and Zanzotto's interest in language and pedagogy. On Pasolini's pedagogy see also Enzo Golino, *Pasolini: Il sogno di una cosa. Pedagogia, Eros, Letteratura* (Milan: BUR, 1985). Golino traced the presence of pedagogy in Pasolini's whole literary corpus (cinema production excluded) as a constant and evolving issue informing the poet's creativity. Specifically, Golino proposed to read it as a natural urge ('un maestro naturale') informed by a strong ethical stance. According to Golino's interpretation, Pasolini elevated pedagogy to the level of a civil duty for an entire generation.

75 Zanzotto, *Pedagogia*, 144.

76 Ibid., 142.
77 Tontini, Paolo, '"Non si uccide la poesia!" Frammenti ritrovati di Giovanna Bemporad', *L'arengario: Studio bibliografico*, 2012. http://www.arengario.it/autografi/non-si-uccide-la-poesia-frammenti-ritrovati-di-giovanna-bemporad.
78 On Bemporad's eccentric appearance see Siciliano, *Vita di Pasolini*, 63.
79 Ibid., 4.
80 Ibid., 79.
81 The importance attributed by Pasolini to dramatic skills in teaching clearly emerges from his *Diario di un insegnante* now in Pier Paolo Pasolini, *Romanzi e racconti*, 2 vols, I, 1946–61, ed. Walter Siti and Silvia De Laude (Milan: Mondadori, 1998), 1334–7.
82 Elio Pagliarani, 'Quando lei mi leggeva Montale', *Paese Sera*, 4th March 1981 now in Giovanna Bemporad, *Esercizi vecchi e nuovi* (Milan: Edizioni Archivio Dedalus, 2010), 207–8.
83 Plato, *Phaedrus*, 245a in D. A. Russell and M. Winterbottom eds, *Ancient Literary Criticism: The Principal Texts in New Translations* (Oxford: OUP, 1972), 75. On poetic madness see E. R. Dodds, 'The Blessing of Madness' in *The Greeks and the Irrational* (Berkeley, LA, London: University of California Press, 1973), 64–101.
84 An example to see how Bemporad changed her own voice when performing her translations can be found at: https://www.youtube.com/watch?v=nlQg2oFQPIM (accessed on 10 January 2023).
85 Siciliano, *Vita di Pasolini*, 81–3. In the course of my recent archival research, I discovered that Bemporad translated Greek tragedies during that period. These translations helped shape her poetic image of death and offered the possibility of exploring the archetype. Such an influence on Bemporad's poetic imaginery, hitherto unknown as the translations have not yet been published, is discussed in Chapter 3 of this thesis. On Bemporad's musical skills see also Francesca Cadel, *La lingua dei desideri: il dialetto secondo Pier Paolo Pasolini* (Lecce: Manni, 2002), 254, 261 and 264.
86 Enzo Siciliano, *Pasolini: A biography*, 77–8.

Conclusion

1 Giovanna Bemporad, 'La traduzione dell'Odissea' in *La traduzione del testo poetico*, ed. Buffoni (Milan: Marcos y Marcos, 1989), 239–41.

Bibliography

Abbreviations

BUR: Biblioteca Universale Rizzoli
CEI: Conferenza Episcopale Italiana
CUP: Cambridge University Press
ERI: Edizioni RAI Radiotelevisione Italiana
OUP: Oxford University Press
TAPhA: Transactions and Proceedings of the American Philological
    Association

Audiovisual Material

Omero, *Odissea*, adaptation by Giovanna Bemporad, preface by Giovanni Battista Pighi, screenplay and dialogues by Giampiero Bona, Vittorio Bonicelli, Fabio Carpi, Luciano Codignola, Mario Prosperi, Renzo Rosso for RAI TV co-production, Ortf, Bavaria and Dino De Laurentiis (Turin: ERI, 1968)
Pezzella, Vincenzo, *Giovanna Bemporad: A una forma sorella. Intervista video-ritratto* (Milan: Archivo Dedalus Edizioni, 2011)
Zanzotto, Andrea, *Dalla trascrizione della trasmissione radiofonica 'Giovanna Bemporad e Alda Merini: Conversazione con Andrea Zanzotto' Radio Lugana, 1980*, now in Giovanna Bemporad, *Esercizi vecchi e nuovi* (Milan: Archivio Dedalus, 2010), 205–6

Primary Sources

Bembo, Pietro, 'Prose della volgar lingua' in Carlo Dionisotti (ed.), *Pietro Bembo: Prose e rime* (Turin: Unione Tipografica-Editrice, 1966)
Bemporad, Giovanna, *Esercizi: Poesie e traduzioni* (Venice: Urbani e Pettanello, 1948)
Bemporad, Giovanna, *Poesie e traduzioni* (Fermo: Tipografia La Rapida, 1963)

Bemporad, Giovanna, *Esercizi: Poesie e traduzioni* (Milan: Garzanti, 1980)

Bemporad, Giovanna, 'La traduzione dell'Odissea' in Franco Buffoni (ed.), *La traduzione del testo poetico* (Milan: Marcos y Marcos, 1989), 240–1

Bemporad, Giovanna, 'Pasolini, amico e antagonista' in Davide Ferrari and Gianni Scalia (eds), *Pasolini e Bologna* (Bologna: Edizioni Pendragon, 1998), 101–6

Bemporad, Giovanna, 'Come tradurre Omero' in *Resine: Quaderni Liguri di Cultura* (Genova: Marco Sabatelli Editore, 2005), 13–16

Bemporad, Giovanna, *Esercizi vecchi e nuovi*, ed. Andrea Cirolla (Milan: Edizioni Archivio Dedalus, 2010)

Bemporad, Giovanna, *Esercizi vecchi e nuovi*, ed. Valentina Russi (Bologna: Luca Sossella editore, 2011)

Bignone, Ettore, *Le tragedie di Sofocle*, 3 vols (Florence: Sansoni, 1937–8)

Brioschi, Franco and Landi Patrizia (eds), *Giacomo Leopardi: Epistolario*, 2 vols (Turin: Bollati Boringhieri)

Campbell, Lewis, *Sophocles: The Plays and Fragments*, vol. II (Oxford: Clarendon Press, 1881)

Carson, Anne, 'Screaming in Translation' in *Sophocles: Electra*, trans. Anne Carson (Oxford: OUP, 2001), 41–8

Costa, Giampiero and Scheiwiller, Vanni (eds), *Camillo Sbarbaro 'Trucioli' dispersi* (Milan: Libri Scheiwiller, 1986)

Croce, Benedetto, *La Poesia* (Bari: Laterza, 1953)

Croce, Benedetto, *Estetica come scienza dell'espressione e linguistica generale: Teoria e storia*, ed. G. Galasso (Milan: Adelphi, 1990)

D'Annunzio, Gabriele, 'Discorso agli Ateniesi', *Il Marzocco*, 28 May 1989, now in Gabriele D'Annunzio, *Scritti giornalistici*, ed. Annamaria Andreoli, Federico Roncoroni and Giorgio Zanetti, 2 vols, 2 (Milan: Mondadori, 2003), 460–3

D'Annunzio, Gabriele, 'La rinascenza della tragedia', *La Tribuna*, 2 August 1987, now in Gabriele D'Annunzio, *Scritti giornalistici*, ed. Annamaria Andreoli, Federico Roncoroni and Giorgio Zanetti, 2 vols, 2 (Milan: Mondadori, 2003), 262–5

D'Annunzio, Gabriele, *Lettere ai Treves*, ed. Gianni Oliva, collaborazione di Katia Berardi e Barbara di Serio (Milan: Garzanti, 1999)

D'Annunzio, Gabriele, 'Nella vita e nell'arte: Il caso Wagner I, II, III', *La Tribuna*, 23 July 1893, 3 August 1893, 9 August 1893, now in Gabrile D'Annunzio, *Scritti giornalistici*, ed. Annamaria Andreoli, Federico Roncoroni and Giorgio Zanetti, 2 vols, 2 (Milan: Mondadori, 2003), 233–61

Erfurdt, Carl Gottlob and Hermann, Johann Gottfried, *Sophoclis tragoediae septem ac deperditarum fragmenta emendavit, varietatem lectionis, scholia notasque tum aliorum tum suas adjecit Carolus Gottlob Augustus Erfurdt. Accedit lexicon Sophocleum (Cum adnotationibus G. Hermanni)* (Lipsia: 1822–5)

Eschilo, *Il Prometeo legato*, trans. Emanuele Rapisarda (Turin: Società Editrice Internazionale, 1936)

Eschilo, *Le Coefore*, trans. Manara Valgimigli (Bari: Laterza, 1948)

Eschilo, *La Orestea: Agamennone, Coefore, Eumenidi*, trans. Manara Valgimigli (Florence: Sansoni, 1948)

Eschilo, *Le Coefore*, trans. Salvatore Quasimodo (Milan: Bompiani, 1949)

Eschilo, *Prometeo incatenato*, ed. and trans. Camillo Sbarbaro (Milan: Bompiani, 1949)

Eschyle, *Les Suppliantes – Les Perses – Les septe contre Thèbes – Prométhée enchainé*, ed. and trans. Paul Mazon (Paris: Les Belles Lettres, 1931)

Euripide, *Le Cyclope – Alceste – Medée – Les Héraclides*, ed. and trans. Louis Méridier (Paris: Les Belles Lettres, Paris, 1926)

Euripide, *Alcesti: Il Ciclope di Euripide*, trans. Camillo Sbarbaro (Milan: Bompiani, 1952)

Euripide, *Ecuba*, trans. Salvatore Quasimodo (Urbino: Argalìa, 1962)

Euripide, *Eracle*, trans. Salvatore Quasimodo (Urbino: Argalìa, 1966)

Farris, Giovanni (ed.), *Camillo Sbarbaro: Il mio 'primo vagito'* (Savona: Sabatelli, 1982)

Huysmans, Joris-Karl, *Controcorrente*, trans. Camillo Sbarbaro (Milan: Rusconi, 1972)

Lagorio, Gina and Scheiwiller, Vanni (eds), *Camillo Sbarbaro: L'opera in versi e in prosa* (Milan: Garzanti, 1985)

Nietzsche, Friederich, *The Birth of Tragedy and The Case of Wagner*, trans. Walter Kaufman (New York: Vintage, 1976)

Nietzsche, Friederich, *Daybreak: Thoughts on the Prejudices of Morality*, trans. R. J. Hollingdale, ed. Maudemarie Clark and Brian Letter (Cambridge: CUP, 1997)

Omero, *Odissea*, versione di Giovanna Bemporad, preface by Umberto Abini (Turin: ERI, 1970)

Omero, *Odissea: Canti e Frammenti*, poetical version by Giovanna Bemporad, introduction by Maurizio Perugi (Florence: Le lettere, 1992)

Pasolini, Pier Paolo, 'Dal diario di un insegnante', now in Pier Paolo Pasolini, *Romanzi e racconti*, 2 vols, I, 1946–61, ed. Walter Siti and Silvia De Laude (Milan: Mondadori, 1998), 1334–7

Pasolini, Pier Paolo, 'Poesia della Bemporad' in *Saggi sulla letteratura e sull'arte*, ed. Walter Siti and Silvia De Laude (Milan: Mondadori, 1999), 294–7

Pasolini, Pier Paolo, *Teatro*, ed. Walter Siti and Silvia De Laude (Milan: Mondadori, 2001)

Plato, *Phaedrus*, 245a in *Ancient Literary Criticism: The Principal Texts in New Translations*, ed. D. A. Russell and M. Winterbottom (Oxford: OUP, 1972), 75

Quasimodo, Salvatore, *Tragici greci tradotti da Salvatore Quasimodo: Le coefore di Eschilo, Elettra di Sofocle, Edipo re di Sofocle* (Milan: Mondadori, 1963)

Sanguineti, Edoardo, *Teatro antico: Traduzioni e ricordi*, ed. Federico Condello and Claudio Longhi (Milan: BUR, 2006)

Sbarbaro, Camillo, *Scampoli* (Florence: Vallecchi, 1960)

Sbarbaro, Camillo, *Ricordo di Giorgio Labò* (Milan: All'insegna del pesce d'oro, 1969)

Sbarbaro, Camillo, *La trama delle lucciole: Lettere ad Angelo Barile (1919–1957)*, ed. Domenico Astengo and Franco Contorbia (Genoa: San Marco dei Giustiniani, 1979)

Sbarbaro, Camillo, *L'opera in versi e in prosa*, ed. Gina Lagorio and Vanni Scheiwiller (Milan: Garzanti, 1985)

Sbarbaro, Camillo, *'Trucioli' dispersi*, ed. Giampiero Costa and Vanni Scheiwiller (Milan: Libri Scheiwiller, 1986)

Scheiwiller, Vanni (ed.), *Camillo Sbarbaro: Poesia e prosa* (Milan: Mondadori, 1979)

Sofocle, *L'Elettra*, trans. Ulisse Agatodemone (Naples: L. Chiurazzi, 1909)

Sofocle, *L'Elettra*, trans. Luigi Alessandro Michelangeli (Bologna: Zanichelli, 1917)

Sofocle, *Elettra*, trans. Giovanni La Magna (Ragusa: Stab. tib. popolare, 1923)

Sofocle, *Le tragedie*, trans. Ettore Romagnoli, 3 vols (Bologna: Zanichelli, 1926)

Sofocle, *Elettra*, trans. Hilda Montesi and Nicola Festa (Rome: Ausonia, 1927)

Sofocle, *Elettra*, trans. Enrico Turolla (Milan: Carlo Signorelli, 1937)

Sofocle, *Antigone*, trans. Camillo Sbarbaro (Milan: Bompiani, 1943)

Sofocle, *Edipo re*, trans. Salvatore Quasimodo (Milan: Bompiani, 1946)

Sofocle, *Antigone*, trans. Placido Cesareo (Turin: Società Editrice Internazionale, 1947)

Sofocle, *Elettra*, trans. Salvatore Quasimodo (Milan: Mondadori, 1954)

Sophocles, *Ajax-Antigone-Oedipe roi-Électre*, ed. and trans. Paul Masqueray (Paris: Les Belles Lettres, 1929)

Sophocles, *Plays and Fragments: Electra*, ed. Richard Claverhouse Jebb, Patricia Elizabeth Easterling and Ruby Blondell (Harvard: Harvard University Press, 1894)

Sophocles, *Electra*, ed. J. H. Kells (Cambridge: CUP, 1973)

Sophocles, *Antigone*, ed. Mark Griffith (Cambridge: CUP, 1999)

Sophocles, *Plays: Antigone*, ed. R. C. Jebb, P. E. Easterling and R. Blondell (London: Bristol Classical Press, 2004)

Sophoclis, *Fabulae*, ed. Alfred Chilton Pearson (Oxford: E Typographeo Clarendoniano, 1923)

Ungaretti, Giuseppe, 'Difesa dell'endecasillabo' in *Vita di un uomo: Saggi e interventi*, ed. Mario Diacono and Luciano Rebay (Milan: Mondadori, 1974), 154–69

Virgilio, *Dall'Eneide*, trans. Giovanna Bemporad, introduction by Luca Canali (Rome: Forcom, 2000)

Virgilio, *Bucoliche*, trans. Giovanna Bemporad, introduction by Caterina Paoli (Urbino: QuattroVenti, 2023)

Von Hofmannsthal, Hugo, *Elettra*, trans. Giovanna Bemporad (Milan: Garzanti, 1981)

Woolf, Virginia, 'On Not Knowing Greek' in *The Common Reader* (London: Hogarth Press, 1925), 3–18

Secondary Sources

Ackerman, Robert, *J.G. Frazer: His Life and Work* (Cambridge: CUP, 1990)

Ackerman, Robert, *The Myth and Ritual School: J. G. Frazer and the Cambridge Ritualists* (New York: Routledge, 2002)

Angeleri, Carla and Costa, Giampiero (eds), *Bibliografia degli scritti di Camillo Sbarbaro* (Milan: All'insegna del pesce d'oro, 1986)

Avanzolini, Maurizio, 'L'eterno nemico: Dalla censura libraria all'applicazione delle leggi razziali: il Ventennio fascista nella Biblioteca dell'Archiginnasio', *L'Archiginnasio*, Bollettino della Biblioteca Comunale di Bologna, CXIV (2019), 487–618

Avezzù, Guido, *Sofocle, Euripide, Hofmannsthal, Yourcenar. Elettra. Variazioni sul mito* (Venice: Marsilio, 2002)

Avezzù, Guido, 'Text and transmission' in A. Markantonatos (ed.), *Brill's Companion to Sophocles* (Leiden: Brill, 2012), 39–58

Baldazzi, Anna, *Bibliografia della critica dannunziana nei periodici italiani dal 1880 al 1938* (Rome: Cooperativa scrittori, 1977)

Bàrberi Squarotti, Giorgio, *Camillo Sbarbaro* (Milan: Mursia, 1972)

Bàrberi Squarotti, Giorgio, *Le sorti del 'tragico': Il Novecento italiano: romanzo e teatro* (Ravenna: Longo Editore, 1978)

Barile, Angelo, *Al paese dei vasai: Santi, artisti, scrittori, paesi di Liguria* (Savona: Sabatelli, 1970), 117–21

Barile, Angelo, 'Testimonianza per Camillo Sbarbaro', *Il Letimbro*, 34 (1978): 3

Beard, Mary, *The Invention of Jane Harrison* (Cambridge, MA: Harvard University Press, 2002)

Benjamin, Walter, 'The Task of the Translator' in *Illuminations* (London: Pimlico, 1999), 70–82

Benucci Serva, Anna (ed.), *Cara Giovanna: Lettere di Camillo Sbarbaro a Giovanna Bemporad (1952-1964)* (Milan: Edizioni Archivio del '900, 2004)

Berman, Antoine, *L' épreuve de l'étranger* (Paris: Gallimard, 1984)

Berman, Antoine, *La traduction et la lettre ou l' auberge du lointain* (Paris: Éditions du Seuil, 1999)

Bernal, Martin, *Black Athena: The Afroasiatic Roots of Classical Civilisation*, vol. I (London: Free Association Books, 1987), 285–8

Bertelli, Lucio, 'J.E. Harrison e "Ritualisti di Cambridge": la riscoperta del "primitivo", *Ítaca: Quaderns Catalans de Cultura Clàssica*, 21 (2005): 111–38

Bevilacqua, Mirko, Divano, Diego and Carrea, Daniela (eds), *Camillo Sbarbaro: Lettere a Enrico Falqui. 1928–1967* (Genoa: Fondazione Giorgio e Lilli Devoto – San Marco dei Giustiniani, 2012)

Bianca, Concetta (ed.), *Remigio Sabbadini: Il metodo degli umanisti* (Rome: Edizioni di Storia e Letteratura, 2018)

Billings, Joshua, *Genealogy of the Tragic: Greek Tragedy and German Philosophy*, (Princeton, NJ: Princeton University Press, 2014)

Bisulca, Paola, 'Il traduttore-attore: Edoardo Sanguineti dietro la maschera degli antichi', Istituto Nazionale del Dramma Antico, http://www.indafondazione.org/it/il-traduttore-attore-edoardo-sanguineti-dietro-la-maschera-degli-antichi/

Bo, Carlo, 'Com'era Sbarbaro' in A. Guerrini (ed.), *Atti del convegno nazionale di studi su Camillo Sbarbaro: Spotorno 6–7 Ottobre 1973* (Genoa: Resine: Quaderni Liguri di cultura, 1974), 7–20

Bo, Carlo, *Il debito con Sbarbaro* in Giorgio Devoto (ed.), *Otto studi* (Genoa: San Marco dei Giustiniani, 2000), 105–18

Boiardi, Franco, 'La riforma della scuola di Gabrio Casati' in *Il parlamento italiano*, vol. 1 (Milan: Nuova CEI Informatica, 1988), 317–18

Bonnefoy, Yves, 'Le paradoxe du traducteur' in *L'autre langue à portée de voix* (Paris: Éditions du Seuil, 2013)

Bonnefoy, Yves, 'Signification et poésie' in *L'autre langue à portée de voix* (Paris: Éditions du Seuil, 2013)

Bonnefoy, Yves, *L'hésitation d'Hamlet et la décision de Shakespeare* (Paris: Seuil, 2015)

Borghetti, Vincenzo and Pecci, Riccardo, *Il bacio della sfinge: D'Annunzio, Pizzetti e Fedra* (Turin: E.D.T. Istituto Nazionale Tostiano, 1998)

Bornmann, Fritz, 'La traduzione dell'Odissea di Vanna Bemporad', *L'Approdo letterario*, XVII, no. 53 (1971)

Braccesi, Lorenzo (ed.), *Gli eroi: antologia dell'epica per la scuola media*, with updated translations from classical poems by Giovanna Bemporad (Bologna: Edizioni scolastiche Patron, 1965)

Bravo, Benedetto, *Giorgio Pasquali e l'eredità del XIX secolo* in M. Bollack and H. Wismann (eds), *Philologie und Hermeneutik im 19. Jahrhundert*, II (Göttingen: Vandenhoeck and Ruprecht, 1983), 333–58

Cadel, Francesca, *La lingua dei desideri: il dialetto secondo Pier Paolo Pasolini* (Lecce: Manni, 2002)

Calder III, William M., 'Werner Jager and Richard Harder: an Erklärung', *Quaderni di storia*, 17 (1983): 99–121

Calder III, William M., 'Werner Jager' in Ward W. Briggs and William M. Calder III (eds), *Classical Scholarship: A Biographical Encyclopedia* (New York: Garland Publishing, 1990), 211–26

Calder III, William M., *The Cambridge Ritualists Reconsidered: Proceedings of the First Old father Conference, Held on the Campus of the University of Illinois at Urbana-Champaign April 27–30 1989, Illinois Classical Studies*, Supplement 2 (Atlanta: Scholars Press, 1991)

Calder III, William M. (ed.), 'Werner Jager Reconsidered', *Illinois Classical Studies*, Supplement 3 (Atlanta: Scholars Press, 1992)

Camilletti, Fabio, *Classicism and Romanticism in Italian Literature: Leopardi's Discourse on Romantic Poetry* (London: Routledge, 2016)

Canfora, Luciano, *Ideologie del classicismo* (Turin: Einaudi, 1980)

Cardinali, Giuliana, 'Ricordo di Gennaro Perrotta' in Bruno Gentili and Agostino Masaracchia (eds), *Giornate di studio su Gennaro Perrotta* (Pisa: Istituti Editoriali e Poligrafici Internazionali, 1996), 117–20

Caruso, Carlo, 'Metri barbari e verso libero' in Carlo Caruso and Juan Rigoli, *Poétiques barbares: Poetiche barbare* (Ravenna: Longo, 1998), 209–30

Casi, Stefano, *I teatri di Pasolini* (Milan: Ubulibri, 2015)

Cavallini, Eleonora (ed.), *Scrittori che traducono scrittori: traduzioni 'd'autore' da classici latini e greci nella letteratura italiana del Novecento* (Alessandria: Edizioni dell'Orso, 2017)

Cianciani, Domenico and Vito, M. Antonietta (eds), *Marguerite Yourcenar – Simon Weil. Elettre. Letture di un mito greco* (Milan: Edizioni Medusa, 2004)

Classen, Carl Joachim, 'Giorgio Pasquali, un italiano come mediatore della scienza tedesca,' *Quaderni di Storia*, 13 no. 26 (1987): 5–23

Condello, Federico, 'Su Pasolini traduttore classico: Sparsi rilievi tra fatti e leggenda', *Semicerchio*, XVLII, no. 2 (2012): 8–17

Condello, Federico and Rodighiero, Andrea (eds), *'Un compito infinito': Testi classici e traduzioni d'autore nel Novecento italiano* (Bologna: Bononia University Press, 2015)

Conte Falcone, Luigi, *Metrica classica e metrica barbara: L'esametro latino e il verso sillabico italiano. Due saggi critici* (Wien: 1855)

Contini, Gianfranco, *Letteratura dell'italia unita: 1861–1968* (Florence: Sansoni, 1968)

Costa, Giampiero, 'Camillo Sbarbaro e Vanni Scheiwiller: lettere all'editore' in Giorgio Devoto and Paolo Zoboli (eds), *Camillo Sbarbaro. Atti della giornata di studio 11 Aprile 2003* (Genoa: Edizioni San Marco dei Giustiniani, 2003), 111–39

Cowan, Marianne, *An Anthology of the Writings of Wilhelm von Humboldt: Humanist without Portfolio* (Detroit: Wayne State University Press, 1963)

Di Battista, Flavia, 'Gabriella Bemporad (1904–1999) e Giovanna Bemporad (1923–2013)' in Anna Baldini and Giulia Marcucci (eds), *La donna invisibile: Traduttrici nell'Italia del primo Novecento* (Macerata: Quodlibet Studio, 2023), 197–208

Di Martino, Giovanna, 'L'*Agamennone* di Eschilo: Italianitàà e Sicilianità alla vigilia della Grande Guerra', *FuturoClassico*, 5 (2019), 174–208

Di Martino, Giovanna, Ioannidou, Eleftheria and Troiani, Sara (eds), 'A Hellenic Modernism: Greek Theatre and Italian Fascism', *Classical Receptions Journal* (OUP), 16, no. 1 (2024)

D'Ina, Gabriella and Zaccaria, Giuseppe (eds), *Caro Bompiani: Lettere con l'editore* (Milan: Bompiani, 2007)

D'Intino, Franco, *Giacomo Leopardi: Poeti greci e latini* (Rome: Salerno Editrice, 1999), VII–LXIII

Dawe, Roger David, *Studies on the Text of Sophocles* (Leiden: Brill, 1973–8)

De Robertis, Giuseppe, 'Fuochi fatui', *Gazzetta di Parma*, 27 September 1956, now in *Altro Novecento* (Florence: Le Monnier, 1962), 197–207

De Sanctis, Francesco, *Leopardi*, ed. Carlo Muscetta and Antonia Perna (Turin: Einaudi, 1983)

Dodds, Eric Robertson, 'Plato, the Irrational Soul, and the Inherited Conglomerate' in *The Greeks and The Irrational* (Los Angeles: University of California Press, 1951), 207–35

Dodds, Eric Robertson, 'The Blessing of Madness' in *The Greeks and the Irrational* (Berkeley, CA: University of California Press, 1973), 64–101

Elsner, Jas, 'Paideia: Ancient Concept and Modern Reception', *International Journal of Classical Tradition*, 20 (2013): 136–52

Ergun, Emek, Kripper, Denise, Meï, Siobhan, Russel, Sandra Joy, Rutkowski, Sarah, Shread, Carolyne and Solberg, Ida Hove, 'Women (Re)Writing Authority: A Roundtable Discussion on Feminist Translation' in Louise Von Flotow and Hala Kamal (eds), *The Routledge Handbook of Translation, Feminism and Gender* (London: Routledge, 2020), 5–15

Falqui, Enrico, 'L'Odissea dal video al testo e la galleria dei traduttori di Omero', *Il Dramma*, 11–12 (novemebre–dicembre, 1970)

Ferrari, F., *Ricerche sul testo di Sofocle* (Pisa: Scuola Normale Superiore, 1983)

Fausto, Giordano, 'Introduction' in Giorgio Pasquali, *Filologia e storia* (Florence: Le Monnier, 1998), III–XXI

Ferreri, Davide (ed.), *Camillo Sbarbaro, Lettere a Lucia: 1931–1967* (Genova: Fondazione Giorgio e Lilli Devoto – San Marco dei Giustiniani, 2007)

Figurelli, Fernando, *La formazione del Leopardi sino al 1819: Lezioni dell'anno accademico 1970–71* (Naples: De Simone, 1971)

Fornaro, Sotera, 'Christian Gottlob Heyne dans l'historie des études classiques', *Revue germanique internationale*, 14 (2011): 15–26

Fowler, Robert, 'Gilbert Murray' in Ward W. Briggs and William M. Calder III (eds), *Classical Scholarship: A Biographical Encyclopaedia* (New York: Garland Publishing, 1990), 321–4

Franco, Carlo, 'Werner Jager in Italia: il contributo di Piero Treves', *Quaderni di storia*, XX, no. 39 (1994): 173–94

Fumaroli, Marc, 'Les abeilles et les araignées' in Anne-Marie Lecoq (ed.), *La Querelle des Anciens et des Modernes: XVII–XVIII siècles* (Paris: Gallimard, 2001), 7–218

Fusillo, Massimo, *La Grecia secondo Pasolini: Mito e cinema* (Florence: La Nuova Italia, 1996), 243–6

Gaborik, Patricia, *Mussolini's Theatre: Fascist Experiments in Art and Politics* (Cambridge: CUP, 2021)

Gardini, Nicola, *Com'è fatta una poesia* (Milan: Sironi, 2007)

Gargiulo, Alfredo, 'Camillo Sbarbaro' in *Letteratura italiana del Novecento* (Florence: LeMonnier, 1943), 171–6

Gentile, Emilio, 'The Theatre of Politics in Fascist Italy' in Günter Berghaus (ed.), *Fascism and Theatre: Comparative Studies on the Aesthetics and Politics of Performance in Europe, 1925–1945* (Oxford: Berghann Books, 1996), 72–93

Gentile, Giovanni, 'Il diritto e il torto delle traduzioni' in *Frammenti di estetica e letteratura* (Lanciano: Carabba, 1920)

Gentili, Bruno and Lomiento, Liana, *Metrica e ritmica: Storia delle forme poetiche della Grecia antica* (Milan: Mondadori Università, 2003)

Gentili, Carlo and Garelli, Gianluca, *Il tragico* (Bologna: Il Mulino, 2010)

Gigante, Marcello, 'Gennaro Perrotta e Benedetto Croce' in Bruno Gentili and Agostino Masaracchia (eds), *Giornate di studio su Gennaro Perrotta* (Pisa: Istituti Editoriali e Poligrafici Internazionali, 1996), 129–52

Giusti, Simone, 'Tradurre per comprendere: Gobetti tra Croce e Gentile' in Simone Giusti, *La congiura stabilita: Dialoghi e comparazioni tra Ottocento e Novecento* (Milan: Franco Angeli, 2005), 39–54

Golino, Enzo, *Pasolini: Il sogno di una cosa. Pedagogia Eros Letteratura* (Milan: Bompiani, 2014), p. 25

Griffin, Roger, 'Fascism's Modernist Revolution: A New Paradigm for the Study of Right-Wing Dictatorships', *Fascism*, 5, no. 2 (2016), 105–29

Guarnieri Corazzol, Adriana, *Musica e letteratura in Italia tra Ottocento e Novecento* (Milan: Sansoni, 2000), 131–66: 163

Harloe, Katherine, *Winckelmann and the Invention of Antiquity: History and Aesthetics in the Age of Altertumswissenschaft* (Oxford: OUP, 2013)

Hyang, Lee and Yun Seong-Woo, Yun, 'Antoine Berman's Philosophical Reflections on Language and Translation: The Possibility of Translating without Platonism', *Filozofia*, 66, no. 4 (2011): 336–46

Ioannidou, Eleftheria, Di Martino, Giovanna, and Troiani, Sara (eds), '(Re)Living Greece and Rome: Performances of Classical Antiquity under Fascism', *Fascism: Journal of Comparative Fascist Studies*, 12, no. 2 (2023)

Jervolino, Domenico, 'Croce, Gentile e Gramsci sulla traduzione' in Giuseppe Cacciatore, Girolamo Cotroneo and Renata Viti Cavaliere (eds), *Croce filosofo: Atti del convegno internazionale di studi in occasione del 50 anniversario della morte*, 2 vols, II (Soveria Mannelli: Rubbettino, 2003), 431–41

Lagorio, Gina, 'Il Ciclope', *Atene e Roma*, n.s. V, 3, (1960): 181–4, now in Gina Lagorio (ed.), *Sbarbaro controcorrente* (Parma: Guanda, 1973), 255–6

Lagorio, Gina, *Sbarbaro controcorrente* (Parma: Guanda, 1973)

Lagorio, Gina, 'L'insegnamento' in *Sbarbaro: Un modo spoglio di esistere* (Milan: Garzanti, 1981), 160

Lagorio, Gina, *Sbarbaro: Un modo spoglio di esistere* (Milan: Garzanti, 1981)

Luperini, Romano, *Il novecento: apparati ideologici, ceto intellettuale, sistemi formali nella letteratura contemporanea* (Turin: Loescher, 1981), 223–44

Macrí, Oreste, 'La traduzione poetica negli anni trenta (e seguenti)' in Franco Buffoni (ed.), *La traduzione del testo poetico* (Milan: Marcos y Marcos, 2004), 243–56

Magi, Paola and Vincenzo, Pezzella (eds), *Carlo Izzo: Lettere a Giovanna Bemporad 1940-1943* (Milan: Archivio Dedalus Edizioni, 2013)

Malabou, Caroline, *Plasticity at the Dusk of Writing: Dialectic, Destruction, Deconstruction*, trans. Carolyn Shread (New York: Columbia University Press, 2009)

Mancini, Massimiliano, *Saggi sulla poesia barbara e altri studi di metrica italiana* (Rome: Manziana Vecchiarelli, 2000)

Masaracchia, Agostino, 'Gli scritti sulla tragedia greca' in Bruno Gentili and Agostino Masaracchia (eds), *Giornate di studio su Gennaro Perrotta* (Pisa: Istituti Editoriali e Poligrafici Internazionali, 1996), 75–92

Mattioli, Emilio, 'Storia della traduzione e poetiche del tradurre (dall'umanesimo al romanticismo)', in Rosita Copioli (ed.), *Tradurre poesia* (Brescia: Paideia, 1983)

Méautis, George, *Sophocle: Essai sur le héros tragique* (Paris: Edition Albin Michel, 1957), 234, 244

Mengaldo, Pier Vincenzo, 'Camillo Sbarbaro' in *Poeti italiani del Novecento* (Milan: Mondadori, 1978), 317–36

Mesturini, Anna Maria, 'Sbarbaro e il Ciclope di Euripide', *Resine* [IV] (1975): 47–54

Mesturini, Anna Maria, 'Antigone secondo Sbarbaro', *Resine* [V] (1976): 18, 3–26

Naldini, Nico, *Pasolini, una vita* (Turin: Einaudi, 1989)

Pagliarani, Elio, 'Quando lei mi leggeva Montale', *Paese Sera*, 4 March 1981, now in Giovanna Bemporad, *Esercizi vecchi e nuovi* (Milan: Edizioni Archivio Dedalus, 2010), 207–8

Pagnanelli, Remo, 'Giovanna Bemporad: poesia e traduzione', *Otto–Novecento*, XII (1988): 213–18

Pasquali, Giorgio, 'Arti e studi in Italia nell'ultimo venticinquennio: Gli studi di greco', *Leonardo*, I (1925): 12, 261–5, now in Fritz Bornmann, Giovanni Pascucci and Sebastiano Timpanaro (eds), *Scritti filologici, II, Letteratura latina Cultura Contemporanea Recensioni*, introduzione di Antonio La Penna (Florence: Olski, 1986), 736–51

Pasquali, Giorgio, *Università e scuola* (Florence: Sansoni, 1950)

Pasquali, Giorgio, *Filologia e Storia* (Florence: Le Monnier, 1998)

Pasquali, Giorgio, *Storia dello spirito tedesco nelle memorie di un contemporaneo* (Milan: Adelphi, 2013)

Paoli, Caterina, 'La voce poetica di Giovanna Bemporad', *Istmi: Tracce di vita letteraria*, 31-2 (2013): 257–73

Paoli, Caterina, 'Giovanna Bemporad: Il mito della poesia', *Poesia: Mensile internazionale di cultura poetica*, 290 (2014): 55–62

Paoli, Caterina, 'Da quale parte il primo fuoco accenda: L'*Orestea* di Eschilo nella traduzione di Giovanni Giudici', *Istmi: Tracce di vita letteraria*, 35 (2015): 463–94

Paoli, Caterina, 'La resa felice degli Esercizi: Giovanna Bemporad e i classici', *Quaderni dell'associazione culturale 'La Luna'*, 4 (2017): 1–26

Paoli, Caterina, 'Translating Virgil at Age Sixteen: Giovanna Bemporad's *Bucolics*' in Helena Sanson (ed.), *Women and Translation in the Italian Tradition* (Paris: Classiques Garnier, 2022), 291–314

Pasolini, Pier Paolo, 'Odissea', *Nuovi Argomenti*, n.s. 22 (1971)

Pasolini, Pier Paolo, 'Dal diario di un insegnante', in Pier Paolo Pasolini, *Romanzi e racconti*, 2 vols, I, 1946–61, ed. Walter Siti and Silvia De Laude (Milan: Mondadori, 1998), 1334–7

Pasolini, Pier Paolo, 'Poesia della Bemporad' in *Saggi sulla letteratura e sull'arte*, 2 vols, I, ed. Walter Siti and Silvia De Laude (Milan: Mondadori, 1999), 294–7

Pavarini, Stefano, *Sbarbaro prosatore Percorsi ermeneutici dal frammento alla prosa d'arte* (Bologna: Il Mulino, 1997)

Perrotta, Gennaro, *Intelligenza di Giorgio Pasquali*, *Primato*, IV, I, 1 (Gennaio, 1934), 7–12

Perugi, Maurizio, 'Odissea', *Paragone*, XXII, 254 (1971): 129–35

Pighi, Giovan Battista, 'L'*Odissea* della Bemporad', *Il Popolo*, 31 (Gennaio, 1971)

Polato, Lorenzo, *Camillo Sbarbaro* (Florence: La Nuova Italia, 1974)

Polato, Lorenzo (ed.), *Camillo Sbarbaro: Pianissimo* (Milan: Il Saggiatore, 1983)

Pontani, Filippomaria, 'Gracili avena': le versioni ultime, Pitagora e Pascoli in *La dorata parmelia. Licheni, poesia e cultura in Camillo Sbarbaro (1888–1967)*, ed. Magurno (Rome: Carocci, 2011), 181–205

Prins, Yopie, *Ladies' Greek: Victorian Translations of Tragedy* (Princeton, NJ: Princeton University Press, 2017)

Prete, Antonio, 'Le pagine di Leopardi sul tradurre', *Testo a Fronte*, III (1991): 131–4

Privitera, Aurelio, 'La storia della letteratura greca di Gennaro Perrotta' in Bruno Gentili and Agostino Masaracchia (eds), *Giornate di studio su Gennaro Perrotta* (Pisa: Istituti Editoriali e Poligrafici Internazionali, 1996), 21–39

Puccini, Davide, *Lettura di Sbarbaro* (Florence: Nuovedizioni Vallecchi, 1974), 137–53

Quasimodo, Alessandro (ed.), *Salvatore Quasimodo: Il poeta a teatro* (Milan: Spirali Edizioni, 1984)

Ramat, Silvio, *Storia della poesia del Novecento italiano* (Milan: Mursia, 1976)

Ramat, Silvio, '"Pianissimo" di Camillo Sbarbaro' in *La poesia italiana 1903–1943: Quarantuno titoli esemplari* (Venice: Marsilio, 1997), 124–35

Rodighiero, Andrea, *La tragedia greca* (Bologna: Il Mulino, 2013)

Rodighiero, Andrea, 'L'Odissea di Giovanna Bemporad' in F. Condello and A. Rodighiero (eds), *'Un compito infinito': Testi classici e traduzioni d'autore nel Novecento italiano* (Bologna: Bononia University Press, 2015), 229–44

Romagnoli, Ettore, 'La musica greca', *La nuova antologia*, s. IV, CXVI [CC] (1905): 800, 650–72, now in *Musica e poesia nell'antica Grecia* (Bari: Laterza, 1911)

Romagnoli, Ettore, *Musica e poesia nell'antica Grecia* (Bari: Laterza, 1911)

Romagnoli, Ettore, *Minerva e lo scimmione* (Bologna: Zanichelli, 1917)

Romagnoli, Ettore, *La diffusione della cultura classica* in *Vigilie Italiche* (Milan: Istituto Editoriale Italiano, 1919)

Romagnoli, Ettore, *Lo scimmione in Italia* (Bologna: Zanichelli, 1919)

Romagnoli, Ettore, *Nel Regno d'Orfeo: Studi sulla lirica e la musica greca* (Bologna: Zanichelli, 1921)

Ronconi, Alessandro, *Il filologo* in *Per Giorgio Pasquali: Studi e testimonianze*, ed. Lanfranco Caretti (Pisa: Nistri-Lischi, 1972), 116–17

Rossi, Luigi Enrico, 'Umanesimo e filologia (A proposito della Storia della filologia classia di Rudolf Pfeiffer)', *Rivista di Filologia e Istruzione Classica*, 104 (1976): 98–117

Rossi, Luigi Enrico, 'L'approccio non classicistico di Pasolini alla tragedia attica' in Tullio De Mauro and Francesco Ferri (eds), *Lezioni su Pasolini* (Ripatransone: Edizioni Sestante, 1997), 123–31

Ruocco, Danilo, 'Salvatore Quasimodo e il teatro' in Alessandro Quasimodo (ed.), *Quasimodo* (Milano: Mazzotta, 1999), 169–81

Russi, Valentina, 'Esercizi di assoluto: La poesia di Giovanna Bempoard', *Esperienze letterarie*, 3, XXXVI (2011): 70–81

Salomoni, Patricia (ed.), *Ritmo, Parole, Musica: Ettore Romagnoli traduttore dei poeti*, Atti del seminario di studi (Rovereto: Edizioni Scripta, 2021)

Savettieri, Cristina, 'Tragedia, tragico e romanzo nel modernismo', *Allegoria*, XXIII (2011): 45–63

Savoca, Giuseppe, *Concordanze delle poesie di Camillo Sbarbaro: concordanza, liste di frequenza, indici* (Florence: Olschki, 1989)

Sbarbaro, Clelia, 'Camillo Sbarbaro nei ricordi della sorella', *Paragone*, XXI, 248 (1970): 130–6

Scheiwiller, Vanni (ed.), 'Pascoli tradotto da Sbarbaro' in *Edizione non venale per gli Amici del Credito Italiani, con due scritti di Eugenio Montale, Manara Valgimigli e tre acqueforti a colori di Enrico Della Torre* (Milan: Scheiwiller, 1984)

Schindel, Ulrich, 'C.G. Heyne' in Ward W. Briggs and William M. Calder III (eds), *Classical Scholarship: A Biographical Encyclopedia* (New York: Garland Publishing, 1990), 176–82

Schleisier, Renate, 'Jane Ellen Harrison' in Ward W. Briggs and William M. Calder III (eds), *Classical Scholarship: A Biographical Encyclopaedia* (New York: Garland Publishing, 1990), 127–41

Schmidt, Dennis J., *On Germans and Other Greeks: Tragedy and Ethical Life* (Bloomington, IN: Indiana University Press, 2001)

Schwart, Barth David, *Pasolini Requiem* (New York: Pantheon Books, 1992)

Siciliano, Enzo, *Vita di Pasolini* (Milan: Rizzoli, 1979)

Solmi, Sergio, *I 'Trucioli' di Sbarbaro* in *Scrittori negli anni* (Milan: Il Saggiatore, 1963), 232–7

Spagnoletti, Giacinto, 'Dal risvolto di copertina di Esercizi 1980', now in Giovanna Bemporad, *Esercizi vecchi e nuovi* (Milan: Archivio Dedalus, 2010)

Stabile, Francesca Romana (ed.), *Un sabotatore: Giorgio Labò* (Rome: Gangemi Editore, 2014)

Steiner, George, *The Death of Tragedy* (London: Faber & Faber, 1961)

Steiner, George, *After Babel: Aspects of Language and Translation* (Oxford: OUP, 1975)

Steiner, George, *Antigones: The Antigone Myth in Western Literature, Art and Thought* (Oxford: OUP, 1984)

Stone, Jennifer, 'Pasolini, Zanzotto, and the question of pedagogy' in Patrick Rumble and Bart Testa (eds), *Pier Paolo Pasolini: Contemporary Perspectives* (Toronto: University of Toronto Press, 1994), 40–53

Szondi, Peter, *An Essay on the Tragic*, trans. Paul Fleming (Stanford, CA: Stanford University Press, 2002)

Taminiaux, Jacques, *Le théâtre des philosophes: La tragédie, l' être, l' action* (Grenoble: Jérôme Million, 1995)

Taxidou, Olga, *Greek Tragedy and Modernist Performance: Hellenism and Theatricality* (Edinburgh: Edinburgh University Press, 2023)

Thibodeau, Martin, *Hegel et la tragédie grecque* (Rennes: Rennes University Press, 2011)

Timpanaro, Sebastiano, 'Recensione a Giorgio Pasquali, *Filologia e storia*, nuova edizione con una premessa di Alessandro Ronconi, Firenze, Le Monnier, 1964, x–96', *Critica Storica*, IV (Messina-Florence: G. D'Anna, 1965), 565–6

Timpanaro, Sebastiano, *La filologia di Giacomo Leopardi* (Rome: Laterza, 1977)

Tontini, Paolo, '"Non si uccide la poesia!": Frammenti ritrovati di Giovanna Bemporad', *L'arengario: Studio bibliografico* (2012), http://www.arengario.it/autografi/non-si-uccide-la-poesia-frammenti-ritrovati-di-giovanna-bemporad

Trevi, Emanuele, 'Giovanna Bemporad: l'*Odissea* di Omero', *Nuovi Argomenti*, 46 (1993), now in Giovanna Bemporad, *Esercizi vecchi e nuovi* (Milan: Archivio Dedalus, 2010)

Trevisan, Giacomo, 'Edipo all'alba "Io griderò chiara e intatta la mia vergona": Studio su "Edipo all'alba" di Pier Paolo Pasolini', *Studi Pasoliniani*, 2 (2008): 37–55

Troiani, Sara, *Dal testo alla scena e ritorno: Ettore Romagnoli e il teatro greco*, Collana Labirinti, Università degli Studi di Trento (Dipartimento di Lettere e Filosofia: Trento, 2022)

Turolla, Enrico, *Saggio sulla poesia di Sofocle* (Bari: Laterza, 1934)

Turyn, Alexander, 'The Sophocles Recension of Manuel Moschopolous', *TAPhA*, 80 (1949): 94–153

Turyn, Alexander, *Studies in the Manuscript Tradition of the Tragedies of Sophocles* (Urbana, IL: Illinois University Press, 1952)

Valensise, Marina (ed.), *Orestea: Atto Secondo* (Milan: Electa, 2021)

Valentini, Valentina, *La tragedia moderna e mediterranea: Sul teatro di Gabriele D'Annunzio* (Milan: Franco Angeli, 1992)

Valgimigli, Manara, 'Del tradurre poesia antica' in *Del tradurre e altri scritti* (Milan: Ricciardi, 1957)

Vallortigara, Laura, '"Nel furore che mi teneva sveglia": La traduzione dell'*Eneide* di Giovanna Bemporad' in Eleonora Cavallini (ed.), *Scrittori che traducono scrittori: traduzioni 'd'autore' da classici latini e greci nella letteratura italiana del Novecento* (Alessandria: Edizioni dell'Orso, 2017), 107–22

Vallortigara, Laura, '"Do People Still Sing?" Traduzioni italiane dell' Eneide nel Novecento', *Enthymema*, 23 (2019): 157–79. http://doi.org/10.13130/2037-2426/11129

Venturi, Lionello et al., *Un sabotatore: Giorgio Labò* (Milan: La Stampa Moderna s.r.l., 1946), with contributions by Lionello Venturi, Mario Labò (the father), Giulo Carlo Argan, Franco Calamandrei, Alberto Lattuada and Antonello Trombadori

Vernant, Jean-Pierre and Vidal-Naquet, Pierre, *Myth and Tragedy in Ancient Greece*, trans. Janet Lloyd (New York: Zone Books, 1990)

Vitelli, Girolamo, *Filologia classica . . . e romantica*, ed. Teresa Lodi (Florence: Le Monnier, 1962), 133–43

Ward, David, 'Introduction to his English translation of the *Manifesto*' in Patrick Rumble and Bart Testa (eds), *Pier Paolo Pasolini: Contemporary Perspectives* (Toronto: University of Toronto Press, 1994), 152–4

Wood, Douglas Kellogg, 'F. M. Cornford' in Ward W. Briggs and William M. Calder III (eds), *Classical Scholarship: A Biographical Encyclopaedia* (New York: Garland Publishing, 1990), 23–36

Worman, Nancy, *Virginia Woolf's Greek Tragedy* (London: Bloomsbury, 2019)

Zampa, Giorgio, *Eugenio Montale: Sulla poesia* (Milan: Mondadori, 1976)

Zanzotto, Andrea, 'Pasolini, "l'Academiuta di lenga furlana", Nico Naldini', in *Aure e disincanti* (Milan: Mondadori, 1994), 283–9

Zanzotto, Andrea, 'Pedagogia' in *Aure e disincanti* (Milan: Mondadori, 1994), 141–51

Zoboli, Paolo, 'Il motivo di un libro (sulle dediche di Sbarbaro)' in Giorgio Devoto and Paolo Zoboli (eds), *Camillo Sbarbaro: Atti della giornata di studio. 11 Aprile 2004* (Genova: San Marco dei Giustiniani, 2003), 69–91

Zoboli, Paolo, *Linea ligure: Sbarbaro, Montale, Caproni* (Novara: Interlinea, 2006)

Zoboli, Paolo, *La rinascita della tragedia: Le versioni della tragedia greca da D'Annunzio a Pasolini* (Lecce: Pensa Multimedia Editore, 2004)

Zoboli, Paolo, *Sbarbaro e i tragici greci* (Milan: Vita e Pensiero, 2005)

Index

Aeschylus 4, 13, 14, 21, 23, 34–5, 39, 49–50, 79, 80, 86
   Agamennon 2, 15, 22, 35
   Eumenides 22, 35
   Persians 46–7
   Prometheus Bound 22–3, 39, 41, 44–7, 57
   Oresteia 33, 35, 86, 168
   The Libation Bearers 86, 168
Angeleri, Carla
   Bibliografia degli scritti di Camillo Sbarbaro 45
Aristostle 27
Athens 21, 35

Baldi, Sergio 28
Baratono, Adelchi 125
Bàrberi Squarotti, Giorgio 27, 40
Barbey d'Aurevilly, Jules Amedée, 45–7
   Due storie diaboliche 45
Barile, Angelo. 134
   Testimonianza per Camillo Sbarbaro 127
Barilli, Anton Giulio
   La signora Autari 132
Beigua 134–5
Benjamin, Walter 7, 60–1, 167
Bembo, Giovanna 94
Bemporad, Giovanna 2–11, 28–31, 33–4, 36–7, 57, 85–124, 154–64, 165–71
   Esercizi: Poesie e traduzioni 86, 88, 106, 113–16, 120–2, 168
Berman, Antoine 7, 19, 61
   Hölderlin: le national et l'étranger 61
   La traduction et la lettre ou l'auberge du lointain 19
Bertelli, Lucio 25
Bigongiari, Piero 28
Blanchot, Maurice 112
Bo, Carlo 3, 5, 58–9, 61, 126–8, 130
Bocca di Magra 48

Bologna 155–7
   Liceo Galvani 3, 155
   University 155
Bompiani, Valentino 45–50, 57–8
Bonnefoy, Yves 7, 11, 30, 98–9
   L'autre langue à portée de voix 99
   L'hésitation d'Hamlet et la décision de Shakespeare 30
Bortotto, Cesare 156–7
Byron, George Gordon 102

Cambridge Ritualists 26
Casarsa 5, 154–60, 162–3
Castellani, Riccardo 156–67
Cicero 147
Croce, Benedetto 10, 17–19, 21–3, 100
   L'estetica come scienza dell'espressione e linguistica generale: Teoria e storia 17
   Poesia 17
Cornford, Francis Macdonald 26
Cornigliano
   Istituto Calsanzio 126
Costa, Giampiero
   Bibliografia degli scritti di Camillo Sbarbaro 45

D'Annunzio, Gabriele 1, 10–14, 23, 26–7, 91
   Discorso agli Ateniesi 14
   La Rinascenza della Tragedia 1, 10, 12–14, 27
   opera dramatica 13
Dante 101, 132–3, 137, 151
De Bosis Vivante, Elena 3, 54
De Chirico, Giorgio 148, 151–2
Della Bianca, Giovanna 94
Delphi
   charioteer of 14
De Robertis, Giuseppe 42–3, 51
Descartes, René 36
Di Costante, Luxardo Lelio 125

D'Intino, Franco 96, 99
discipline
    anthropology 24–7, 35–6, 141
    geology 25
    hermeneutics 19, 23
    philological method 1, 10, 17, 19, 22, 24, 26, 28, 41, 59, 96, 138
    theoretical philosophy 1, 4, 7, 10, 19, 23, 28, 42, 51, 59, 98, 122–4, 169
Duse, Eleonora, 14

education 5, 7, 21, 25, 95, 97, 123–4, 126, 129, 131, 133, 135, 138–43, 149, 153–5, 158, 163
    didactic imagination 157–8
    didactic method 4–5, 7–8, 34, 39, 59, 128, 140, 142, 153, 157, 162
    pedagogy 5, 7–8, 22, 59, 81, 104, 123–4, 128–9, 131, 133–4, 148–9, 151, 153, 158, 159, 166, 169–70
    pedagogia apedagogica 124, 159–60
    metodo della partecipazione 5, 127, 140, 145, 169
    scuola irregolare 4, 154–9
    teacher, 91–2, 123–31, 133–54, 157–8, 161–3, 166, 169–70
    teaching 5, 20–1, 123–7, 129–31, 135, 137–40, 143–7, 150–5, 157–8, 160, 162, 166, 169–70
Errante, Vincenzo 3, 94
Euripides 14, 39, 79–80, 86, 93
    Alcestis 39, 41, 44–7, 65–7, 79–80
    Electra 86
    Medea 93–94
    The Cyclops 40–2, 45–8, 57, 79

Falqui, Enrico 47, 49–50, 53, 58
Fascist ideology 2, 41, 124, 128, 156
    tessera fascista 128
Ferrara 3
Fiammazzo, Pietro 138, 140
    Gocce 137
Florence 3, 143
    Piazza San Marco 142
Foscolo, Ugo 101, 121, 161–2
    Sepolcri 160
Fraccaroli, Giuseppe 20–1
Frazer, James George 26
    Golden Bough 25

Freud, Sigmund
    uncanny 97
    unheimlich 96

Garboli, Cesare 54
Gargallo, Mario Tommaso 2
Gela 21
Genoa 47, 123, 128, 130
    Ilva ironworks 125
    Istituto Arecco 126
    University 125
Gentile, Giovanni 10, 17–19, 21, 23
    Il diritto e il torto delle traduzioni 19
George, Stefan 102
Giordani, Pietro 96, 119
Giusti, Giuseppe 151–2
Goethe (von), Johann Wolfgang 101–2, 161
    Faust 161
Gresino (don), Giacomo 134–8
    Scampoli 135
Griffith, Mark 77
Gruppi di Azione Patriottica (GAP) 144

Harrison, Jane Ellen 26
Hegel, Georg Wilhelm Friedrich
    influence of 41
Heyne, Christian Gottlob 24–5
Herodotus
    Histories 45–6
Hölderlin, Friedrich
    Antigone 61
Hofmannsthal (von), Hugo 102
    Elektra 86, 168
Holy Scriptures 60
Homer 21, 58, 101, 151, 161, 171
    Iliad 95
    Odyssey 3, 86, 101, 124, 167
Horace
    Ars Poetica 53
Humboldt (von), Wilhelm 24–5
Huysmans, Joris-Karl
    À rebours 52

Il Setaccio (journal) 155
Izzo, Carlo 3, 28, 87–95, 101–2
Istituto Nazionale del Dramma Antico (INDA) 1–2, 10, 12, 14–16, 20, 22–3, 27–8, 33–4, 36, 165

Jervolino, Domenico 18

Keats, John 102

Lagorio, Gina 40, 54, 128–9, 135
   Sbarbaro: Un modo spoglio di esistere
      40
La Riviera Ligure (journal) 3, 134
La Voce (journal) 3–4, 170
Labò, Giorgio 144–53
Leopardi, Giacomo 4, 7, 85–8, 95–9, 101,
      110–13, 115, 119–22, 151–2, 161, 168
   A Silvia 120
   Zibaldone 96
Liceo Galvani *see* Bologna
Liddell-Scott-Jones (LSJ) 115
Lido di Venezia 160–1
Longanesi, Leo 50
Luzi, Mario 28

Machiavelli, Niccolò 131
Macrì, Oreste 28
Madame de Staël
   De l'esprit des traductions 1
Maestroni, Ettore 128–9
Mallarmé, Stéphane 112
Matapan 62
Méautis, George 105
Mesturini, Anna Maria 40–2
metrics
   barbaric metrics / *metrica barbara* 90
   hendecasyllable / *endecasillabo* 3– 4,
      16–17, 23, 31–2, 44, 78, 82, 87–8, 90,
      92, 94, 96, 100–4, 108–9, 113, 117,
      162, 167
   hexameter / *esametro* 90, 101
   five-syllable line / *quinario* 87, 109
   prosody 87–9, 95, 102, 138
   seven-syllabe line / *settenario* 87
Milan 45–6
Montaigne (de), Michel 139
Montale, Eugenio 3, 81, 161
Monte Rosa 134–5
Monviso 134–5
movements
   Aestheticism (Aesthetic interpretation)
      2, 4, 5, 10, 11, 16, 17, 20, 22, 26, 28,
      30, 33, 59, 61, 165
   Baroque 85–6

Classicism 16, 22, 34
Hellenism 15, 16
Hellenocentrism 24, 27
Hermeticism 3–4, 28, 170
Humanism 1
Idealism 11, 17, 22, 27
Liberty 85–6
Romanticism 1, 16, 22, 80
Murray, Gilbert 26
Mycenae / Micene 14

Naquet, Pierre *see* Vidal-Naquet, Pierre
Naldini, Domenico (Nico) 154–7
Nietzsche, Friederich 1, 13, 15–16, 26–7,
      140–2
   The Birth of Tragedy 27
Noli 62
Novalis 101–2

Ovid
   Epistula ex Ponto 53

Pagliarani, Elio 160–1
Pagnanelli, Remo 106, 112–13, 116
Parronchi, Alessandro 28
partisans 150, 152
Pascoli, Giovanni 53–4, 88
   Canti di Castelvecchio 54
   Pomponia Grecina 42, 45
   Thallusa 42, 45
Pasolini, Guido 154–5, 160
Pasolini, Pier Paolo 3, 5, 7, 11, 33–6, 101,
      116, 123–4, 154–62, 169–70
   Diario di un insegnante 34, 160
   Lettera del traduttore 34
   Manifesto del nuovo teatro 35
   Oresteia 33, 35
   The Ashes of Gramsci 34
Pasquali, Giorgio 10–11, 19–22, 26
Perrotta, Gennaro 10, 22–3
   I tragici greci 22
   Storia della letteratura greca 22
Petrarch 101
   Familiar Letters 46
Pindar 20–1, 142–3
Plato 25, 89, 139
   Phaedrus 161
Poggioli, Renato 28
Polato, Lorenzo 40, 43, 53

Pompeius Macer 53
Pontani, Filippomaria 53-4
Pontus 53
Pordenone 156
Praz, Mario 3, 28, 94
Procopio of Cesarea
    Gothic War 46
Pythagoras
    Golden Verses 42, 45

Quasimodo, Salvatore 5, 11, 36-7, 40, 100
    Lirici greci 40

Ramat, Silvio 44
Rapallo 144
rhetoric
    Altertumswissenschaft 24
    amplification / *amplificato* 59, 99, 103
    analogon 112
    antinomy 2, 129, 133
    aphorismatic nature 40, 43
    ars (iners) poetica 53, 131
    catalysing element 116
    cenacolo letterario 162
    comparative method 24
    comunione letteraria 155, 161
    criticism 1, 4, 19, 22, 28-9, 95, 139-40, 151-2
    Demiurge 2, 16-17
    emprise philologique 19
    equals 114
    eruditi and *estetizzanti* 2
    etymologizing literalness 61
    flourishes / *svolazzi* 50, 59
    lexicon 95, 115, 117, 122
    melos 87, 95, 102, 116
    metaphorical element or expression 39, 45, 48-9, 51, 56, 64-6, 75-6, 81-2, 95, 99, 105-7, 113, 115, 117-20, 131, 135-6, 139, 144, 167-8
    metapoetic element 4, 6, 29, 40, 82, 115-16, 167
    music 2, 15, 27, 87-8, 91-3, 95, 101-3, 107, 160-2
    mythopoietic act 67
    omniritmia 16-17
    ordo verborum 32
    paradox 97-9, 138-40
    poetica dell'aderenza 57, 166
    poetic inspiration 1, 52, 57, 88, 99, 124
    psychological element 43-4, 80, 86, 104, 113, 144
    ratio studiorum 25
    rhetorical devices 60-1, 75, 82
    rhetorical figure 153
    sarcasm 76, 78, 82, 138,
    satirical drama 45
    scrittura sotto dettatura 45, 167
    stile legato 48-9, 51
    symbolistic element or meaning 12, 15, 17-18, 29, 35, 53, 82, 106-7, 109-10, 115-16, 119-21, 131, 133, 135, 144, 148, 151, 161-2, 167-8
    the core of tragedy / *il punto centrale della tragedia* 61
    theoretical element or meaning 1, 4, 7, 10, 19, 23, 28, 42, 51, 59, 98, 122-4, 169
    tropes 83, 88, 112, 114-15, 166
    untranslatability 17-18
    verisimiglianza 79
    vernacular, popular or colloquial language 1, 34
    vital source of inspiration 139
Rilke, Rainer Maria 4, 97-8, 102, 112
Rodocanachi, Lucia 47-9, 51, 58
Romagnoli, Ettore 1, 2, 10-11, 14-17, 19-23, 26-7
Rome 3, 13

Saba, Umberto 101
San Giovanni di Casarsa 156-7
Sanguineti, Edoardo 5, 11, 36-7
Santa Margherita Ligure 3
Sappho 131
Savona 132
Sbarbaro, Camillo 2-11, 28-33, 36, 37, 39-71, 73-83, 123-54, 160-1, 165-70
    Cartoline in franchigia 44, 62, 134
    Fuochi fatui 39-40, 42-4, 46, 51, 53-6, 60, 78, 81-3, 127-8, 131, 134, 138, 141, 167-8
    Pianissimo 40, 44, 53, 61, 64-6, 69-71, 73, 76, 79, 81-3, 168
    Ricordo di Giorgio Labò 144
    Trama delle lucciole 129
    Trucioli dispersi 44, 140, 150
Sbarbaro, Clelia 125
Schelling, Friedrich 27

Sereni, Vittorio 28
Shakespeare, William 11, 93, 101–2
   Macbeth 92
Scheiwiller, Vanni 3, 40
Schopenauer, Arthur
   influence of 15
Shelley, Percy Bysshe 102
Siciliano, Enzo 155, 157, 159–60
Siena
   Villa Solaia 2
Socrates 139, 162
Solmi, Sergio 44
Sophocles 14, 21, 29, 31–2, 39–40, 47–50,
   56, 60, 79–80, 86, 88, 96–7, 102, 114,
   116, 120, 165, 168, 170
   Antigone 6–7, 12, 34, 39–40, 45, 60, 62,
      65, 70, 80, 91–2, 123, 127, 166
   Electra 6–7, 31, 58, 86–8, 96, 99–100,
      102–3, 115–16, 118, 120–2, 166–8
   Oedipus at Colonus 92
   Oedipus Rex 22
   Women of Trachis 22
Steiner, George 17–18, 60, 69–70, 83
Spotorno 49, 53
Szondi, Peter 6
   An Essay on the Tragic 27

theatre
   Albano 14
   Athens (Dionysus) 12
   Bayreuth 13, 14
   Orange (Roman theatre) 12
   Syracuse 2, 10, 14–15, 23, 27, 33, 36
Thebes 74–5, 92
Tolstoy, Leo
   Resurrection / Resurrezione 132
topics
   archetypes 1, 13, 44, 60, 61, 85, 113
   Admetus 65–6
   antiqui huomini 131
   Aphrodite 63–4
   Apollo 160–1
   Ares 74
   Argo, 75, 86
   Athena 35
   beauty (idea of) 13, 119, 151, 160
   classical civilization 10, 15, 20, 24–7,
      124, 139, 169
   Clytemnestra 108–9, 116
   compagna di destino 33, 69, 74
   connoisseurs 139
   Danae 91–2
   Dionysus 36, 74
   death 32, 35, 63, 65–8, 71–3, 76, 106,
      108, 110–13, 115–21, 130, 144, 153,
      162, 168
   end *see* death
   Erinyes 105
   Eros 54, 63–6, 72, 108
   ethics 5, 8, 60, 130, 154, 159, 169
   flights 50, 75
   Grundton 61
   Haemon 63,
   Ismene 33, 61, 69, 73
   Kreon 63, 67, 76, 77
   lament 12, 13, 31, 65, 67, 104–5, 107,
      109–10, 113, 115–16, 120–1, 167–8
   landscape 112, 119
   light 12, 67, 74–5, 89, 104–7, 110–12,
      118, 120, 148
   melancholy 120, 137
   memory / *ricordo* 44, 54, 62, 73, 78–9,
      109–11, 117, 119–21, 151
   methaphysical interpretation 56, 112
   morality 60, 140–2
   Muse 20
   nature 73, 106 113, 119
   nest / *nido* 54, 66, 67, 72
   other (concept of) 26, 52, 57, 60
   Orestes 104, 106–7, 109–11, 113, 116,
      118, 120–1, 168
   Orphic elements 112
   pain 33, 36, 41, 61, 70–4, 76, 107,
      110–12, 118, 120, 140
   Persephone 73
   pleasure / *diletto* 51, 71, 73, 112, 127,
      130, 132, 146
   prejudice 19, 140
   Pythia 161
   ricordo 109–10
   santità laica 97
   scarti 143
   shadow / *ombra* 106, 111, 113, 117–18,
      120, 168
   silence 117, 144–5
   sleep / *sonno* 66–8, 70, 111–13, 117–19,
      121, 131
   solitude 110–11, 120

subjugation / *soggezione* 50
symbol 12, 15, 17–18, 29, 35, 53, 106–7,
    109–10, 115–16, 119–21, 131, 133,
    135, 144, 148, 151, 161–2, 167–8
thalamus 108
thanatos 108
varied populace / *gente diversa* 12
Victory 74
water 57, 119, 121
Zeus 33, 69, 74
topoi *see* topics
Traina, Alfonso 54
translation
    amplificatio 59, 99, 103
    continuation model 114
    execution of her inner Self / *esecuzione
        dell'intimo* 114
    humanistic-symbolistic idea 29
    interlinear
    larvatus prodeo 36
    literal 57–60, 127, 167
    periodo delle frenetiche traduzioni 42,
        45, 55
    poetic virtues / *pregi poetici* 41
    prose translation 16–18, 21, 32, 34,
        39–40, 42, 44–5, 57, 76, 78–80, 82,
        100, 119, 166
    rewriting / *riscrittura* 48
    rhythmic translation 4, 11, 16–17,
        29–32, 37, 44, 51, 56, 68, 74–5, 85,
        87–9, 92, 94–6, 100–3, 105, 108–9,
        113, 121, 166–7, 170
    sister figure / *forma sorella* 106–7, 116,
        121–2, 168
    theorization 15
    very free translation / *traduzione
        liberissima* 42
    transcriber writing under dictation 81
    translator (role and activity of) 2–7,
        10–11, 16–17, 21, 28–31, 36–7,
        39–40, 43, 48–9, 51, 53, 56, 60–2, 64,
        80, 82–3, 85, 87, 93, 98–9, 103–4,
        114, 124, 131, 165–8, 170
    verse translation 12, 16–17, 20, 31, 41–2,
        44, 57, 74–5, 78, 88, 90, 92, 94, 100–1,
        103, 105, 107–9, 119, 163, 167

versification 75, 87
walking on the rope / *camminare sulla
    corda* 46–8, 51, 53, 56, 167
transnational 1, 29
Traverso, Leone 3–4, 28–9, 94
Treves, Piero 14
Trevigli [Treviglio] 45–6
Turolla, Enrico 100
    Biblioteche di letteratura 100

Udine 154, 156–7
Ungaretti, Giuseppe 3, 88, 90, 101
    Sentimento del tempo 101

Valgimigli, Manara 10, 21–2
    Del tradurre la poesia antica 21
Varazze 132
Varigotti 62
Venice 3, 89, 92, 93, 161
Vernant, Jean-Pierre, 26, 36, 171
Vettori, Francesco 131
Vicenza 22
Vidal-Naquet, Pierre 26, 36, 171
Virgil 85–6
    Aeneid 3, 34, 155
    Georgics 90
Viserba 160
Vittorini, Demetrio 48
Vittorini, Elio 45–6, 48–9
Vivante family 3

Wagner, Richard 13–14
Wilamowitz-Moellendorff (von), Ulrich
    26
Winckelmann, Johann Joachim 16
Woolf, Virginia 112

Xenophon
    Anabasis 46

Zanzotto, Andrea 114, 124, 157–8
Zoboli, Paolo 13, 41–2, 53–4, 100
    La rinascita della tragedia 9
    Sbarbaro e i tragici greci 41
Zola, Émile
    Germinal 57

www.ingramcontent.com/pod-product-compliance
Lightning Source LLC
Chambersburg PA
CBHW071829300426
44116CB00009B/1487